Grace in Season

Grace in Season

The Riches of the Gospel in Seventy Sermons

J. Augustine Di Noia, O.P.

With a Foreword by
AQUINAS GUILBEAU, O.P.

CLUNY MEDIA

Cluny Media edition, 2019

For more information regarding this title
or any other Cluny Media publication,
please write to info@clunymedia.com, or to
Cluny Media, P.O. Box 1664, Providence, RI, 02901

⚜ VISIT US ONLINE AT WWW.CLUNYMEDIA.COM ⚜

Library of Congress Control Number: 2019951412

ISBN: 978-1950970384

Cover design by Clarke & Clarke
Cover image: Johannes Vermeer, *Woman Holding a Balance*,
c. 1664, oil on canvas
Courtesy of Wikimedia Commons

CONTENTS

Dedicated to Father Thomas Dominic Rover, O.P.
Professor of Homiletics, Poet, Playwright, and Spiritual Guide

✻✻

❧ FOREWORD

THE WORD OF GOD FINDS A SPECIAL HOME in the chapels of Dominican priories. There, choir and sanctuary combine to host a near-perpetual service—an enduring *leitourgia*—of sacred scripture. Arranged around these chapels in rows of stalls, consecrated men— friars preachers—contemplate the sacred page in their private prayer, chant the inspired Word in the Divine Office, listen to the proclamation of the Old and New Testaments at Mass, and receive instruction in the scriptures' meaning through daily preaching. Such is the friars' continuous service to the Word in choir. In the sanctuary, their service is less frequent but complementary: it perfects their service in choir. The Word that a friar preaches from the pulpit is the Word that he first hears, studies, and praises in his stall. Taken together, the friars' service to the Word in choir and in the sanctuary realizes St. Paul's counsel to Timothy: "Devote yourself to the reading of scripture, to preaching and teaching" (1 Tim. 4:13). In Dominican chapels, the Word of God— studied, chanted, proclaimed, and preached—seldom rests.

This effect is the result of some design. When St. Dominic founded the Order of Preachers in the thirteenth century, he established a form of religious life dedicated to the study and proclamation of the Word of God. The life of his friars unites into a single whole—under the guidance of the Rule of St. Augustine—the fraternity of the apostolic band, the perpetual prayer of the desert fathers, the liturgical worship of monks, and the arduous study of teachers, all for the purpose of providing the Church with preachers at once urbane but poor, passionate but chaste, creative but obedient, whose signature is their devotion to the Word of God manifest in the intelligence and beauty of their preaching. By the classical form of their life, Dominican friars contemplate the Word; in response to the contemporary needs of the faithful, they preach it. Launched in study, forged in contemplation, and honed in praise, the friars' preaching aims to exhibit the Word of God in all of its saving truth.

Archbishop J. Augustine Di Noia, O.P., first adopted the rhythms of Dominican preaching at the Order's *studium* in Washington, DC. In the chapel of the Dominican House of Studies, the young Br. Augustine was immersed in the Word of God as it was studied, chanted, proclaimed, and preached. In the chapel's choir, he prayed and sang the Word. In the chapel's sanctuary, he preached it. As providence would ordain for his priestly life, the seed and the fruit of Fr. Augustine's preaching would suffer little separation: he would preach regularly at the House of Studies, first as a professor assigned there, and then as an archbishop home from Rome for the holidays. Like so many apples fallen close to their tree, a number of Archbishop Di Noia's homilies preached in the priory chapel have been included in the present collection. In the chapel of the House of Studies, the Word of God—served by the words of Archbishop Di Noia—has seldom rested.

Stirred restless by the restless Word, Archbishop Di Noia has gleaned in his Dominican prayer the insights that inform his preaching. These insights are remarkable for their penetration into the Christian mysteries, as well as for the poetic quality of their expression. Archbishop Di Noia's Christmas and Easter homilies provide excellent examples of his Dominican talent. In his Christmas preaching, Archbishop Di Noia presents the drama of the Incarnation as something at once mystical and accessible. He reminds us of "the restlessness that God has for us" (p. 36), which is a mark of God's being an "adventurer of love" calling us into the "blazing furnace of the Godhead" (p. 19). As "our champion in the struggle against sin" (p. 13), God "bends recklessly low to seek us" in a "stunning condescension" (p. 14–15): God becomes Emmanuel in the babe of Bethlehem. "Gazing at this baby," the archbishop reminds us, "we see with what love God undertakes to execute his plan to draw us into the communion of Trinitarian life" (p. 24). Archbishop Di Noia thus urges us to "run like the shepherds to find and adore the Infant Savior" (p. 30).

Because Archbishop Di Noia appreciates how Christ's earthly life traces an "arc from Bethlehem to Golgotha" (p. 9), his Christmas preaching flows naturally into his Easter preaching. There, the same wonder that Archbishop Di Noia expresses over the Incarnation marks his treatment of the Paschal Mystery. With awe, he observes that, because "no one has ever desired anything more than God desires to share the communion of his Trinitarian love with us" (p. 69), we see on Good Friday and Easter Sunday "God's astonishing mercy" (p. 46) on display. Jesus "takes to the Cross as a king to his throne" (p. 58), and thereby—through "the enormous power of the flow of blood and water from the pierced side of Christ" (p. 114)—the sinful human heart gains as its "sole conqueror…Christ the King, Christ crucified, risen and seated at the right hand of the Father" (p. 66). In response to the "supreme delicacy of divine providence" (p. 82) at work in the Paschal Mystery, we the baptized look longingly to Christ our King in glory, and "we pray that His glorious wounds will guard and keep us" (p. 69). Secure in the promise of the resurrection, guarded by Christ's wounds, we pilgrims travel through the present vale of tears fortified with the "laughter of redemption" (p. 80).

The joy that Archbishop Di Noia expresses in his Christmas and Easter homilies pervades his preaching on other occasions, many examples of which are also collected in this volume. He spotlights the joy of the Gospel—so often recalled by Pope Francis—awaiting discovery in the feasts and solemnities of Ordinary Time, in the observances of civic holidays, in the ordinations of new priests, and even in the funerals of relatives and friends. As Archbishop Di Noia is keen to show, no human moment escapes the timeless providence of the restless Word. This is a cause of joy: Every season has its grace.

Dominicans preach not just to Dominicans, of course, but to everyone. Thanks to this collection of Archbishop Di Noia's homilies, many of which he preached to Dominicans, all can enjoy the fruits of his restless contemplation of the Word. May *Grace in Season* deepen the faith and increase the joy of all who read it. May it serve, too, as a special help to preachers, who might find here a model for gently but effectively subjecting the vain restlessness of the world to the merciful restlessness of the Word.

~ Very Rev. Aquinas Guilbeau, O.P.
Prior, Dominican House of Studies
Washington, DC
Our Lady of the Rosary, 2019

❧ PREFACE

In the words of the Second Vatican Council, "The sermon...
should draw its content mainly from scriptural and liturgical sources,
and its character should be that of a proclamation of God's wonderful
works in the history of salvation, the mystery of Christ, ever made present and active within us, especially in the celebration of the liturgy."
Since the Council, the consistent teaching of the Church has been that
which distinguishes the homily from other forms of instruction is its
liturgical context.

The *Introduction to the Lectionary* spells out this critically important point:

> Through the course of the liturgical year the homily sets forth
> the mysteries of faith and the standards of the Christian life
> on the basis of the sacred text.... The purpose of the homily
> at Mass is that the spoken word of God and the liturgy of
> the Eucharist may together become "a proclamation of God's
> wonderful works in the history of salvation, the mystery of
> Christ." Through the readings and homily Christ's paschal
> mystery is proclaimed; through the sacrifice of the Mass it
> becomes present. Moreover Christ himself is always present and active in the preaching of his Church. Whether the
> homily explains the text of the Sacred Scriptures proclaimed in

the readings or some other text of the Liturgy, it must always lead the community of the faithful to celebrate the Eucharist actively, "so that they may hold fast in their lives to what they have grasped by faith." From this living explanation, the word of God proclaimed in the readings and the Church's celebration of the day's Liturgy will have greater impact. But this demands that the homily be truly the fruit of meditation, carefully prepared, neither too long nor too short, and suited to all those present, even children and the uneducated.

Clearly, then, the homily is more than a matter of simply "preaching about the readings." The homilist should speak about the readings and prayers in such a way that their meaning is found in the death and Resurrection of the Lord. The homily reflects on the meaning of the readings and prayers of a given celebration in light of the paschal mystery, and it leads the assembly to the Eucharistic celebration in which they have communion in the paschal mystery itself.

In effect, living a life shaped by the liturgy of the Church and the place of the Scriptures therein is a school of spirituality. In this school, the grace of the Holy Spirit forms us so that we might understand the gifts bestowed on us by God. In preaching, we will, in the words of St. Paul, "impart this in words not taught by human wisdom but taught by the Spirit, interpreting spiritual truths to those who possess the Spirit" (1 Cor. 2:13). As our meditation on the word of God is shaped more and more by the Church's faith, we can then interpret daily experience through the lens of the paschal mystery with greater facility.

"When the Son of man comes, will he find faith on earth?" (Luke 18:8) An affirmative answer to that question will depend in some measure on the homily. Does our preaching nourish and deepen faith? Much Catholic preaching today addresses itself to the biblical readings in the liturgy, but often this is reduced to sharing some insights gained from biblical commentaries and then offering a moral exhortation for us to be more like Jesus. This may be "practical," but it is not sufficient. If Christ is seen to be simply a good person who provides us with an example to follow, and we do not base our preaching on the faith of the Church, then the question as to whether Christ will find faith on the earth when he returns makes us uncomfortable, and if it does not, it should.

In preaching, Pope Francis tells us, "the heart of its message will always be the same: the God who revealed his immense love in the crucified and risen Christ" (*Evangelii Gaudium*, §11). This revelation is founded on the truth that Jesus Christ is the Son of God incarnate, the Second Person of the Holy Trinity. If we do not speak about the mysteries of the faith on the one occasion every week at which most people have an opportunity to learn about them, there is the danger that when the Son of man returns he will not find faith in the hearts of members of his Body. If that faith is lacking because we contented ourselves with offering them some instructive background on the biblical readings and a dose of moral uplift, we will have much to answer for. As we follow Christ from Bethlehem to Golgotha and beyond, the biblical texts and the writings of the Fathers and saints also cluster around the mysteries of Christ in the incarnation, life, death and Resurrection of the Lord, and the gift of the Holy Spirit.

Preaching must be directed to the needs of a particular community with its unique culture and circumstances. Listen again to *Evangelii Gaudium*:

> The same Spirit who inspired the Gospels and who acts in the Church also inspires the preacher to hear the faith of God's people and to find the right way to preach at each Eucharist. Christian preaching thus finds in the heart of people and their culture a source of living water, which helps the preacher to know what must be said and how to say it. Just as all of us like to be spoken to in our mother tongue, so too in the faith we like to be spoken to in our "mother culture," our native language (cf. 2 Macc. 7:21, 27), and our heart is better disposed to listen. This language is a kind of music which inspires encouragement, strength and enthusiasm.

Sermons are meant to be preached and heard within the liturgical celebration where the words of the celebrant move us to active participation in the praise of God and in the Holy Sacrifice of Christ who suffered and rose from the dead for our sakes. Thus the experience of hearing a sermon within a worshipping community is different from reading it in the privacy of our home.

This volume contains seventy sermons that were preached and heard only once. They take on a new life in the form of a book and are offered here as aids to reflection, meditation, and prayer. If preachers find in them some inspiration for the preparation of their own sermons, that is all to the good. There is no end to the sheer delight that we experience when we read about the wonders of God's love for us. This is a grace that comes to us in season as we move through the liturgical year, moving us to hope, to repentance, to good works, and to give glory to God. While there is surely no substitute for hearing the word preached to us, it has been the experience of Christians through the centuries that having at hand a collection of sermons to read and ponder at leisure can lead us to a deepened understanding of the mystery of salvation and stir us to the love of God.

This book is dedicated to the memory of Thomas Dominic Rover, O.P., who was a teacher of homiletics and whose "poetic use of language and dramatist's sense of timing could hold an entire congregation spellbound as his sermons worked their way to a studied climax. One could say that the Holy Spirit spoke easily through him." The preacher of the sermons in this volume owes a debt of gratitude to Fr. Rover's teaching and example.

~ Archbishop J. Augustine Di Noia, O.P.
Vatican City
St. Ignatius of Antioch, 2019

PART I

Christmas Season

❧ SERMON 1

His Blessings Flow Far as the Curse Is Found

"No MORE LET SINS AND SORROWS GROW, / Nor thorns infest the ground; / He comes to make his blessings flow / Far as the curse is found, / Far as the curse is found."

Like many other carols, this rarely sung verse of "Joy to the World" leads us into the profound mystery of the Christmas feast. In the little child whose birth we celebrate tonight, we gaze on the face of our Champion in a struggle that could not be won without him. Listen to St. Leo the Great: "For unless [Christ] the new man, by being made *in the likeness of sinful humanity*, had taken on himself the nature of our first parents, unless he had stooped to be one in substance with his mother while sharing the Father's substance and, being alone free from sin, united our nature to his, the whole human race would still be held captive under the dominion of Satan."

For this child, the road that begins tonight in Bethlehem continues on to Golgotha and beyond to glory. The enchanting beauty that surrounds us on this feast of the Nativity of our Lord celebrates the glory of the Champion of our salvation. But between the Nativity and the glory there was the Cross, the passion and the death of our precious Savior. With Mary tonight we gaze with joy on the child over whose ruined body we shall later shed bitter tears. The Father of heaven and earth did not hesitate to allow his only-begotten Son to become the Son of Mary in order to make his blessings flow far as the curse is found.

From Bethlehem to Golgotha: as another carol reminds us, the destiny of this child is prefigured in the harsh circumstances of his birth: "In the bleak midwinter, / frosty wind made moan, / Earth stood hard as iron, water like a stone; / Snow had fallen, snow on snow, / snow on snow, / In the bleak midwinter, long ago." The mighty Conqueror comes into the world in piercing cold, in a stable "because there was no room for them in the inn." "In the bleak midwinter / a stable place sufficed / for the Lord God Almighty, Jesus Christ."

Tonight, already knowing the destiny of this child, we find ourselves at the absolute center of the Christmas mystery. What Mary and Joseph, the angels and archangels, the shepherds and now, brothers and sisters in Christ, all of us—what they and we behold with nearly breathless wonder is the birth of the one who, taking on our humanity, will lay down his life for us in the Sacrifice of the Cross so that we can become sharers in his divinity. This wonderful exchange restores us to life, making possible things otherwise completely beyond our reach and imagination: namely, participation in the divine life, and forgiveness and healing of our sins.

St. Leo reminds us: "The Conqueror's victory would have profited us nothing if the battle had been fought outside our human condition." Born into our human nature, Christ makes it possible for us to be reborn as his brothers and sisters in the communion of Trinitarian love. By assuming our human frailty, the sinless one is victorious within the very arena of earthly existence where we lay under the curse, condemned to sin and death.

Not from outside, but from within this arena, he comes to make his blessings flow. Like a flowing river, the uncontainable surge of his grace streams into every crevice and corner of our lives sweeping away our sins and sorrows, and all the thorns that infect the ground. How far? Far as the curse is found, deep into the dark fissures of our hearts where the thorns of envy and malice, pride and lust, greed, hatred and despair would find a niche and thrive. How far then do his blessings flow? Far as the curse is found.

As far, even, as the world of unbelief. When exhorted to "put Christ back into Christmas," I ask myself: "But who could have taken him out of Christmas?" It would be better to speak of revealing or uncovering his ineffaceable presence at the very heart of Christmas. Is it not possible with the eyes of faith to see in every Christmas tree, in every wreath, in every exchange of gifts, in every instance of generosity to the needy, in every family reunion of loved ones from far and near—to see in every Christmas celebration, even of those who do not acknowledge him, remote outposts of his blessings that flow as far as the curse is found?

Consider those who would see Christ erased from their so-called "Holiday Season." They are of two sorts.

There are those who want to see God everywhere else but uniquely in Christ. They are confounded by the claim that God is specifically located in a particular person—with a birthday and a birthplace, a nationality, a genealogy, and a biography, as summarized in the Apostles' Creed, of one "who was conceived by the Holy Spirit, born of the Virgin Mary, suffered under Pontius Pilate, was crucified, died, and was buried...[and] on the third day rose from the dead."

Then there are those, far more interesting, who think of God as, at best, a construct of the social psyche. God is not everywhere but nowhere. Yet they are content to join their cause with the first group. Together they are determined to expunge from the public square every sign of precisely this mysterious divine particularity—every crèche, every Christmas tree, every wreath, every carol.

What makes this second group interesting is that, like the demons, they spy the real truth about Christmas as much as they hate it: Christ cannot be erased from Christmas, nor can the flow of his blessings be interrupted or blocked, except in the truly impenitent heart. Christmas itself would have to fade away. Not very likely.

But we who believe in him must embrace his blessings and shake off the attachments to sin that keep us mired in the realm of the curse. We must strive to keep our hearts pure, to confess our sins regularly, not just twice a year in Advent and Lent, so that we allow the devil no point of entry into our hearts and minds, souls and bodies. We cannot change the world. But we can open our hearts resolutely to the Christmas grace.

* * *

The Dominican friars sang Christmas carols at various locations in downtown Washington last week. On Thursday evening when we were singing Christmas carols at the corner of 12th and G Streets—just across from Macy's, a New Yorker cannot fail to mention—something marvelous happened.

All of a sudden, we were joined by a homeless woman who sang a couple of carols along with us, assuring us that she could sing alto or bass. We were at the end of our caroling, and ready to leave. She ignored her friend waving her away from this strange group of twenty-odd black-and-white-robed friars. She had one request before we parted ways. Would we sing "Silent Night" for Newtown? When we had done so, she nodded, turned away smiling, and said: "For Newtown." She understands the meaning of Christmas, I thought. Like this good woman, the Holy Mother of God would, in effect, be homeless on Christmas night, prefiguring the terrible day on Golgotha when her son, naked to the world, would give his life for us. Tonight, my brothers and sisters in Christ, may we be one with Mary and Joseph, the shepherds and that cheerful homeless lady, as in faith, hope and love, we confess and sing that he comes to make his blessings flow, far as the curse is found.

❧ SERMON 2

Christ Was Born for This

TODAY WE SING: "Good Christian men rejoice / With heart and soul and voice. / Give ye heed to what we say, / Jesus Christ is born today. / Ox and ass before him bow, / for he is in the manger now. / Christ is born today. Christ is born today."

The spell of this birth—in the form of poinsettias, wreaths, garlands, lights, music, family celebrations, gift-giving—penetrates the remote corners of our aggressively secular age. There is this wondrous grace: Christ is born today. God has become one of us, upsetting all human expectations of what is possible and impossible, of what can be and what cannot be. The Son of God has come in the flesh—a pure, stunning, and, as we say, amazing grace. Who could have foreseen it, planned for it, or arranged it? What purely human conditions could have made way for it? None. Christ is born today—notwithstanding human unreadiness and skepticism—Christ is born today.

God, who desires to share the love and communion of his life with us, makes himself accessible in the incarnate humanity of his only-begotten Son—"that we might share in the divinity of Christ who humbled himself to share in our humanity" (Collect). When regarding this event we take the God's-eye-view that our faith makes possible, we see how fitting it is that God should make his Son "like us in all things but sin," drawing us into the communion of his divine life along humanly accessible pathways suffused with his grace: words, gestures, objects, sacraments—tangible, visible, audible, persons and things, full of human and divine significance. "No one has ever seen God. The only Son, God, who is at the Father's side, has revealed him" (John 1:18). But there is more. We also sing: "Good Christian men, rejoice, / with hearts and souls and voice. / Now ye hear of endless bliss, / Jesus Christ was born for this. / He hath opened heaven's door, and man is blessed evermore. / Christ was born for this," we sing, "Christ was born for this."

Born for what? In his depiction of the Nativity, the sixteenth century Italian artist Lorenzo Lotto painted a crucifix into a niche in the background behind the kneeling figure of St. Joseph. Christ was born for this, Lotto seems to tell us—for the Cross. In Liz Lemon Swindle's beautiful Madonna and Child—entitled "Be It Unto Me"— Mary looks out with a certain apprehension into a future beyond the viewer's sight, while the Child's raised eyebrows wrinkle his forehead. One artist's crucifix in the niche parallels the other's Cross on the horizon. For over the peaceful scene of the Nativity falls the shadow of the Cross. The Christian tradition has almost universally seen in the harsh circumstances of Christ's birth "at midnight, in Bethlehem, in piercing cold" a prefiguring of the brutal circumstances of his death on the Cross. "Ox and ass before him bow; and he is in the manger now." But in the future the wood of the Cross will take the place of the wood of the manger. Be it done unto to me, indeed. He willingly embraces the Cross for our sakes, by his perfect obedience erasing the deadly effects of our disobedience. "He hath opened heaven's door, and man is blest forevermore." "Christ was born for this," we sing, "Christ was born for this."

But there is yet more to sing about: "Good Christian men, rejoice, / with hearts and souls and voice. / Now ye need not fear the grave. Jesus Christ was born to save. / Calls you one and calls you all, to gain his everlasting hall. / Christ was born to save," we sing, "Christ was born to save."

Thus we have, in the first place, the grace of the "Nativity of our Lord Jesus Christ according to the flesh" (Roman Martyrology), and then, through his Cross, "the purification from sins" (Hebrews 1:3). Now we have the glory. "And the Word became flesh and made his dwelling among us, and we saw his glory, the glory of the Father's only Son, full of grace and truth" (John 1:14). And "he took his place at the right hand of the Majesty on high" (Hebrews 1:4). We have grace of the Incarnation, the victory of the Cross, and the Resurrection and life everlasting. This is the full meaning of Christmas, the arc from Bethlehem to Golgotha, and beyond. "Now ye hear of endless bliss. Jesus Christ was born for this."

We give up the forceful proclamation of this mystery, my brothers and sisters in Christ, and we are left with a pitiful dry husk of moral maxims and human wisdom. At the heart of the Christmas story is not merely a wonderful moral ideal but the person of Jesus Christ and the salvation and new life he makes possible for us. "Now ye need not fear the grave. Jesus Christ was born to save."

* * *

"Good Christian Men Rejoice" is the English title of the carol "In Dulci Jubilo," attributed to the fourteenth-century German Dominican mystic, Blessed Henry Suso. The original text is a delightful mix—a "macaronic" alternation—of Latin and medieval German. The melody is at least seven hundred years old. In his autobiography, Blessed Henry tells us that an angel came to him in a vision, bringing him heavenly joys, exhorting him to cast all sorrow from his mind and to join with the angels in a heavenly dance and in a joyous song about the infant Jesus: "In Dulci Jubilo! Good Christian men rejoice!"

❧ SERMON 3

O Marvelous Exchange

We REJOICE ON THIS CHRISTMAS MORNING in the "marvelous exchange—*O admirabile commercium*—[by which] man's Creator has become man, born of a virgin, [and] we have been made sharers in the divinity of Christ who humbled himself to share in our humanity" (Collect). The mystery of the Incarnation, borne to us in the sights and sounds of the Christmas liturgy, fills our hearts with joy. For us and for our salvation, God, who is infinite and omnipresent, creator of the universe, transcending and yet present in every part of it, nonetheless squeezes himself, as it were, into a tiny babe—"God's infinity / Dwindled to infancy." And not only that. As the opening of the Letter to the Hebrews affirms, God does this in a way that unsurpassably locates and identifies him with this child, and uniquely so with respect to all other conceivable manifestations or divine appearances before or afterwards.

The ineffaceable particularity of the Incarnation has seemed a quaint belief to some, a preposterous one to others, and, to the more polite and theologically up-to-date, nothing but a comforting myth. We do not make it easy for them, do we? We confess not merely that God is present in this child (God who is after all present everywhere), but more robustly that God the Son personally assumed the human nature of, and is thus uniquely—hypostatically, the tradition affirms—joined to this child. For some, this is hard to swallow: How can the

11

unbounded be contained or the infinite be made particular? We can confront the incredulity of unbelievers only with faith seeking the inexhaustible intelligibility of divine wisdom. Given what God has revealed to us about his purposes, beginning with the first chapter of Genesis, the mystery of the Incarnation makes—dare we say it?—perfectly good divine sense, and perfectly good human sense too. And for two reasons.

In the first place, by faith we know that God wants to share the communion of his Trinitarian life with us. In other words, he wants to make us his sons and daughters—in short, as the Christian tradition has not hesitated to say, his intimate friends. How better to accomplish this than by becoming one of us. While a shared human nature is fundamental to our relationships with others, it is only with particular human beings that we can have such relationships. Even a generous love for humankind as a whole is no substitute for knowing and loving particular people whom we can see, hear, address, touch, hold, and kiss. These people have names, they live somewhere, they have ethnic and social backgrounds, and so on. To bring us into the communion of Trinitarian life, God first enters into the round of human existence and thus, as Aquinas loved to say, he adapts his action to our nature. He even has a mother whose "hand leaves his light / Sifted to suit our sight." At the same time, God adapts our nature to his. "A Boy is born in Bethlehem," we sing, "Wherefore rejoice Jerusalem / The Father's Word on high doth take / A mortal form for mortals' sake / … He took our flesh, to man akin / In all things like us, save in sin / That he might make our mortal race, alleluia / Like God and like himself by grace, alleluia, alleluia." How could we share in the communion of Trinitarian life if we were not made sharers—"partakers"—of the divine nature (cf. 2 Peter 1:4)? Listen to St. Athanasius: "The Son of God became man so that we might become God."

From the divine point of view, then, the Incarnation makes perfectly good sense for this reason: "Our Lord Jesus Christ, the Word of God, of his boundless love became what we are that he might make us what he himself is" (St. Irenaeus). But there is a second reason. Not only must our human nature be elevated, but the sin and death that oppress us must be overcome. To be at home in the communion of the Blessed Trinity we need to be redeemed as well as divinized. What the Son is by nature we become by the twofold grace of adoption, that fills us with joy, and redemption, that dispels our sadness. "There cannot rightly be any room for sorrow," insists St. Leo the Great in the first Christmas sermon of his pontificate, "in a place where life has been born. By dispelling fear of death, life fills us with joy about the promised eternity.... [T]he Word of God, God the Son of God, who 'in the beginning was with God, through whom all things were made and without whom was made nothing,' to free human beings from eternal death was himself made human."

Viewed with the eyes of faith, the mystery of the Incarnation again displays how exquisitely tailored to the human condition are the divine provisions for our redemption. "In the conflict undertaken on our behalf," declares St. Leo, "battle was joined on the most remarkably fair terms. Omnipotent Lord engages...[the devil], *not in his own majesty but in our lowliness*, bringing against him the very same form and the very same nature [that had been overcome], partaker indeed in our mortality but wholly without sin." The work of redemption engages the fullness of divine power, without which it would be futile, exercised at the same time, and indeed fittingly, from within the very zone in need of remedy. Our champion in the struggle against sin is one like us in all things but sin—and one who, though succumbing to death for a time, conquered it by his resurrection and thereby won for us eternal life.

"He took our flesh, to man akin / In all things like us, save in sin / That he might make our mortal race / Like God and like himself by grace / Now lies he in a manger poor / Whose kingdom shall for aye endure / This day let joyful praises flow, alleluia / *Benedicamus Domino*, alleluia, alleluia."

❧ SERMON 4

No Room for Sorrow

IN THE DAYS BEFORE CHRISTMAS we prayed that, with the coming of the divine Messiah, sadness would flee away. Today our prayer is answered: sadness has fled, and sorrow gives way to joy. "Hark! Your sentinels raise a cry. Together they shout for joy" (Isaiah 52:8). "There can be no room for sorrow," insists St. Leo, "in a place where life has been born." The new life is that of the only-begotten Son of God, born of the flesh of the Blessed Virgin Mary, born truly God and truly man. The summons to rejoice comes from the very hosts of heaven. "Joyful all ye nations rise," they cry out, "join the triumph of the skies."

The great reason for our joy at Christmas lies in this: In the new life born today God's immense love for us is made manifest. "Nothing is so needful for our hope," wrote St. Augustine, "than for us to be shown how much God loves us. And what is a better sign of this than the Son of God deigning to share our nature?" This unmistakable gesture of love both amazes us and radically alters our prospects.

On the one hand, we are utterly amazed. We gaze in wonder at the child in the manger. "It would be less amazing that a human being should advance to divine things than that God should descend to human ones." The human search for God we can understand. To want to enjoy some share in the divine life—whether or not such a thing were possible—seems reasonable. But, while we might plausibly seek a higher form of life in this way, God bends recklessly low to seek us out and indeed to take up human nature. "Mild he lays his glory by / Pleased as man with man to dwell / Jesus, our Emmanuel." As amazing as this may be, all the more so is God's purpose in this stunning condescension. We awake on Christmas morn to the wonderful news that his boundless love has opened to the human race a whole new future. Christ assumes our nature, and God becomes man *that we might become God*. The Gospel of John could not be clearer: "The Word was made flesh, and dwelt among us.... To those who...accept him he gave power to become children of God, to those who believe in his name, who were born not by natural generation nor by human choice nor by a man's decision but of God." Christ is "Born to raise the sons of earth / Born to give them second birth."

Our first birth joins us to a natural family, while our second to a divine family. In our first birth we experience the love of our fathers and mothers, of our brothers and sisters, while in the second birth we share the Trinitarian love of the Father, Son, and Holy Spirit. The human family welcomes us after our first birth, while the holy Church on earth with the communion of saints in heaven celebrates our second birth.

The arc that sweeps the Son of God from Bethlehem to Golgotha and beyond to the "right hand of the Majesty on high" manifests the specific Christmas grace. Today our second birth is revealed to be a reconciliation that makes us wholly pleasing in God's sight (cf. Offertory Prayer). The human nature that is ordered by the Incarnation to a participation in the life of the Blessed Trinity does not come innocent to the threshold of the Holy of Holies. It is wounded by sin and destined to die. But God's love for us is not thwarted by this obstacle. It encompasses a plan to undo the damage to human nature caused by sin. "It has come about through his great power that the Son of God took up human substance *along with its need*—to rebuild that nature which he created and to abolish the death which he did not make." Thus, in the Collect of today's Mass, we address God as he "who wonderfully created the dignity of human nature and still more wonderfully restored it."

In his great love for us, God did not hesitate to send his own Son, "for what else could have covered our sins but his sinlessness? Where else could we…have found the means of holiness except in the Son of God alone?" The Incarnation is for our redemption. "For unless the new man, by being made in the likeness of sinful humanity, had taken on himself the nature of our first parents…the whole human race would still be held captive under the dominion of Satan. The Conqueror's victory would have profited us nothing if the battle had been fought outside our human condition." St. Thomas gives the reason for this with characteristic conciseness: "One who was merely a man could not make satisfaction for the entire human race. And how could God? It was fitting for Jesus Christ to be both God and man. St. Leo says: '… Unless he were truly God, he could not provide a cure; unless he were truly man, he could not offer an example.'" Hear St. Leo again: "Nature could find no remedy since it would not be able to alter its condition by its own powers." And yet again: "We could not be released from the chains of eternal death had he not become lowly in our condition while remaining at the same time omnipotent in his own."

My brothers and sisters in Christ, leave behind all the troubles and sorrows you have brought with you this morning: they are banished by the grace of Christmas. Behold the future of a life reconciled with God through the Incarnation of his only-begotten Son. Listen to the heavenly hosts who summon us to rejoice: "Hark! The herald angels sing, / 'Glory to the newborn King. / Peace on earth and mercy mild, / God and sinners reconciled.'" Through Christ our Lord. Amen.

❧ Sermon 5

Let No Tongue on Earth Be Silent

"Let no tongue on earth be silent, / every voice in concert sing, / Evermore and evermore." Let us together keep Christmas as the festival of the Nativity of the only-begotten Son of God according to the flesh. Let us worship God, the adventurer of love, who so loved our poor human nature that he placed it imperishably for all eternity in the very midst of the blazing furnace of his Godhead. God was not satisfied to be in himself, as it were, but in addition willed to be a human being. Now that God himself belongs to it as a brother, humankind is not just an anonymous multitude but a sacred family.

"To those who accept him Christ gave the power to become children of God." The Son of God became a son of man so that the sons and daughters of man could become the children of God. O amazing goodness of God! "Of the Father's love begotten," Christ was born the only Son, but would not remain so. He did not hesitate to admit joint heirs to his inheritance, brothers and sisters by adoption who would share in his inheritance without lessening its worth. According to St. Augustine, the Word was made flesh in order that so apparently incredible a grace—that men should be born of God—would not alarm or surprise us: why marvel that men are born of God when God himself was born of man?

How partial must any mere humanism seem when, in and through the Son of the Father and of the Virgin, man is to become God and thus infinitely more than man. The Incarnation has radically transformed the shape and direction of human history. In Jesus of Nazareth, *delivered to us as Christ and Lord,* the human race has experienced in its earthly history a definitive and unsurpassable coming of God in the flesh. While "in times past God spoke in partial ways to our ancestors through the prophets, in these last days he has spoken to us through the Son." While retaining his ineffable mystery, in Jesus of Nazareth God has expressed himself as Word wholly and irrevocably. "This is he whom seers in old time / Chanted of with one accord; / Whom the voices of the prophets / Promised in faithful word; / Now he shines the long expected / Let creation praise its Lord, / Evermore and evermore." The sorrow and tragedy of human history—of which we continue, day in and day out, to be the dismayed witnesses—must after all have a blessed outcome if God takes part in it himself.

This monumental transformation of human existence, even if fully visible only to the eyes of faith, could not have remained completely hidden. "We saw his glory, the glory as of the only-begotten Son of the Father." The Nativity of the only-begotten Son according to the flesh was humble and mysterious, to be sure. This birth came in conditions of ignorance, superstition, and cruelty, greed and hatred, lust and hypocrisy—indeed, conditions not unlike our own. But his birth was not unknown or unacknowledged. All creatures recognized their Lord: the angels summoned the shepherds and the star alerted the Magi. The very universe itself shouted louder than any trumpet that the king of heaven had come. Devils fled—St. John Chrysostom said in a homily— diseases were healed, graves gave up their dead, and souls were brought out of wickedness to the outmost height of virtue. "For the Lord has bared his holy arm in the sight of all the nations and all the ends of the earth behold the salvation of our God." Thus, we must sing: "Let no tongue on earth be silent, / every voice in concert sing, / Evermore and evermore."

No one is excluded from the joy of Christmas. According to St. Leo the Great, all share the same reason for rejoicing. Our Lord, victorious over sin and death, finding no man free from sin, came to free us all. Let the saint rejoice, and the sinner be glad. Let the unbeliever take courage as he is summoned to life. During Advent, we prayed that Christ would show himself to those who have never known him, to let them see his saving work, and to let them see his glory. Perhaps in the popular celebration of Christmas we can discern at least a partial answer to our prayers for those who do not yet believe in Christ.

Christmas is the single biggest event on the planet, and nothing affects so many people around the world every year as Christmas does. Most Americans—Christians, adherents of other faiths, and non-believers—celebrate Christmas. The Christmas tree, the wreath, gift-giving, an almost universally observed legal holiday, the merriment, even the public crèche—these can seem to be manifestations of a merely secular spirit of Christmas. But Jesus Christ, not the winter solstice, is unquestionably the reason for the season. This allegedly secular festival would not exist apart from the fact that the birth of Christ is celebrated on this day and in this season. Put Christ back into Christmas, some like to say. But who has the power to take him out of Christmas? God has come to us and no one can take him away from us, for Christ the Lord is now our brother. Many aspects of the popular celebration of Christmas seem to represent little more than cultural ritual, to be sure, but there are unmistakably religious undertones. Otherwise, why would activist atheists campaign so ferociously against every hint of Christmas observance in public spaces?

Whether it be "White Christmas" or "Blue Christmas," "I'll Be Home for Christmas" or "All I Want for Christmas"—popular Christmas music is full of unrequited love, disappointment and, above all, longing. The desire to find the perfect gift for a loved one, to meet the perfect companion for life, to have the perfect family, to enjoy a perfectly peaceful life with one's family, friends, and neighbors—all this Christmastide nostalgia and yearning cannot fail to appear to the eyes of faith as an expression of the longing for him that God has planted in every human heart. Even an unbeliever might ask himself in an unguarded moment if in his heart of hearts there does not lay the unlikely courage to believe in Christmas. As Pope Benedict XVI wrote:

"Just as stars are visible long after they have become extinct, since their erstwhile light is still on its way to us, so this mystery frequently offers warmth and hope even to those who are no longer able to believe in it." Like La Befana—the mythical Italian figure who brings presents to children at Epiphany as she searches for the Christ child whom she refused to visit when invited to do so by the shepherds and the Magi but now seems never to be able to find—like her, many unbelievers, immersed in the observances of the Christmas festival, search for a fulfilment that annually slips from their grasp because they cannot find their way to the Christ child. Christmas is a time when many who consider themselves non-believers feel a stirring of the spirit. Whether it starts at the mall or on the Hallmark Channel, it not infrequently leads them to church at Christmas time. To a Catholic sensibility, even the apparently shallow aspects of the popular Christmas celebration might possess a certain truth and depth after all. The seeming pretense of the secular festival is then not the ultimate truth about it. Behind it stands the holy and silent truth that God has in fact come and celebrates Christmas with us.

Brothers and sisters in Christ, God made Christmas without consulting us. There is nothing for us to do for the time allotted to its annual celebration but to fall under its spell, to yield our hearts to its enchantments, to sing the Christmas songs and carols, to love our neighbor and be merry, to "venerate with integrity of faith the mystery of so wondrous an Incarnation," and to worship and give fervent thanks to God, Father, Son, and Holy Spirit for the amazing love that has been shown to the human race—that for men to be born of God, God did not hesitate to be born of man. "O ye heights of heaven adore him; / Angel hosts, his praises sing; / Powers, dominions, bow before him, / and extol our God and King! / Let no tongue on earth be silent, / Every voice in concert sing, / Evermore and evermore!" Amen.

❧ Sermon 6

He Came to Earth to Lead Us to the Stars

"He that is the Word of the most high God," we sang, "deigns to take a body unto himself; he assumes our flesh." *Carne sumpta* (Laetabundus). He, who is the Word, who in the beginning was God and was with God, he through whom all things came to be and without whom nothing came to be, he is today the child born for us and the son given to us. Begotten of God before time began, he now begins to be in time, begotten of the flesh in the womb of the Blessed Virgin Mary. "The Virgin's womb has given us the King of Kings! O wonderful mystery!" we sang. *Res miranda!* (Laetabundus).

About this, the Christmas festival leaves us in no doubt. *Puer natus est nobis.* "He was a baby and a child, so that you may become a perfect human being," St. Ambrose writes: "He was wrapped in swaddling clothes so that you may be freed from the snares of death. He was in a manger so that you may be at the altar. He was on earth that you may be in the stars. He had no place in the inn, so that you may have many mansions in the heavens. He, being rich, became poor for your sakes, that through his poverty you might be rich.... He chose to lack for himself that he may abound for all."

"He was a baby and a child, so that you may become a perfect human being." This is the great truth of Christmas. Christ takes our nature in order to share his nature with us. "Sacred Infant, all divine / What a tender love was Thine, / Thus to come from highest bliss /

Down to such a world as this." "The Word was made flesh, and dwelt among us. To those who... accept him he gave power to become children of God." Here we are at the very heart of the Christmas mystery. Gazing at this baby, this child, we see with what love God undertakes to execute his plan to draw us into the communion of Trinitarian life. Assuming our humanity unto himself and sharing his divinity with us, Christ makes it possible for us to participate by adoption in the divine life that belongs to him, with the Father and the Holy Spirit, by nature. "Our Lord Jesus Christ, the Word of God, of his boundless love became what we are that he might make us what he himself is."

Only the sinfulness of the human race could block the participation in the divine life that God desires for us. Thus was this holy Child "wrapped in swaddling clothes so that you may be freed from the snares of death." Swaddling clothes. There are various theories about the practice of tightly wrapping infants in cloth or blankets after birth. Perhaps, as some suggest, the practice prolongs the sense of comfort and safety afforded by the womb. Be that as it may. The eyes of faith allow us to see what St. Ambrose sees in the swaddling clothes: they may be seen to symbolize the bonds of sin and death that Christ came to loose. He who is without sin allows himself to be regarded as a sinner, taking on the bonds of sin symbolized by the swaddling clothes, in order to free us from sin and death. He accomplishes *purification from sins*—the curse of Adam's sin and our own personal sins—all that would block us from participation of the life of the all holy God. "He comes to make his blessings flow / Far as the curse is found / Far as the curse is found."

With St. Ambrose, we look again at the Christ Child on this Christmas morning: "He was in a manger so that you may be at the altar." What is the manger but the feed box or trough for horses and cattle? At feed time, of course, the manger would be full of hay or oats or other types of fodder. Now the manger is empty and there is room for an infant child "Lo, within a manger lies / he who built the starry skies." An empty manger becomes the first crib of the Lord of the universe. Fodder gives way to the bread of angels. Approaching the manger now—his table—we find not fodder but the bread from heaven. It is not the ox and ass nearby who are to be fed, but we who are to receive the heavenly bread at the altar as we celebrate the eucharistic sacrifice that is the Christ Child's everlasting gift to us. Thus can the Prayer over the Offerings of today's Mass beg God to "make acceptable our oblation on this solemn day when you inaugurated for us the fullness of divine worship" (Prayer over the Offerings).

The Incarnation, the Paschal Mystery, the Eucharistic Sacrifice of the Mass, the other Sacraments, the sacred Liturgy—the many facets of the Christmas festival reveal these mysteries to the eyes of faith and prepare us for the enjoyment of eternal bliss. Following the arc from Bethlehem to Golgotha, and beyond, we are swept along with Christ from earthly to heavenly realms. As a child and a babe and a man, "he was on earth that you may be in the stars." We are to share in the glory that is his, through whom God "has spoken to us" and "whom he made heir of all things, the refulgence of his glory." "He had no place in the inn, so that you may have many mansions in the heavens." The Lord of Creation, he through whom "all things came to be, and without whom nothing came to be," has no proper dwelling for his nativity, but he makes a place for us in the heavenly realms. "He chose to lack for himself that he may abound for all." "From his fullness we have all received, grace upon grace."

Wonderful indeed are the mysteries that Christmas unfolds before the eyes of faith! "Break forth, O beauteous heavenly light. / This Child, now weak in infancy, our confidence and joy shall be. / He comes in human flesh to dwell / our God with us, Immanuel." Amen.

❧ SERMON 7

Christ at the Heart of the Holy Family

MANY YEARS AGO, there was a cartoon that featured a man answering a questionnaire about Christmas. The first question asks: "Were you disappointed in Christmas this year?" He checks off the box marked "yes." "Would Christmas be less of a disappointment if there were no exchange of gifts?" His answer: yes. "Would it be less of a disappointment if there were no contact with the family?" His answer: yes. "Was this Christmas more disappointing than last? 5%? 10%? 15%?" His answer: "More." The last question is a fill-in-the-blank: "What in your opinion is the best way to celebrate Christmas?" His answer: "Hide!"

The cartoon is funny, and like all good cartoons, it reflects a common experience. Since, for many reasons, things never seem to turn out the way we hope or imagine they will, the Christmas holidays can be a difficult and disappointing time. There is a troubled and anxious side to the holidays, the side where the money runs out, where family tensions run high, where absent or deceased loved ones are missed, and so on. In one recent article, the writer advised that the best Christmas present would be a set of airline tickets.

Actually, this is a good day to confront the difficult side of the Christmas holidays. The feast of the Holy Family seems like an "in-between" Sunday, with Christmas past and New Year's Day yet to come. It is a day when the depressing side of the holiday season might well be felt more acutely—not least because for many people the chief disappointments of the Christmas season are associated with family interactions.

In fact, very much like ourselves and our families, the Holy Family was no stranger to sorrow and difficulties. Consider just how many hardships Jesus, Mary, and Joseph faced right from the very start. There were, in the first place, the harsh circumstances of his birth—so harsh, in fact, that the Christian tradition has not hesitated to see in these circumstances a prefiguration of the passion and death of Christ. Then there is the hurried flight into Egypt, when the very life of their child was in danger. This year the feast of the Holy Family happens to fall on the very day, December 28, when the Church normally celebrates the feast of the Holy Innocents, the young boys whom King Herod massacred in order to be sure that the Infant Jesus would be killed as well. Not to be forgotten is the journey home from Jerusalem when Jesus remained behind to talk with the teachers of the law, while Mary and Joseph "searched in sorrow" for him until they found him in the Temple. And finally, in this morning's Gospel, we hear the ominous words of Simeon: "Behold, this child is destined for the fall and rise of many in Israel, and to be a sign that will be contradicted—and you yourself a sword will pierce—so that the thoughts of many hearts may be revealed." No surprise that tradition listed these early events in the life of the Holy Family among the "Seven Sorrows" of our Lady.

As we ponder the difficulties that the Holy Family faced, we begin to look at things through the eyes of faith, like Abraham, and Simeon, and Anna, and Mary and Joseph. When we do this, we can see that today is not just an in-between Sunday, but a critical opportunity to get beyond the more superficial aspects of the holiday season and to grasp the true meaning of Christmas—even if we may have found the celebrations, humanly speaking, disappointing. For, at Christmas, we celebrate nothing less than the birth of the Savior of the world.

By entering deeply into the mystery of the Incarnation, we can look beyond our vague disappointments to seize hold of the saving grace which is Christ himself, who experienced for our sakes all the sorrows and disappointments of human life—everything but sin, but nonetheless even unto death—precisely in order to overcome their power to harm us. Our Savior came to take upon himself and to conquer the sin that is the ultimate source of all our disappointments and sadness. Like the sword that pieced the heart of Mary, the grace of the Incarnation penetrates beneath our moods and feelings—happy or sad—to touch our souls.

The rejoicing this grace brings us can—and normally will—find expression in tangible ways in the liturgical and familial celebrations that make Christmas such a special and wonderful time of the year. But even in the absence of the good feelings we call the "Christmas spirit," when we confess our sins, resolve to follow Christ faithfully, and receive his body and blood in the Holy Eucharist, we are transformed in the very core of our beings, whatever our particular feelings may be at the moment.

What is more, the feast of the Holy Family teaches us that there are no perfect families—not even the Holy Family itself. Naturally, it is appropriate to take it as a model of the family, but not because it represents some unattainable idyllic state of familial bliss. On the contrary, we have seen that the Holy Family experienced sorrows and difficulties, some of them—like having to take flight to save the life of their child—more grave than anything any of us are ever likely to face. Moreover, Joseph and Mary were as much in need of the grace of Christ as we are. By the Immaculate Conception, Mary was preserved from the stain of sin by the foreseen merits of her Son, and St. Joseph was freed from sin by a special grace.

It is precisely Christ's presence that is the source of a loving family life—in the Holy Family and in every other family. The ordered and peaceful family that Sirach describes is possible only where Christ is present. It is not for non-existent perfect people or perfect families that the only-begotten Son of God came in the flesh, and was crucified under Pontius Pilate, buried and risen from the dead, but for us who are sinful and troubled. Christ came not for those who are well but for those who ill. He can find room in our hearts and in our imperfect families as well if we but unlock the doors and welcome him in.

While our opening cartoon captures a real problem, it offers quite the wrong solution. The last thing we should want to do is hide. Rather, we should run like the shepherds to find and adore the Infant Savior, to rest always in the company of the Holy Family, and, through the intercession of the Holy Mother of God and St. Joseph her spouse, to experience the full reality of the grace of Christmas and to share it with others. Through Christ our Lord. Amen.

❧ SERMON 8

My Father's House

"SEE WHAT LOVE THE FATHER HAS BESTOWED on us that we may be called children of God...We are God's children now; what we shall be has not yet been revealed. We do know that when it is revealed we shall be like him, for we shall see him as he is." Here St. John is speaking of the divine desire that is at the heart of all the Christmas celebrations, including today's feast of the Holy Family: nothing less than God's desire to share the communion of Trinitarian life with us. In the Incarnation Christ becomes one of us so that he can make us like himself, adopting us in the Holy Spirit as children—sons and daughters—of the Father.

Thus we sing at Christmas: "The Father's Word on high doth take / A mortal form for mortals' sake / ... He took our flesh, to man akin / In all things like us, save in sin / That he might make our mortal race / Like God and like himself by grace." St. Athanasius puts it with characteristic directness: "the Son of God became man so that we might become God"—always with the objective of making us sharers in the communion of the Father, Son, and Holy Spirit. This is what Christmas is all about.

How can we understand it? Well, we know that a shared human nature is basic to all our relationships with other people. We can't have a relationship with human nature in the abstract, can we? It is only with particular human beings that we can have such relationships. There is

no substitute for knowing and loving particular people whom we can
see, hear, address, touch, hold, and kiss. These people have names, they
have families, they live somewhere, they have ethnic and social backgrounds, and so on.

Something like this is also true of our relationship with the Triune
God. To bring us into the communion of Trinitarian life, God the Son
of God first enters into the round of human existence and thus begins to
adapt his saving action to our nature. We come to know Christ as a fellow
human, born of the Virgin Mary by the power of the Holy Spirit, like us
in all things but sin. We can hear him and see him—or at least imagine
what he might look like. He has a voice that we can listen to, and he has
arms that can embrace us. The Gospel genealogy lays out his ancestry
for us. We know that his grandparents were called Joachim and Ann,
and that Mary and Joseph are his virgin mother and his foster father. We
know that he was born in Bethlehem and lived in Palestine under Roman
rule. We know that he was Jewish and spoke Aramaic. There can be no
doubt that Jesus is a fellow human being, and yet very God.

In order to draw us into his own divine life, Christ is among us as
really and truly one of us. To be sure, we can't deny that God could have
accomplished our salvation in other ways, but given our human nature
and given his purposes known to us only by faith, to make it possible
for us to meet him and know him personally makes a lot of sense. God
adapts himself to us, always with the objective of making us his children and *thus adapting our nature to his.* For how could we share in the
communion of Trinitarian life if we were not made sharers—"partakers"—of the divine nature (cf. 2 Peter 1:4)? What the Son of God is by
nature, we become by the grace of adoption.

We can see that Jesus's social and family ties are among the circumstances of his life that significantly establish his humanity for us. He
has a family just as we do. During these Christmas days, we have been
spiritually and liturgically present with the Holy Family at his birth,
gazing with love at the infant Jesus asleep in the hay, with Mary and
Joseph at his side, with the ox and ass, with the shepherds below and
the angels above.

Today the scene shifts. It's twelve years on. Jesus has traveled with Mary and Joseph to the temple in Jerusalem for the feast of Passover—a momentous pilgrimage for him this year because the coming of adolescence initiates a period of more intense formation in the Jewish faith. It is on the return journey from Jerusalem to Nazareth that a very serious family crisis develops when Jesus appears to be lost: "The boy Jesus remained behind in Jerusalem, but his parents did not know it." We can imagine their dismay. "Thinking that he was in the caravan, they journeyed for a day and looked for him among their relatives and acquaintances, but not finding him, they returned to Jerusalem to look for him. After three days they found him in the temple, sitting in the midst of the teachers, listening to them and asking him questions, and all who heard him were astounded at his understanding and his answers."

After three days, during Passover, with the paschal mystery thus already on the horizon, Christ's first words recorded in the Gospel express his divine sonship and his dedication to his Father's will. We are deeply struck by what he has to say when for the first time we hear him speak. The dramatic circumstances of his parents' anguished search for him accentuate the absolute determination with which the twelve-year-old Jesus embraces the divine plan for our salvation. Jesus replies to Mary and Joseph: "Why were you looking for me? Did you know not know that I must be in my Father's house?" Venerable Bede is on the mark when he writes that, notwithstanding the seemingly sharp tone of this reply, Christ "does not upbraid them…for searching for their son, but he raises the eyes of their souls to appreciate what he owes him whose Eternal Father he is." When for the first time we hear God the Son of God speak, we understand that he is clearly thinking of his Father *and* clearly thinking of us. What is it that he owes to his eternal Father other than to fulfill the work of our salvation by which we come to share the divinity of Christ who humbled himself to share in our humanity?

And, my dear friends in Christ, he did indeed humble himself. "He went down with [Mary and Joseph] and came to Nazareth, and was obedient to them." For our sake, the Lord of the universe, just like an ordinary human child, was subject to his earthly parents, and thereby acknowledged their authority as sharing in the authority of his Father. "And Jesus advanced in wisdom and age and favor before God and man." During these years of his so-called hidden life before the start of his public ministry, Jesus worked with St. Joseph as a carpenter in Nazareth, living an ordinary life as a devoted son and, moreover, consecrating family life as a sign of the communion of Trinitarian love. Christ's human family is made holy by his presence in its midst. The primary lesson of the feast of the Holy Family, *as celebrated within Christmastide*, lies here. Just as the incarnate only-begotten Son of God makes his family holy, so he wants to make our families holy as well. This purpose fits with the whole economy of salvation by which he comes to share our humanity in order to accomplish something that is completely beyond our capacities, namely, that, sharing in his divinity, we become children of the Father. The feast of the Holy Family is not simply intended to present an example to be imitated or a model to be reproduced, but the possibility of Christ's transforming grace made actual in our own families. When approving the feast of the Holy Family, Pope Leo XIII wrote: "When a merciful God determined to complete the work of human reparation which the world had awaited throughout long ages, he so established and designed the whole, that from its very inception, it would show to the world the sublime pattern of a divinely constituted family. In this [Holy Family] all men should see the perfect example of domestic unity, and of all virtues and holiness." May our families be made holy by the eternal source of all created communion, the Father, Son, and Holy Spirit dwelling with us. Amen.

❧ SERMON 9

Christ Manifested to the Whole World

HAIL TO OUR LORD JESUS CHRIST, "manifested by the star / to the sages from afar," to whom we raise today "songs of thankfulness and praise." Christ today manifested to the sages from afar, and thus to the whole world, as the fulfilment of the promises made to Israel, promises that touch not only Israel and the Church, but every human heart. Christ made manifest as the unique and universal Savior of the world whom the Church today confesses, proclaims, and celebrates in this solemn mystery of the Epiphany.

In our day, we are happy to confess and celebrate but timid to proclaim this mystery. To ascribe a uniquely salvific role, *universal in scope*, to Jesus Christ seems to constitute an affront to the communities of other religious founders. According to the modern mentality, all religions express some experience of the "transcendent"—however it may be named and described. In the culture of pluralism that surrounds and to some extent even infects us, the idea prevails that no religion can claim to possess a privileged description of a reality in itself incomprehensible and ineffable to all equally, nor to afford unique access to a realm in principle available to all equally.

It must be stated forthrightly that the mystery we celebrate on Epiphany Sunday—namely, Christ's unique role as universal savior—in no way entails a devaluation of the world's religions. For one thing, as Pope Benedict XVI has often pointed out, the religions of the world are monuments to the human search for God. As such, they are worthy of respect and study because of the immense cultural richness of their witness to the desire for God planted in every human heart. But, my dear friends in Christ, the Christian faith attests not principally to the human search for God, but over and above to God's search for us. In his Epiphany homily on Friday, Pope Benedict XVI employed a striking phrase to express this when he spoke of the *"inquietudine di Dio"*— the restlessness that God has for us. No doubt, he was thinking of St. Augustine's description of us as having hearts restless for God. Pope Benedict boldly applied this idea to God, who is restless in his desire to share with us nothing less than a communion of life, a participation in the divine Trinitarian life. We may think of the star that the Wise Men followed as a kind of supernova, according to Pope Benedict, a sign of God's bursting love for us.

This is the basic starting point for understanding the unique role of Jesus Christ in the salvation of the human race. For the idea that God wants to share the communion of his life with persons who are not God cannot come from anyone but God himself. The initiative here is strictly on God's side, both to reconcile us because of sin and to make possible a kind of life that would not only be impossible for us but unthinkable as well. Salvation in this comprehensive sense is not something that can be arranged or organized by human beings. It cannot come from the created order, for the created order has neither the resources to achieve nor the imagination to conceive such a destiny for human persons.

Arians, neo-Arians, and their fellow travelers throughout history have been more than willing to acknowledge that Jesus is a savior of sorts—as if salvation were "nothing more than a minor adjustment internal to the contingent order...that one creature performs in relation to others." But given that salvation in the Christian sense of the term involves both reconciliation of sinners and the elevation of creaturely persons to a new kind of life, it cannot come from within this world.

Saviors are a dime a dozen when one fails to grasp what is really at stake in the divinely willed salvation. We need to be delivered not just from error, or suffering, or desire, or warfare, or injustice, or poverty. To understand what the Christian faith means and promises by salvation, we must grasp both the peril of the human condition as well as the glory that is human destiny in the economy of salvation.

God desires to share his life with us. If the salvation that the triune God wills for the entire human race entails communion with the Father, Son, and Holy Spirit, then the creaturely and sinful obstacles to this communion must be overcome. It has never been claimed of anyone but Jesus Christ that he could and did overcome these obstacles, and that he could and did make us sharers in his divine life. This is at the heart of our celebrations of Christmas and Epiphany. "For today you have revealed the mystery of our salvation in Christ as a light for the nations, and, when he appeared in our mortal nature, you made us new by the glory of his immortal nature" (Preface of the Epiphany of the Lord). Through Christ we are both healed of sin and raised to an adoptive participation in the life of the Blessed Trinity—and nothing less.

The obstacles to this participation in divine life are either overcome, or they are not. If they are not overcome, then Christians have nothing for which to hope, for themselves or for others. In that case, they will hawk an empty universal salvation on the highways of the world. If Christians abandon the proclamation of Christ's unique and universal mediatorship as the divine, only-begotten Son of the Father, they will have no other mediatorship with which to replace it. We need the Savior who is not just any savior.

How persons who are not now explicit believers in Christ can actually come to share in the salvation that God desires for the human race and that Christ alone makes possible is too large a topic for a sermon. It has been the object of a great deal of serious and largely fruitful theological reflection. For ourselves, however, beyond obeying Christ's command to preach the Gospel to all nations, we should not be more anxious about the salvation of those who have not yet heard it than we are about ourselves who have. Ours is the greater peril.

Nonetheless, my dear friends in Christ, if Christians—in the wholly admirable desire to be respectful of non-believers—no longer proclaim Christ's unique and universal mediatorship in making ulti-mate communion with the Blessed Trinity a real possibility for created persons, then the problem of how non-Christians can share in it is not resolved: it simply evaporates. For Christians to have a truly universal hope and confidence in the salvation of persons who are not Christians, they have to affirm the unique role of Christ in bringing this salvation about, not just for Christians but for others as well.

God gave to the "sages from afar" the grace and the joy to follow the star, to have sought and beheld this great mystery. Let us join them today, "As with joyful steps they sped / to that lowly manger bed; There to bend the knee before / him whom heav'n and earth adore," to the glory of the Father, Son, and Holy Spirit. Amen.

❧ SERMON 10

Consecrated to His Father's Service

TODAY, AT THE PRESENTATION OF THE LORD in the Temple at Jerusalem, we hear Simeon exclaim: "Master, you are now dismissing your servant in peace, according to your word; for my eyes have seen your salvation, which you have prepared in the presence of all peoples, a light for revelation to the Gentiles and for glory to your people Israel." Spoken just forty days after the Nativity of Christ in Bethlehem, these are words that could have been uttered after his crucifixion and death just as well as after his birth. For they are words that encompass the whole work of salvation—even if, when Simeon utters them, its completion still lies in the future. "This child is destined for the falling and rising of many in Israel," Simeon tells Mary his Mother, "and to be a sign that will be opposed so that the inner thoughts of many will be revealed—and a sword will pierce your own soul too" (Luke 2:30–33).

The ancient feast of the Presentation of the Lord links Christmas and Easter. At Christmas we celebrate the coming in the flesh of the only-begotten Son of God whose sacrifice for our sake we will celebrate at Easter. Just as Samuel was consecrated to the Lord—"to remain in his house forever"—by his mother Hannah, so Christ who is born of the flesh of the Blessed Virgin Mary is presented by her and by blessed Joseph her spouse to be eternally dedicated to God, "the first to open the womb" who gives his life to save those otherwise doomed to die (cf. Exodus 13:1). Taking on our nature and condition in all things but sin, the sinless High Priest will offer the perfect sacrifice that takes away the sins of the world (cf. Hebrews 2:14–18). Today Simeon hails as the Savior of the world the one who, entering for the first time into the place of sacrifice, will offer his own sacrifice on the Cross.

Simeon's words—joining the mystery of the Incarnation to the mystery of the Pasch—are uttered in the Temple, where, twelve years on, Jesus is to be found once again. He has traveled to Jerusalem with Mary and Joseph for the feast of Passover—a momentous pilgrimage for someone on the threshold of adolescence. When *for the first time we hear him speak*, we are struck by what he has to say: Christ's first words recorded in the Gospel at once express his divine sonship and his dedication to his Father's will. Of Mary and Joseph, he asks: "Why were you looking for me?"—and then, echoing the words of Hannah, he reminds them of the deep meaning of his Presentation in the Temple twelve years before—"Did you know not know that *I must be in my Father's house?*" The dramatic circumstances of his parents' anguished search for him serve to accentuate the determination—dare we not say the love?—with which the twelveyear-old Jesus embraces the divine plan for our salvation.

Thus are the words of Simeon's prophecy in effect confirmed by our Lord's own words. Consecrated to his Father's service at the Presentation in the Temple, Jesus embraces the work of our salvation that will take him from the wood of the manger to the wood of the Cross—from Bethlehem to Golgotha, and beyond, to the right hand of the Father in glory. My brothers and sisters, the salvation Christ won for us follows the same arc. Consecrated to the Father in Baptism, we are daily being transformed by sacramental grace and by the gifts of the Holy Spirit in order to become more and more like Christ whom the Father loves and in whom we are in turn loved by the Father. We "who have received a spirit of adoption" are "children of God, and if children, then heirs, heirs of God, and joint heirs with Christ—if, in fact, we suffer with him so that we may also be glorified with him." The salvation won for us by the passion, death, and resurrection of Christ consists precisely in the transformation—the configuration to Christ—that we shall undergo in order for our adoption and our participation in the life of the Blessed Trinity to be fully realized.

Today we sing of the salvation which Simeon foresees and acclaims: "Jesus, by thy presentation, / Thou, who didst for us endure, / Make us see our great salvation, / Seal us with thy promise sure. / And present us in thy glory / To thy Father, cleansed and pure."

* * *

The Feast of the Presentation is a particularly auspicious day for an episcopal ordination—the moment when a worthy priest is presented to God to be consecrated perpetually to apostolic service in his holy Church. More intensely configured to Christ by episcopal ordination, the new bishop follows him along the path from Bethlehem to Golgotha, becoming ever more closely united with him in the ministry of pastoral charity for the people of God. As Pope St. John Paul II wrote in the apostolic exhortation *Pastores Gregis*, "Each Bishop is configured to Christ in order to love the Church with the love of Christ the Bridegroom, and in order to be in the Church a minister of her unity." Because in this precious moment the bishop becomes nothing less than the instrument of Christ's saving work in the world, each one of us who participate in the episcopal ordination tomorrow evening can declare, with Simeon, "my eyes have seen your salvation, which you have prepared in the presence of all peoples, a light for revelation to the Gentiles and for glory to your people Israel." Amen.

❧ PART II ❧

Holy Week and Easter Season

❧ SERMON 11

Palm Sunday and *Passion Sunday*

P ALM SUNDAY OR PASSION SUNDAY? The fact that we use both titles for the Sunday of Holy Week actually reflects something of the history of today's festival. It seeks to combine, at the start of the week, the commemoration of Christ's triumphal entry into Jerusalem with the celebration of the events of his passion, death, and resurrection that fall on the days of the week's end. Sparing you the details of this fascinating history in which the liturgical traditions of Jerusalem and Rome have come to be intertwined, let's consider rather how this liturgical conjunction of palm and passion introduces us to the deep spiritual significance not only of Christ's role in this momentous week but also of our own place in the paschal mystery.

Christ lays aside the glory that Palm Sunday celebrates in order to take on the aspect of one condemned. For our part, at the start of the week, we can rightly acclaim his triumphant entry. For we know how this story will end and so can rejoice this morning with palms in hand. "Together let us meet Christ," writes St. Andrew of Crete, "who is going of his own accord to that holy and blessed passion to complete the mystery of our salvation." But at the end of the week? Alas, we who have rejoiced at Christ's triumphant entry will find ourselves among his accusers. For today is not just Palm Sunday, but it is also Passion Sunday.

To grasp the significance of this juxtaposition, consider the question: Who is responsible for the passion and death of Christ? On the face of things, no person, acting alone, could have brought it about. The envy of the leading Pharisees, the betrayal of Judas, the denial of Peter, the cowardly flight of the disciples, the false accusations of the Sanhedrin, the venality of Herod, the vacillation of Pilate, the mockery of the crowd, the cruelty of the soldiers, and so on—all of these *together* bring Christ to the Cross.

The narrative of Christ's Passion conveys in a dramatic mode that it was not just one sin nor the sin of just one person, but these many sins and the guilt of these many persons that brought Jesus to the Cross. The narrative recounts how the sins of all these people conspire to bring about the suffering and death of Christ, and, by implication, how all sins, including ours, are involved. The narrative may be taken to signify that *all sins* and *all persons* are complicit in this terrible deed. Christ literally *dies* under the weight of all this sin. Concentrated in this one, toxic dose, it kills him.

We who are happy to place ourselves among the crowd that acclaims his glory must not be surprised to find ourselves in the crowd that calls for his condemnation. For it is always a serious misreading of the Passion narrative either to try to assign blame to one character or group (for example, the Jews), or, even worse, to try to exempt oneself from blame. If I am not one of the blameworthy, then how can I be among those who share in the benefits of Christ's passion? This is why the Church's liturgy gives to the congregation the parts of the Passion narrative spoken by the Sanhedrin, by Judas, by Pilate, by Herod, by the crowd. It is only by seeing ourselves among the guilty that we will be able, through God's astonishing mercy, to find ourselves numbered among the forgiven and reconciled.

But there is more. The pure, the spotless, the sinless One *takes our place* here. He rides into Jerusalem fully aware of the Cross he is to embrace. He "who knew no sin" (2 Corinthians 5:21) allows himself to be judged and condemned by all the guilty *for their sake*. He never takes up his own defense. He never says—as he rightly could and as we who love him almost long for him to do—to declare, "No, you are making a mistake; I'm innocent of all these charges that have been brought against me." How could he, when it is precisely in order to take the place of sinners that he has come?

Why is this? Because in the unfolding design of the divine mercy, there is also the divine justice. God did not take the unreconciled human condition lightly, but in all seriousness. He undertook to rectify this human situation from within, through his only Son who, becoming one of us, could take our place as sinners and, making reparation for our sin, reconciled us with God. In obedience, Christ embraced this design of divine righteousness and mercy. Thus, while it is entirely true that all the actors in this drama are indeed guilty of the passion and death of Christ, they acted out a design permitted by the Father and embraced obediently and, above all else, lovingly by his Son.

Having been killed by all the sins and all the guilt, accumulating from the beginning to the end of time, the Risen Christ now stands definitively triumphant over sin and the death it inevitably brings.

The triumphant entry into Jerusalem in which we participate today anticipates the glory that will be revealed at the end. St Andrew of Crete again: "Come then, let us run with him as he presses on to his passion. Let us imitate those who have gone out to meet him, not scattering olive branches or garments or palms in his path but spreading ourselves before him as best we can, with humility of soul and upright purpose."

Palm Sunday *and*, not *or*, Passion Sunday. To understand that all sin has been crushed is very important for each who enter into these mysteries today: beholding the Risen Christ, who has died to sin but is now triumphantly alive, we know that, if all sins have been crushed, then *our sins* have surely lost their power to destroy us. This is what the Passion narrative conveys: not just some kinds of sins, nor just some people's sins, are vanquished in their power to destroy us. If we believe in him, repent, receive his forgiveness, and thus *die to our sins*, we will surely share in his Resurrection and the new life it assures—the communion of life and love that God so much desires to share with us.

✳ ✳ ✳

Dearest sisters in St. Dominic, as you begin today your first Holy Week in this new monastery, recall that the events of the passion, death, and resurrection of Christ have always evoked an intense piety in Dominican hearts—and especially those of our contemplative nuns. The names of Margaret of Hungary, Agnes of Montepulciano, and Catherine d'Ricci among others spring immediately to mind. This Dominican piety is intensely personal, characterized by a powerful desire to participate—to find one's place, as I have suggested—in this mystery. Through the intercession of his sorrowful Mother—who alone of the *dramatis personae* in the Passion had no responsibility for his death—may the grace of Christ ensure that, as every Holy Week here is marked with intense devotion, the nuns of the monastery now and in the future will ride with Christ into the glory reserved for those who have shared in his sufferings. Amen.

❧ SERMON 12

Palm Sunday: Past and Present

WITH THE LITURGY OF PALM SUNDAY, we are drawn into the most solemn week of the liturgical year when we commemorate the mysteries of Christ's Passion. These mysteries are not recalled during Holy Week simply as a series of past events. Certainly, they are that, and importantly so: In these events, things happened in Jerusalem that altered—absolutely and irreversibly—the course of history and the conditions of human existence. With the passion, death, and resurrection of Jesus, nothing could be as it had been before in the relations of the human race with the Triune God. Fittingly, the mysteries are celebrated in their proper chronological order—recounted with exquisitely reverent detail in the passion narratives of the Gospels—not as if we were in suspense as to their final outcome, but precisely in view of the triumphant Easter morning for which they form the prelude and through which we will draw joyfully from the overflowing Paschal grace.

Thus the force of these mysteries lies not merely in the past, but in the way they draw us to God and become vehicles for his grace now, today, in these days, throughout our lives—"not as things past and abolished, but as things present, living, and even eternal, from which also we have to gather a present and eternal fruit." In the celebration and contemplation of these mysteries, St. Bernard reminds us, we are drawn to God, who, though "by nature incomprehensible and unthinkable...wished to be understood, to be seen, to be thought of."

How? Through his nativity, his preaching, his prayer, his crucifixion, his death (in which he "grew pale"), his rising from the dead on the third day, his post-resurrection sojourn with his apostles, and finally his ascension into the sanctuary of heaven where he would make room for us as well. "Whatever of all this I consider, it is God I am considering," St. Bernard says, and "in all this, he is my God."

Palm Sunday is the first day of this most solemn week of the liturgical year during which we celebrate the mysteries of Christ's passion, death, and resurrection. Christ lays aside the glory that Palm Sunday celebrates in order to take on the aspect of one condemned. For our part, at the start of the week, we can rightly acclaim his triumphant entry. For we know how this story will end and so can rejoice this morning with palms in hand. "Together let us meet Christ," writes St. Andrew of Crete, "who is going of his own accord to that holy and blessed passion to complete the mystery of our salvation."

The beautiful alternate collect for Friday of the fifth week of Lent encourages us to turn to the Holy Mother of God as we enter into the celebration of these mysteries—she whom Pope John Paul II called an "incomparable model" for the contemplation of the mystery of Christ's passion. "O God, who in this season give your Church the grace to imitate devoutly the Blessed Virgin Mary in contemplating the Passion of Christ, grant, we pray, through her intercession, that we may cling more firmly each day to your only-begotten Son and come at last to the fullness of his grace" in communion with the Father, Son, and Holy Spirit. Amen.

❧ SERMON 13

God Greatly Exalted Him

IT IS NO IRONY THAT THE WEEK in which we celebrate with sorrow and tears the Passion and Death of Christ should be introduced by his triumphant entry into Jerusalem. The Church's liturgy anticipates the climax of this most solemn week that in fact ends in the victory of Christ over sin and death. Everything in between must be seen in the light of the triumph of which Palm Sunday is the foretaste and Easter Sunday the reality.

Already in the very manner of Christ's triumphant entry we can discern the central elements of the nature of the victory to come.

Mounted humbly on an ass yet welcomed as a king—"behold your king comes to you meek and riding on an ass"—Christ is "going of his own accord to that holy and blessed passion to complete the mystery of our salvation." His hour has come, and he embraces his Father's will for our salvation with determination and yet also with that precious divine condescension that characterizes these mysteries. "And so he comes, willingly taking the road to Jerusalem, he who came down from the heights for us, to raise us who lie in the depths to exaltation with him."

This combination of obedience and humility is manifest in the entry into Jerusalem as much as it is absolutely fundamental to the victory that Christ wins for us. For in his passion and death are thrown down and crushed the pride and disobedience at the heart of our downfall. "He humbled himself, becoming obedient to the point of death, even death on a cross," we heard this morning and will hear repeatedly during the liturgies of this week. "Because of this, God greatly exalted him, and bestowed on him the name which is above every name, that at the name of Jesus every knee should bend."

Whereas, in our experience, the consequences of our pride and disobedience—"our extreme lowliness"—have seemed tragically insurmountable, precisely by succumbing to them in his passion and death, Christ overcomes them in his resurrection and glory. This stunning reversal is at the heart of the story that the passion narrative recounts—and fittingly so on Palm Sunday, a day that functions as a kind of prologue to all that has, liturgically speaking, yet to transpire.

Not only does Christ overcome the consequences of our sins, but he also raises us to his own level. He becomes like us in order to make us like unto him. "Taking the form of a slave, and coming in human likeness, and found human in appearance," Christ "is pleased to come and live with us and to raise us up or bring us back to him through his kinship with us.... Because of his love for man he will not cease until he has raised man's nature from the ground, from one degree of glory to another, and has manifested it with himself on high."

We are here at the very heart of the Paschal Mystery. As we have joined our voices to the hosannas at Christ's triumphant entry into Jerusalem on this Palm Sunday—waving, as it were, "the spiritual branches of our soul"—let us now enter with a contemplative spirit into the profound silence of these days of Holy Week, praying fervently to share fully in the blessings our victorious Savior won for us by the shedding of his blood.

❧ SERMON 14

When Jesus Came to Jerusalem as a Child

As we commemorate the triumphant entry of our Lord into Jerusalem on Palm Sunday, recall that this would not have been his first visit to the city. Jesus spent much of his public life in Jerusalem—praying in the Temple, teaching, preaching, and performing miracles. But of particular significance on Palm Sunday—as we begin Holy Week—are his two childhood visits to Jerusalem.

As an infant no more than forty days old, Jesus was first brought to the Temple in Jerusalem by Mary and Joseph in observance of the Mosaic Law that prescribed the redemption and presentation of the firstborn son. "Every male that opens the womb shall be called holy to the Lord" (Exodus 13:2). To be sure, it was not strictly necessary to fulfill these obligations of the Law in the Temple itself. But for St. Luke's Gospel Christ's very first entry into the Temple is full of deep significance: He is presented to God, to whom he now belongs completely—more precisely *offered*, a term that signaled the sacrificial character of the action. With prophetic intuition, Simeon and Anna recognized this and grasped the true identity and destiny of this child.

At the time of his next recorded visit to Jerusalem Jesus was twelve years old. The Torah prescribed that every Jew should travel to the Temple for the three great feasts—Passover, Pentecost, and Tabernacles (Cf. Exodus 23:17; 34:23f.; Deuteronomy 16:16f.). Mary and Joseph piously brought Jesus to the Temple on his first Passover pilgrimage a year earlier than the prescribed age of thirteen. On their return journey, his parents were alarmed to discover that Jesus was not among the group of travelers. Unbeknownst to them, he had remained in Jerusalem, and when they returned there, they found him in discussion with the teachers in the Temple (cf. Luke 2:46). To their anguished inquiry about his behavior, Jesus replied: "Why were you searching for me? Did you not know that I must be in my Father's house?" (Luke 2:49)

It is about twenty years later now, and on Palm Sunday our Lord enters Jerusalem for the last time, not just in order to observe the Passover feast but to bring it to its completion in himself. The determination to be in his Father's house, expressed all those years before, foreshadowed the determination with which he would embrace his own Passover now. "When the days grew near for him to be taken up, he set his face to go to Jerusalem" (Luke 9:51). What was foreseen by Simeon and Anna is now to be fulfilled: "See, we are going up to Jerusalem, and everything that is written about the Son of Man by the prophets will be accomplished" (Luke 18:31).

How clearly do those earlier childhood visits to the Temple in Jerusalem point to the deepest meaning of Christ's entry into Jerusalem on Palm Sunday *and* of the events to follow: nothing less than the consummation of all the sacrifices of the Old Covenant in his own perfect sacrifice. St. John Fisher wrote: "Jesus Christ is our high priest and his precious body is our sacrifice, which he offered on the altar of the Cross for the salvation of all men. The blood, poured out for our redemption, was not that of calves or goats, as in the old law, but the blood of the most innocent lamb, Jesus Christ our Savior."

Recalling the Suffering Servant Songs of Isaiah, Simeon had acclaimed the child he held in his arms "a light for revelation to the Gentiles and for glory to your people Israel" (Luke 2:32). Abundantly fulfilling all the expectations of the prophets about the Messiah, the passion, death, and resurrection of Christ that we celebrate in Holy Week complete what divine love had willed for us from the beginning: "First he offered sacrifice here on earth when he underwent his most bitter death. Then, clothed with the new garment of immortality he entered the holy of holies taking his own blood, that is he went to heaven; and there he showed forth before the throne of his Father that blood of great price which he had poured out seven times for all sinful men." We rejoice today that "this sacrifice is so pleasing and acceptable to God that as soon as he sees it he cannot but take pity on us immediately and show mercy to all who are repentant."

❧ Sermon 15

Exaltation Hidden in Humiliation

Today we celebrate the exaltation and humiliation of the on-ly-begotten Son of God in his humanity. For today our Lord enters Jerusalem riding on a colt. On Good Friday he will leave Jerusalem behind—indeed he will be *led out* of the city, carrying a cross.

Today's entry is triumphal. "Ride on! Ride on in majesty," we sing. For Jesus enters Jerusalem as does a king. Claiming a king's rights, he rides a requisitioned colt "on which no one has ever sat." He is welcomed by "the whole multitude of his disciples [who]...praise God aloud with joy for all the mighty deeds they had seen." As for a king, the people spread their cloaks on the road as he approaches from Mt. Olivet, and they proclaim: "Blessed is the king who comes in the name of the Lord." The triumphal entry into Jerusalem fulfills the words of the prophet Zechariah: "Rejoice greatly, O daughter Zion! Shout aloud, O daughter Jerusalem! Lo, your king comes to you; triumphant and riding on a donkey" (9:9). Our commemoration of this entry expresses its triumphal character: "All glory, laud and honor to you, Redeemer King."

Christ's triumphal entry into Jerusalem reminds us of the victory processions of the ancient world when the populace hailed the return of conquering heroes after a successful military campaign. Yet today is different. Normally, the victory parade takes place after the battle is won, but Christ's "last and fiercest strife" lies ahead. It is a battle still to be joined. Because we have been here before, we know that victory lies in the future. Our songs today anticipate the triumph of our glorious champion king. "Ride on! ride on in majesty! / Hark! all the tribes Hosanna cry; / O Savior meek, pursue thy road / with palms and scattered garments strowed. / Ride on! ride on in majesty / In lowly pomp ride on to die; / O Christ, thy triumphs now begin / o'er captive death and conquered sin."

No surprise then that, on Good Friday, our Lord's departure from Jerusalem will be an event in marked contrast to his triumphal entry. His royal title will be mocked, not celebrated. The crowd that accompanies him will be weeping rather than cheering: "A great number of people followed him, and among them were women who were beating their breasts and wailing for him" for his "last and fiercest strife is nigh." The angels "of the sky look down with sad and wondering eyes / to see the approaching sacrifice." Lament rather than rejoicing will be on display.

In the triumphal entry and the tearful leave-taking, the eyes of faith discern one continuous journey from Mt. Olivet to Mt. Calvary, and beyond to the empty tomb. For the entry into Jerusalem marks the opening scene of the final act of the drama of our salvation. He who willed to be hailed as king, for our sake willingly allows himself to be led to the place where he takes to the Cross as a king to his throne. The humiliation of his being led out of the city only *seems* to erase the exaltation of his triumphant entry. Is not his humility already revealed in his majesty—the "Savior meek" who rode into Jerusalem "in lowly pomp" on the back of a colt? And does not the humiliation of the Cross conceal the exaltation of victory, the triumph "o'er captive death and conquered sin"? "Ride on! ride on in majesty! / In lowly pomp ride on to die; / bow thy meek head to mortal pain, / Then take O God thy power and reign."

My brothers and sisters in Christ, today we celebrate the humiliation and exaltation of the only-begotten Son of God in his humanity *for our sake*. According to St. Leo, "This whole mystery…was a dispensation of mercy and act of love. With such chains are we held bound that only by this grace can we be released. Condescension by the divinity therefore becomes our advancement" unto the glory of the Blessed Trinity, Father, Son, and Holy Spirit. Amen.

❧ SERMON 16

Entering Jerusalem with Christ

INGREDIENTE DOMINO IN SANCTAM CIVITATEM. "As the Lord entered the Holy City, the children of the Hebrews proclaimed the resurrection of life, and, waving olive branches, they loudly praised the Lord: Hosanna in the highest." The procession this morning paused at the entrance of the chapel before we sang these words. Only as we crossed the threshold did we chant the antiphon *Ingrediente Domino*. Just as the Lord entered the holy city, we likewise entered the chapel bearing palms and singing the words that the Gospels attribute to the crowd on that occasion. In this way, we are able to reenact liturgically the Lord's triumphal entry into Jerusalem. We commemorate the Lord's action by repeating it.

This pattern of repetition is characteristic of the Church's liturgy. In every Mass, of course, we commemorate the Last Supper: the words of consecration repeat exactly the words spoken by our Lord at the institution of the Eucharist. But this feature of the liturgy stands out very clearly in the celebrations of Holy Week. These celebrations invite us to participate not just spiritually but physically in the events of the passion, death, and resurrection of Christ that we celebrate. Today, the procession with palms and the reading of the Passion in parts; on Holy Thursday, the washing of the feet and the procession to the place of reservation of the Blessed Sacrament; on Good Friday, the adoration of the Cross as it is gradually unveiled for our prayerful gaze and then the veneration of the Cross by each member of the congregation.

This dramatic aspect of the liturgies of Holy Week makes it easy to see how the mystery plays emerged in the medieval period. People could not resist the drama they saw in the events of Christ's life and they were eager to play the parts of the major and minor figures. The sacred liturgy of the Church is not a play, of course, no matter how exalted the subject. But we do have parts to play in it.

Consider just one of the roles we play in today's liturgy. The congregation takes the part of the crowd. On Palm Sunday, we join the exultant welcome that Christ receives upon his entry into Jerusalem. But we also join the crowd that calls for his crucifixion. It makes us very uncomfortable to recite the chilling words of the crowd in the passion narrative: "Let his blood be upon us and upon our children." Taking the part of the crowd in this way has a profound significance in the liturgy. To be sure, our sins are the cause of the crucifixion of Christ. But this is a destiny he embraces in obedience to his Father who so loves us that he wills to save us from these very sins by the death of his only-begotten Son. In effect, in our role as the crowd, we both call for his condemnation and pray for the benefits his obedient acceptance of this terrible fate occasions for us. Amazing. Thus the terrible phrase "Let his blood be upon us and upon our children" is not just an imprecation but a prayer. That his blood be poured upon us to cleanse us of our sins is precisely what we want and so desperately need.

The celebrations of Holy Week give us opportunities at every turn to participate in the celebration of the Paschal Mystery not just as onlookers but as actors in the events commemorated. We are there—albeit liturgically and sacramentally—but nonetheless really. This is a special grace of the Holy Week liturgies: so profoundly to enter into the mysteries of Christ's passion as to receive their benefits in the depths of our hearts and to imitate in our lives the pattern of the death and resurrection of Jesus Christ, our beloved Savior and Lord. Amen.

❧ SERMON 17

Every Knee Should Bend

ON PALM SUNDAY, the liturgy allows us to greet our Lord and Savior as he truly deserves to be greeted and as our love for him prompts us to do every day—triumphantly, with a procession of palms and branches, and hymns, and praise. For "at the name of Jesus every knee should bend, of those in heaven and on earth, and every tongue confess that Jesus Christ is Lord, to the glory of God the Father."

All the more so today should Christ be greeted triumphantly, when, standing at the edge of Lent and at the threshold of Easter, we enter Holy Week through the gates of Passion Sunday to join the rejoicing crowd flowing through the gates of Jerusalem singing "Hosanna—save us—Son of David!"

For he enters Jerusalem precisely in order to save us, to accomplish that astonishing plan of divine condescension by which the King of the universe takes possession of our hearts while riding on an ass. "Christ Jesus, though he was in the form of God, did not regard equality with God something to be grasped." He, to whom divinity belonged by nature, did not need to acquire his dominion by seizing it. "Rather, he emptied himself, taking the form of a slave, coming in human likeness." He emptied himself by contracting the ineffable glory of his Godhead within our small compass, taking the form of a slave but not losing the form of God, enhancing the human without diminishing the divine.

"And found in human appearance, he humbled himself, becoming obedient to the point of death, even death on a cross." He became man and willingly undertook the saving work on our behalf. It was a great thing that he became a slave, but a greater thing by far to undergo death for our sake, to be rejected and reviled on Golgotha by the very crowd that sang his praises as he entered Jerusalem. The last words spoken there are the centurion's: "Truly this was the Son of God." Today we rejoice to make them our own.

"Because of this, God highly exalted him and bestowed on him the name which is above every other name." "It is obvious that what is highest is in need of no exaltation. Only what is lowly can be lifted to an exalted state, becoming now what it was not before. Being united to the Lord the human nature is lifted up to share in his divinity. What is exalted is that which has been lifted up from lowliness."

Even as we sing our Hosannas this morning, we know that Christ's glory does not consist in his being worshiped by us. It is God the Father, to his own glory, who "highly exalted him and bestowed on him the name which is above every other name." In the words of St. Athanasius, "The glory of the Father is that the human race not only was created but was re-created when lost. It was given life again when dead.... For the powers in heaven also, the angels and archangels, worship him and now worship the Lord 'in the name of Jesus.' This joy and exaltation belongs to human beings, because the Son of God, having himself become a human being, is now worshiped. The heavenly powers are not offended when they behold all of us being led into our heavenly abode as we share in his body. This could not have happened in any other way. It happened only because, 'being in the form of God and taking the form of a slave, he humbled himself,' agreeing to assume our bodily condition 'even to death.'"

Because God has exalted our beloved Savior in his passion, death, and resurrection, we take up the eternal refrain in a special way on Palm Sunday so that "at the name of Jesus every knee should bend...in heaven and on earth, and every tongue confess that Jesus Christ is Lord, to the glory of God the Father." Amen.

❧ SERMON 18

Palms and Ashes

"At last the feast of our Lord's Passion has arrived, the feast that we have desired and the entire world has longed for." And, as always, we observe the feast of the Lord's Passion with the blessing of palms and bearing these palms in a solemn procession to commemorate our Lord's triumphal entry into Jerusalem.

Palms serve as a remarkable symbolic link uniting the season of Lent with Passiontide and Easter. At the beginning of Lent, our foreheads were marked with the ashes of the palms we had blessed on Palm Sunday a year ago, and the palms we bear today we will see again as ashes on Ash Wednesday a year from now.

The palms we bear today signal the joy we feel as we commence the liturgical celebration of the longed-for feast of the Passion of our Lord. Our celebration of his triumphant entry into Jerusalem is a liturgical anticipation of the victory to come on Good Friday and Easter Sunday. The king's triumphal entry into a city—typically, a conquered city—usually occurs *after* the victory is won. But, because faith is at work in our commemoration of these events, the liturgy replicates the scriptural order of events. The triumphal procession of our King takes place before the actual victory is accomplished. It prefigures the assured victory of the only-begotten Son of God, creator and king of the universe, over the otherwise invincible reign of sin and death.

The palms we bear today will become the ashes we receive on Ash Wednesday next year. In palms-to-ashes lies something of the deep mystery of these solemn feasts. There is hardly a square inch of territory on this earth that has not at one time or another fallen to some king or other in history. But there is one unconquered territory that has eluded all the emperors and kings of history, and that is the human heart whose sole conqueror can be Christ the King, Christ crucified, risen and seated at the right hand of the Father.

Who among us can dare to say that the Jerusalem of our hearts has been fully conquered by the crucified and risen Christ whose victory we happily celebrate today? In a real sense, our experience reflects the scriptural and liturgical sequence of events: Christ won the definitive victory over sin and death in his Passion and Resurrection, and merits to be hailed as King on Palm Sunday. But for his victory over sin and death to take hold in my heart and yours requires a lifetime of prayer and repentance for which Lent is merely a preparation. In this way, in the repeated cycle of Lent, to Passiontide, and on to Easter and Pentecost, the liturgy draws us every year into the pattern of Christ's victory: Like palms-to-ashes, we are continually dying to sin but never losing hope that we will rise with him in glory.

Over the coming months these palms will lose their green color and their pliability; they will become dry and brittle, and finally, as Ash Wednesday approaches, they will be gathered and reduced to ashes. Just so do things unfold in Holy Week. Leaving the triumphant entry into Jerusalem behind, we will soon arrive at the agony in the garden, the betrayal of Judas, the rough arrest of our Lord, a show trial before the Sanhedrin, the crowd whose joyful hosannas become a malign call for his crucifixion, the sentence of death before a reluctant Pilate, the scourging, the carrying of the Cross, the crucifixion and, finally, the death of the only-begotten Son in the flesh. Palms to ashes.

The ashes we receive on Ash Wednesday remind us that our hearts have yet to be conquered. The palms we receive today remind us that our victorious royal champion is already at the gates of our hearts. "The whole order of events that the Gospel narrative fully describes must be received by the faithful hearing it," declared St. Leo the Great, "so that by a saving faith in the actions then completed during the time of our Lord's passion, we should understand not only the forgiveness of sins to have been accomplished by Christ, but also the pattern of justice to have been set forth."

❦ SERMON 19

O Happy Fault

"O HAPPY FAULT. O necessary sin of Adam, which gained for us so great a Redeemer." Dear brothers and sisters in Christ, thus sings the soaring anthem the *Exsultet* in this solemn Easter Vigil tonight. But we must confess that these two words—"happy" and "fault"—do not seem to belong together. To what depths of faith does their juxtaposition point us? To know the answer, we must adopt a divine perspective. A daring move, no doubt, but one to which faith itself invites us. When we take the God's-eye view, what do we see?

We see that no one has ever desired anything more than God desires to share the communion of his Trinitarian love with us. This desire gave rise to a plan, a design, of grace and salvation. According to St. Irenaeus, "For those who pleased him he set down, like an architect, his plan of salvation." Astonishingly, at the very start, this divine desire was met with rejection, at Satan's prompting, on the part of the first human beings to whom it was expressed. But not the obstacle of human disobedience could thwart the plan born of God's desire to share his life with us. For already this plan embraced the steps that God—undeterred because ever-merciful—would undertake to repair the damage caused by the initial rejection of his love. "Yes, the plan of our salvation / Had to have it ordered so: / Thus the multiform deceiver's / Art by art would overthrow, / And from thence would bring the healing / Whence the harm brought by the foe."

Tonight we have heard, in the nine readings of the Easter Vigil, the key passages of Holy Scripture apart from which none of this would be intelligible. There unfolds before us the ravishing canvas of the whole history of this divine plan from the moment of creation until now. The plan includes the remedy for sin—exquisitely fashioned by the divine "art"—fit to the nature of the harm and the nature of the offenders.

There unfolds before us tonight a canvas framed at one end by the disobedience of Adam and at the other by the perfect obedience of Christ the New Adam. In the complex pattern of figuration that weaves through this canvas, Christ is always and everywhere both anticipated and present. For he is "the Passover of our salvation...present in many so as to endure many things. In Abel he was slain; in Isaac bound; in Jacob a stranger; in Joseph sold; in Moses exposed; in David persecuted; in the prophets dishonoured," and on the Cross victorious. So precious is the remedy for Adam's fault that on this night of all nights the Church has dared to call that fault a *happy* one. "O happy fault. O necessary sin of Adam, which gained for us so great a Redeemer." Tonight we celebrate our Redeemer's triumph over the sin of Adam and the numberless other sins that jeopardized but could never wreck the plan of divine love. "For Christ has ransomed us with his blood and paid for us the price of Adam's sin to the eternal Father" (*Exsultet*).

Granted that the fault is a happy one, but what sort of fault could have entailed the dire consequences for the human race which Christian revelation ascribes to it and, moreover, that required such a remedy? What sort of fault could it have been? How could God have allowed its tragic sequels, not excluding the death of his only-begotten Son? What failure on our part could have disrupted and nearly derailed the designs of divine providence?

With regard to Adam's fault, consider these mundane analogies. If, in a fit of anger I smash my friend's priceless Japanese vase, even if he forgives me, we can never make the vase whole again, and even if we are successful at repairing it, it will always be a vase that once was whole and has now been put back together. Much more serious examples come to mind. Suppose my friend tells me something in confidence, and I go off and reveal this secret to someone else. Even if he forgives me, we cannot repair the damage I have caused, if nothing else, by undermining my friend's confidence in me: he will think twice before telling me any more secrets!

From your own experience, you can multiply examples of these seemingly irreparable harms—bad things that we do or say that cause consequences that cannot be undone, even when there is genuine regret and sincere forgiveness on all sides. Now suppose that the sin of Adam—that we have become accustomed, somewhat paradoxically, to calling both the original sin *and* the happy fault—suppose that this sin was an instance of an "irreparable harm," something not susceptible of an easy fix. In order to think along these lines, we must avoid viewing the fault committed by the first human beings—whom the Book of Genesis names Adam and Eve—as merely the transgression of some arbitrary limit or the failure of some capricious test sent to them by divine whimsy.

On the contrary, we must understand that something infinitely important was at stake, and that the fault constituted an implicit rejection—traditionally named disobedience—on the part of these first human beings, of the divine invitation to share the communion of Trinitarian life. God could have but did not just make everything better on the spot. Rather, he accommodated himself to the nature of the deed and thus to the human nature of its perpetrators—"art by art would overthrow." We know from the Scriptures that he immediately undertook to remedy this otherwise irreparable harm, but it was a remedy fit to our nature and to the nature of the fault, and it would take time—a lot of time and a lot of preparation for the human race. "When mankind was estranged from him by disobedience, God our Savior made a plan for raising us from our fall and restoring us to friendship with himself." The sin of Adam and all other sin—which might have provoked only the wrath of a divine judgment and thus have been well and truly irreparable—prompted instead an act of infinite mercy in the sending of our Redeemer, prophesied and prefigured by a great line of ancestors stretching from Abraham through Moses to David, born of the Virgin Mary, for our sake crucified under Pontius Pilate, who suffered, died and was buried, and who is tonight triumphantly proclaimed and confessed to be risen again.

Not for nothing, then, has the Church dared to call this sin of Adam "a happy fault." And not for nothing does the Church celebrate these mysteries in the annual round of the sacred Liturgy from Advent to Pentecost. In this way, each one of us can learn to locate the meaning of his or her existence within the immense framework of this great plan of salvation which found a way to repair the irreparable and to save the utterly lost. According to the divine plan for our salvation, "Christ came in the flesh, he showed us the gospel way of life, he suffered, died on the Cross, was buried and rose from the dead. He did this so that we could be saved by imitation of him, and recover our original status as sons of God by adoption."

The passage of our Redeemer—His Passover or "*passio*"—from Bethlehem to Golgotha and beyond: this pattern we must continually retrace and imitate if we are to be remade in his image and thus, despite Adam's fault and, moreover, *our* faults, we may come to share in the communion which God so greatly desires to consummate with us. In the sacrament of Baptism we imitate his death by setting aside our sins, and, fortified by the Holy Eucharist and the Sacrament of Penance, in the daily struggle to follow him faithfully we beg his forgiveness and continually shake off our attachment to sin.

Dear friends in Christ, now we have the answer that comes from looking at things as God sees them. He undertook to clear away the wreckage our sins would otherwise have entailed for us by fitting the remedy to our nature—by sending a Redeemer like us in all things but sin, and yet unlike us in having the power to overcome all the obstacles to the blessed communion God desires to share with us. Not for nothing do we sing: "O happy fault.... What good would life have been to us had Christ not come as our Redeemer?"

❧ SERMON 20

Hail the God of My Salvation

"O God of my salvation, hail to thee, / O Jesus sweetest love, all hail to thee; / O venerable breast, I worship thee; / O dwelling place of love, I fly to thee, / With trembling touch, adore and worship thee." This is the opening verse of a beautiful medieval poem entitled *Salvator mundi salutare* and dedicated to the *membra Jesu nostri*, each of the seven verses being addressed to a different part of Christ's crucified body: *ad pedes, ad genua, ad manus, ad latus, ad pectus, ad cor, ad faciem* (feet, knees, hands, side, chest, heart, and head).

But tonight, in praising our Savior with the words, "O God of my salvation, hail to thee," no longer is it the Lord's crucified body that we address. It is gone from view. Where is it? The angel tells us: "I know that you are seeking the crucified Jesus, but he is not here; he has been raised just as he said." The angel even shows us: "Come!" he says, "See the place where he lay; he is not here." At once fearful and overjoyed, we hasten to tell the disciples the news. Lo and behold, Jesus meets us on our way and greets us. "O Jesus, sweetest love, all hail to thee." We approach, and, falling to our knees, we embrace his feet. Our crucified Jesus is alive. "O risen Lord: with trembling touch, we worship and adore thee," we sing to his glorified body. We pray that his glorious wounds will guard and keep us.

Knowing full well that we have reason to be frightened, Jesus reassures us, "Do not be afraid. Tell my disciples to hasten to Galilee where they will see me." He is happy to see us and eager to see his disciples. So are we. "O dwelling place of love, we fly to thee." We find the disciples and tell them. But not all of them understand. Later in the day, when two of them meet Jesus on the road to Emmaus, it is obvious that they do not recognize him, and, what is more, that they are puzzled by what we told them. "It is now the third day since our leaders handed him over to be crucified, and some women of our group have astounded us: they were at the tomb early this morning, and when they did not find his body there, they came back and told us that angels said that he was alive." Overjoyed and jubilant to see Jesus alive as we are, it turns out that there are many things we have not understood. The risen Jesus is eager to explain these things to us. He wants to tell us about all that he has done for us.

But the key is very different from that of Good Friday. There are no more accusations. No censures or reproof. The question, "what more could I have done for you?" introduces, not a lament, but an exultant demonstration of the successive wonders of his love. As on Good Friday, these wonders are recounted in song, the *Improperia* yielding now to the *Exsultet*. Not reproaches, tonight, but a jubilant Easter Proclamation. The resplendent glow of the Paschal Candle throws everything into a new light—the light of Christ which dispels all darkness, anxiety, and confusion.

The Paschal Candle stands for the risen Christ who is here—very much here—tonight. The crucified body has given way to the glorified body. Much transformed now—he appears and disappears, he is no longer subject to the restrictions of space, he enters rooms where the doors are closed, and so on—Jesus nonetheless resumes his familiar role as our Teacher. "Was it not necessary that the Messiah should suffer these things and so enter into his glory?" he asks. Then, beginning with Moses and all the prophets, he interprets for us all the things about himself that are contained in the scriptures: Genesis, Exodus, Isaiah, Baruch, Ezekiel, the Psalms, Paul, Matthew.

The passages from the Old Testament are as much about our risen Lord as those from the New. Christ teaches us tonight that he is at the center of all the events they recount. Moreover, while it is true that he speaks to us about things that happened in the past, we are not here simply to recall past events, albeit in an atmosphere of appropriate spiritual emotion. Christ is present here, and because he was present in the events we recall tonight, all these events are made present in him who has now triumphantly fulfilled all that they promised and prefigured.

"I am the Passover of your salvation," he might well say, paraphrasing a famous sermon of St. Melito of Sardis: "I was present in many so as to endure many things. In Abel I was slain; in Isaac bound; in Jacob, a stranger; in Joseph sold; in Moses exposed; in David persecuted; in the prophets dishonoured. I became incarnate of the Virgin. Not a bone of mine was broken on the tree. I was buried in the earth, but rose from the dead, and was lifted up to the heights of heaven."

In the blessing of the baptismal water the liturgical narration of these events makes them present to us here and now. The "types" of baptism recounted in the prayer of blessing—the Spirit breathing over the waters at creation, the waters of the Deluge, the parting of the waters of the Red Sea, the waters of the Jordan, and the water that flowed from the side of Christ—are fulfilled in the sacrament of Baptism whose water draws its potency, so to speak, from Christ's action in all these past events.

According to St. Leo the Great, "All that the Son of God did and taught for the reconciliation of the world is not simply known to us through the historical record of the past; we also experience it through the power of his present works."

What are his present works? In a nutshell, our salvation. Through the power of the Holy Spirit, we are transformed into his image over the course of our lifetimes as each year we traverse the arc of events from Bethlehem to Golgotha, and beyond. For the Sacrament of Baptism is completed by the Sacrament of Confirmation which brings the Holy Spirit to us in a powerful infusion of grace. Just as the Son proceeds from the Father whose love for him is the Holy Spirit, so that same Holy Spirit at work in us transforms us into the image of the Son so that we can be loved as he is loved by the Father. During this most sacred

Triduum, our paschal journey with Christ began at the table of the Last Supper. "O God of my salvation, hail to thee." From Gethsemane, we followed him to Golgotha. "O Jesus, sweetest love, all hail to thee." Now we have reached the climax of his *pasch* at the table of the Easter Vigil. We looked for the crucified Jesus at the tomb, but do not find him. Like the disciples on the road to Emmaus, we will find him here, at this table. Now he is at table with us. And at this table, he will feed us. He takes bread, blesses it, and breaks it, and gives it to us. Our eyes are opened and we recognize him. "Were not our hearts burning within us while he was opening the Scriptures to us!" we exclaim. Our crucified and risen Jesus makes himself known to us, and, more importantly, gives himself to us, in the breaking of the bread—in the expiatory sacrifice that is at the heart of our paschal communion with the Father, Son, and Holy Spirit, and with one another in them. "O risen Lord: with trembling touch, we worship and adore thee."

❧ SERMON 21

Mary Magdalen, the Apostola Apostolorum

On Easter morning, in many Orthodox and Eastern Catholic homes, family members exchange red-colored eggs with the greeting, "Cristos anesti"—"Christ is risen" to which the proper response is, "Truly he is risen!"

This tradition traces to St. Mary Magdalene. After meeting the risen Christ in the garden, legend has it that she traveled to Rome in order to proclaim the Resurrection there. Gaining an audience with Tiberius Caesar, she exclaimed to him: "Christ is risen!" According to tradition, Tiberius laughed and, pointing to an egg, declared that it was as likely that Christ rose from the dead as it would be for that egg to turn red. When Mary Magdalene touched the egg, naturally, it turned a bright red, symbolizing the grace of the Resurrection communicated through the Precious Blood of Christ. Hence the Eastern Christian tradition, where in icons St. Mary Magdalen often appears holding an egg.

The practice of coloring Easter eggs spread from the East to England during medieval times and gradually involved many highly decorated varieties and hues. In 1290, King Edward I purchased four hundred and fifty eggs to be painted and gold-leafed as Easter gifts. Perhaps the most famous decorated Easter eggs in history were those created for Tsar Alexander III in 1883 by the famous goldsmith, Pierre Fabergé—a priceless fifty-seven of which have survived. Even chocolate Easter eggs—which first appeared in Germany and France in the early

1800s—owe their beginnings to the tradition of that miraculous red egg of St. Mary Magdalen.

As we can see with our own eyes at Eastertime, the legend has been remarkably durable. And well it should be. Is it so hard to believe that Mary Magdalen really did travel to Rome to proclaim the Resurrection of Christ to the emperor Tiberius and that she made that egg turn red? As the first witness to the Resurrection, she was also the first to bear the message of the Resurrection to others. While the Synoptic Gospels each recount her presence at the tomb after the Resurrection, only St. John's Gospel reports that she went to the tomb alone at first, and in turn announced to the Apostles that she had found the tomb empty. What is more, she then encountered our risen Lord himself in the form of a caretaker or gardener. In this way, St. John's Gospel gives singular preeminence to Mary Magdalene: She is the first to see the empty tomb, the first to announce the Resurrection and the first to encounter the Risen Lord.

Thus, it came about that, already in the second century, St. Mary Magdalen received the title *apostola apostolorum* from Hippolytus—to be followed by St. Ambrose, St. Augustine, and St. Thomas Aquinas. Her special role in the proclamation of the Risen Christ gave rise to an intimate connection between St. Mary Magdalen and the Dominican friars: very early on, she became, along with St. Catherine of Alexandria (who debated pagan philosophers), co-patroness of the Order.

In our own time, both Pope Saint John Paul II and Pope Benedict XVI drew attention to the distinctive apostolic role that St. Mary Magdalen fulfilled. Pope John Paul wrote that her role as the first to see the Risen Christ "in a sense crowns all that has been said previously about Christ entrusting divine truths to women as well as men."

Pope Benedict stated that "the Gospels...tell us that the women, unlike the Twelve, did not abandon Jesus in the hour of his Passion.... Among them, Mary Magdalene stands out in particular. Not only was she present at the Passion, but she was also the first witness and herald of the Risen One.... St. Thomas Aquinas [said of her]: 'Just as a woman had announced the words of death to the first man, so also a woman was the first to announce to the Apostles the words of life....'"

For his part, in one of his daily meditations, Pope Francis draws attention to the fact that, after the departure of Peter and John, the Gospel of St. John reports that Mary Magdalen "remained at the tomb weeping." Thus, when Christ appears, she sees him through her tears. According to Pope Francis, these tears recall those with which she washed the feet of Christ as he forgave all her sins because she loved so much. It is remarkable, in the Pope's view, that she expressed her desire for forgiveness not with words but simply with tears. Now, as she remained at the tomb weeping, these tears were the medium through which she would see her Risen Lord.

Have we received the gift of tears that prepare our eyes to see the Lord? the Pope asks. There are tears of joy, but there are also tears of pain, of sorrow, of repentance. Sometimes in life, the pope says, the eyeglasses with which to see the Lord are our tears. Our understanding of the passion, death, and resurrection is expressed by the tears that, like St. Mary Magdalen's, prepare us to see the Lord. Knowing how much we, and those whom we love, and the whole wretched broken world need the redemption that Christ has brought to us—this is the knowledge, this gift of tears, turned St. Mary Magdalen into the *apostola apostolorum*.

* * *

Brothers and sisters in Christ, our final word on Easter Sunday morning cannot be about tears. It would be against tradition! If you have laughed, or at least smiled at the story of St. Mary Magdalen's red egg, we will have fulfilled a requirement for Easter sermons dating to fifteenth century Bavaria. The preacher was expected to insert amusing stories into his Easter sermon that would cause the congregation to laugh (*Ostermärlein*)—in the end, of course, without failing to draw some appropriately edifying lesson. Since this Easter laughter gave rise to abuses of the word of God (one can only imagine), it was prohibited by Pope Clement X in the seventeenth century and again in the eighteenth century by Emperor Maximilian III and the bishops of Bavaria.

Alas. Pope Benedict XVI, himself a native Bavarian, draws attention to the scriptural basis of this *risus paschalis*—the paschal laughter, as it is called: "Jesus is Isaac, who, risen from the dead, comes down from the mountain with the laughter of joy on his face. All the words of the Risen One manifest this joy—this laughter of redemption: if you see what I see and have seen...you will laugh!" Abraham's willingness to sacrifice his son together with the unanticipated divine deliverance of Isaac prefigure the redemption won for us by Christ.

Laughter—not the skeptical laughter of Tiberius but the laughter of redemption—rightly expresses the joy that we experience in the knowledge that, through Christ's death and resurrection, sin and death, suffering and sorrow, have lost their power to overcome and destroy us. "I have seen the Lord," exclaimed St. Mary Magdalen. Through tears of joy and with the laughter of redemption, let us join on this Easter morning in her jubilant salutation: *Christ is risen! Truly he is risen!*

❦ SERMON 22

Awake O Sleeper

THERE IS A NOTABLE CONTRAST BETWEEN Eastern and Western iconography of the Resurrection. In Western art, Christ is typically depicted in the very act of rising from the tomb, surrounded by prone soldiers who are either asleep, or amazed at what they are witnessing. In Eastern iconography, however, what is depicted is not the Resurrection as such, but Christ at the moment when, with his Cross, he breaks open the gates of hell and reaches out to Adam and Eve, with St. John the Baptist standing to the side. The scene is perfectly described in a passage from an ancient homily for Holy Saturday: "Truly [Christ] goes to seek out our first parent like a lost sheep; he wishes to visit those who sit in darkness and in the shadow of death. He goes to free the prisoner Adam and his fellow-prisoner Eve from their pains—He who is God and Adam's son. The Lord goes in to them holding his victorious weapon, his Cross."

Fitting, is it not, that the very first beneficiaries of Christ's triumph over sin and death should be Adam and Eve? For did we not sing last night at the Easter Vigil that it was the "happy fault" of Adam that brought us "so great a Redeemer" (*Exsultet*)? Undeterred by Adam's disobedience, God refused to let the human race wreck his plan to share his life with us. He sent his only Son to reconcile Adam and Eve, and all of us, to him so that we could again share in this marvelous gift of his grace.

The supreme delicacy of divine providence, so neatly captured in Eastern iconography—that Adam and Eve, who lost this gift, should be the first to have it restored to them—provides a profound insight both into the nature of their fault and into that of the divine remedy.

In his analysis of the nature of another fault—that of the fallen angels—St. Thomas Aquinas asks what sort of sin that could have been. Eliminating those capital sins which can be committed only by persons with bodies, he is left with the spiritual sin of pride: It is traditionally said that the sin of the fallen angels was that they wanted to be like God. But what is wrong with wanting to be like God, Aquinas asks; this seems to be an altogether admirable thing to desire. Their sin lay, he concludes, in their wanting to possess this likeness to God, not as his gift, *but as their due.*

The parable of the wicked husbandmen (Matthew 21:33–44) dramatizes just this sort of sin—by no means restricted to the angelic realm. The parable recounts the story of a landlord who sends servants to his vineyard to collect from the tenants his share of the harvest. The tenants treat the servants badly—beating, stoning, and even killing them. In the end, the landlord sends his son, thinking that the tenants will respect him. But when the tenants see the son, they say to themselves, "This is the heir; come let us kill him and get the inheritance." The situation here is one in which tenants could realistically expect to inherit the property of an absentee landlord upon the death of the last heir. Seeing the son, the tenants in this parable presume (wrongly) that the landowner is dead, and they kill the son and heir in order to get the vineyard for themselves—thus taking by violence what would eventually have been theirs as an inheritance, or, more to the point, as a kind of gift.

Here we are close to the nature of sin—not only that of the fallen angels, but also that of Adam and Eve as it is recounted in the book of Genesis. Indeed, it is precisely the Devil, in the form of the serpent, who suggests to Adam and Eve the very sin that caused his own downfall. Encouraging them to eat from the only tree in the garden which God has forbidden to them, he concludes enticingly: "For God knows that when you eat of it your eyes will be opened and you will be like God, knowing good and evil" (Genesis 3:5).

This primordial sin of wanting to take from God what could only be given as a gift is tantamount to a rejection of the gift as such, the gift that would be nothing less than a share in his own divine life. Who can have the communion of life with God as his due? Only the Father, Son, and Holy Spirit. No creaturely person—angelic or human—clearly. To become "like" God in this sense can only come as a gift.

Christian revelation teaches us that this original sin on the part of our first parents had inescapable consequences for their descendants, and that God—accommodating our salvation to the nature of the fault, and thus to our human nature—mercifully willed to take the time needed to prepare us for the coming of our "great Redeemer." At the center of the whole history of divine love is Christ who by his perfect obedience to the Father overcomes the sin and death that result from the human unwillingness to receive from God what he would willingly bestow and now graciously restores in his Son. Gazing at the icon of the Resurrection, how can we fail to be touched by the sight of Christ reaching out to Adam and Eve in an unmistakable sign of restoration and reconciliation? Already forgiven by God, they now know the nature of their sin and are happy to receive as a gift the redemption that Christ is so eager to bestow on them and on us.

On this Easter morning, we can understand that the words which the already-quoted ancient homily puts into the mouth of Christ are directed not only to Adam and Eve but also to us: "Awake, O sleeper, and arise from the dead, and Christ shall give you light. I am your God, who for your sake became your son, who for you and your descendants now speak and command with authority those in prison: Come forth, and those in darkness: Have light, and those who sleep: Rise." Driven from the land of paradise, we will be installed "no longer in paradise but on the throne of heaven.... The cherubim throne has been prepared, the bearers are ready and waiting, the bridal chamber is in order, the food is provided, the everlasting houses and rooms are in readiness, the treasures of good things have been opened; the kingdom of heaven has been prepared before the ages."

❧ SERMON 23

Gazing with Mary on the Risen Christ

THE EYES OF ALL THIS MORNING are fixed on the face of the risen Christ: Mary Magdalen's, the disciples', ours, and those of the whole Church. What about his Holy Mother's? An ancient Latin poet imagines that it was to the Blessed Virgin Mary that the Risen Christ first appeared: "Before her eyes the Lord first stood / And presented himself openly in the light, so that his good mother, / Spreading abroad the news of his great miracles, the one who was / The way by which he once came to us, might also signal his return." Pope St. John Paul II thought there might be something to this: "The Blessed Virgin too was probably a privileged witness of Christ's Resurrection, completing in this way her participation in all the essential moments of the paschal mystery." The Gospel Resurrection accounts, of course, do not report an appearance of Christ to his Mother Mary. But we do not have to take a position on this disputed question to imagine an early appearance of Christ to his Holy Mother, to hear the news of his Resurrection from her lips, and to contemplate his face through her eyes.

From the very first moment of Christ's conception, according to Pope John Paul, the "eyes of her heart were already turned to him" and thereafter her "gaze, ever filled with adoration and wonder, would never leave him." "No one has ever devoted himself to the contemplation of the face of Christ as faithfully as Mary." Why? Because "in a unique way the face of the Son belongs to Mary. It was in her womb that Christ was formed, receiving from her a human resemblance which points to an even greater spiritual closeness." The *Regina coeli* invokes precisely Mary's divine maternity to *identify* the Risen One: *Quia quem meruisti portare, Alleluia / Resurrexit sicut dixit, Alleluia.* Who has risen from the dead? The one whom she merited to bear. The "gaze of sorrow" of the *Stabat Mater* is now "transformed into a *gaze radiant with the joy of the Resurrection*" because it is from the face of the one formed in her womb that the glory of the resurrection now blazes forth.

At Christmas we sang: "O that birth forever blessed, / When the Virgin full of grace, / By the Holy Ghost conceiving, / Bore the Savior of our race; / And the Babe, the world's Redeemer, / First revealed his sacred face, / Evermore and evermore." On the morning of the Resurrection, gazing at the face of her Risen Son, Mary can still see the sacred face of her infant Son as he lay in her arms on the night of his birth. So can we, as she draws us into the depths of these mysteries. A pious Jewish maiden, Mary would have been familiar with the whole array of prophecy and tradition that foretold the identity and mission of the child who was to become the Savior of the world. She knew that "He comes to make his blessings flow / Far as the curse is found." She would have known the texts we heard at the Easter Vigil that recall the whole complex web of prefiguration and typology that render the Paschal Mystery intelligible to the eyes of faith. Christ endured every kind of suffering in those who prefigured him: "In Abel he was slain, in Isaac bound, in Jacob exiled, in Joseph sold, in Moses exposed to die… sacrificed in the Passover lamb, persecuted in David, dishonored in the prophets." Discerning all this from the beginning, with the passing years Mary came to an ever deeper knowledge of the saving mission that would climax in the crucifixion, death, and resurrection of her Son.

Surely she must have felt some premonition of the future ordeal of the Passion in the very chill and hardship of the circumstances surrounding his birth when "Earth stood hard as iron, / Water like a stone." The tradition of the Christmas song demonstrates an uncanny intuition of Mary's prophetic sense of what the future would hold for her Son.

After his death Jesus lay in Mary's arms again when she received his body as he was taken down from the Cross. Perhaps she participated in the preparation of his body for burial. As the Gospel of St. John records, Joseph of Arimathea was assisted by Nicodemus who brought aloes and myrrh, according to Jewish custom, to be folded into the white linen burial cloth. Not swaddling clothes this time, but a burial cloth instead. Perhaps at that moment Mary recalled the visit of the Wise Men from the East, the prefigured meaning of whose precious aromatic gifts could now be recognized. "Myrrh is mine, its bitter perfume / Breathes a life of gathering gloom; / Sorrowing, sighing, bleeding, dying, / Sealed in the stone cold tomb."

In Mary's gaze, the face of the infant Christ blends with the face of the suffering Christ and the face of the Risen Christ. Sharing this morning in Mary's contemplative gaze and devoutly imagining her Easter witness, we learn to celebrate the mysteries of Christ in the present tense, for their deepest meanings coexist with and interpenetrate one another. No surprise then that the feast of the Nativity should come to mind in the midst of our celebration of the Paschal Mystery.

For to hear the message of the Resurrection from Mary's lips, as it were, is to contemplate the full sweep of the *passio Christi*—from Bethlehem to Golgotha, and beyond to the right hand of the Father— to learn the meaning of these mysteries for the Church and for ourselves under her tutelage, and not only to learn about them but to receive through her intercession the powerful grace they impart. Expert in the mysteries of Christ, Mary never fails to turn our eyes to what is most important for us to see and grasp there, and "to be open to the grace which Christ won for us by the mysteries of his life, death and resurrection."

The Resurrection of Christ is in a real sense the fulfillment of the Annunciation when Mary's *fiat* opened the way to our redemption, and her own. The body of our risen Lord—the same body he offered in sacrifice on the Cross—was the body he received from Mary in the womb. What is more, Easter has made her what we hope to be as well. "Welcoming the risen Jesus, Mary is…a sign and anticipation of humanity which hopes to achieve its fulfilment through the resurrection of the dead." Our Lady is the first one to share in the resurrection of her Son, the first fruits, as it were, of Easter: Assumed into heaven and now reigning as Queen of Heaven, she anticipates the resurrection of our bodies and the life of bliss to come. How easy it is to imagine with the *Carmen Paschale* that she who was "the way by which he once came to us, might also signal his return."

At Easter, we call on Mary to rejoice—*Regina coeli, laetare*—thus "prolonging in time the 'rejoice' that the Angel addressed to her at the Annunciation." While the (probably Franciscan) author of this wonderful antiphon is unknown, there is a beautiful legend that Pope St. Gregory the Great—as he followed barefoot in procession with St. Luke's icon of Mary—heard angels singing the first lines, and added what would become the antiphon's concluding line: "*Ora pro nobis Deum, Alleluia.*"

Queen of heaven, rejoice, and pray for us to God. May God grant that through the intercession of the Blessed Virgin Mary we who this Easter morning have heard the news of the Resurrection from her lips and "who in this season have received the grace to imitate [her] devoutly in contemplating the Passion of Christ…cling more firmly each day to your only-begotten Son and come at last to the fullness of his grace. Amen"

❧ SERMON 24

Light Shines in the Darkness

THIS EASTER MORNING, we rejoice in the Resurrection of our Lord
Jesus Christ from the dead, and we behold and are the witnesses that
the light shines in the darkness and the darkness has not overcome it.
For two thousand years the Church has recalled her Risen Lord on this
day, and for nearly seventeen hundred of those years she has done so by
the solemn lighting of the Paschal candle. For this pillar of light stands
for the Risen Lord, victorious over darkness.

During Lent, we kept watch with Christ as he contended with
the powers of darkness which appear to triumph on Good Friday.
They seem to extinguish the light. The Tenebrae services capture this
moment, as one by one the candles are extinguished, until at the end
only one remains, and that last candle is carried away leaving the sanctuary and the body of the church in utter darkness to mark the seeming
victory of darkness over the light. But the light of Christ cannot be
finally extinguished. This we see at the Easter Vigil as the candle of
wax dispels the night and pierces the darkness. The light shines in the
darkness, and the darkness cannot overcome it.

But we must not think of this dualistically, as if the equally
matched forces of light and darkness were in a contest whose outcome
is as yet unknown. While it is true that during Holy Week we recapit-
ulate the conflict, the tension, the suffering, the betrayal and all that
leads to the seeming triumph of darkness over light on Good Friday,

nonetheless we already know that Christ's victory is definitive and irreversible.

The Easter celebrations invoke the very earliest verses of Genesis to underscore this point: darkness hovered over the deep, and God separated light from darkness. The panorama on which to behold the now brightly burning Paschal Candle is nothing less the entire history of creation from beginning to end—with the darkness finally dispelled by our Risen Lord. The Easter liturgy thus locates the events of Christ's passion, death, and resurrection in the broadest conceivable framework of knowledge, thought and imagination.

The victory of darkness was transitory. An ancient Church Father reminds us that, when they come for him in the Garden, the powers of darkness carry weapons, torches and lanterns. "The sons of darkness come, bearing light in their hands through which they would reveal the true light to others." But at a glance from the true Light, they drop their torches: for a brief moment, darkness falls to the ground. "In order that the Light might accomplish what it came for, the darkness gets back up. He gives the darkness power over himself. The Light permits himself to be seized by darkness." Perhaps the powers of darkness imagine that they have indeed triumphed when they behold the Son of God nailed to the Cross. Who knows whether they rejoiced or—with a premonition of their ultimate defeat—wept? We understand now that the darkness must seem to have been victorious—for otherwise how could we know that it was in fact defeated by the blazing light bursting from the tomb? "The Light permits himself to be seized by darkness, to be led away, to be hung on the Cross, to be killed, in order that, stripped of the cloud of flesh, he might restore the splendor of his majesty." We are no longer in suspense about the outcome, for with our own eyes we see the light shining in the darkness. From the very beginning of Advent—to speak in terms of the great liturgical cycle that today reaches its climax—we have known that the people who walked in darkness have seen a great light (cf. Isaiah 9:2).

But what about the struggle against the darkness in our hearts? Here the outcome does not seem to be assured. It is no surprise that the Scriptures associate darkness with sin. "The way of the wicked is like darkness" (Proverbs 4:19). Why is this? Because sin is the absence of the holiness that should be there; vice is the absence of virtue. Lust, envy, sloth, anger, pride, gluttony—these seem like positive forces in us, but in fact they are the lack of something—the absence of chastity, the absence of love for another's good, and so on. Thus, sin and vice constitute and emptiness, a blank, a kind of darkness which is the absence of light, "the gloom of sin" (*Exsultet*).

Although we experience our struggle with sin as a contest between darkness and light whose outcome is not yet clear to us, the Paschal Candle is the sign that this contest is already in principle won for us. The conquest of this darkness in us is the work of Christ. "He called you out of darkness into his own marvelous light" (1 Peter 2:9).

The struggle against our darkness is Christ's struggle before ever it becomes ours. In our struggle against sin we have not yet resisted to the point of shedding our blood (cf. Hebrews 12:4). Christ is the "pioneer" (Hebrews 12:1) in this struggle. Before we ever thought about our sins, or the harm they do us and others, or the affront they are to God, before we ever thought to repent of them and beg God's mercy and forgiveness for them—Christ had already borne them and died for them. Like the Israelites at the Red Sea who realized that "the Lord was fighting for them against the Egyptians" (Exodus 14:25), we see that the struggle against our darkness is Christ's struggle first.

Each of us was baptized with the light of the Paschal Candle shining over us, and our parents or godparents held in our stead a small candle lighted from that flame. As we renew our baptismal promises and renounce the darkness of sin this morning, we will each hold a taper lighted from the flame of the Paschal Candle. In this way, we embrace again Christ's struggle against the darkness in our hearts. Holding these tapers in our hands this morning is a way of affirming that we cannot face this darkness on our own. How foolish it would be to try! How foolish it would be to march forth against the darkness without turning to our triumphantly victorious ally, Christ, who leads us from darkness into the splendor of his own light.

It follows that we must "live as children of the light, exhibiting the fruit of the light" (Ephesians 5:8–9). In our witness to Christ, in the quality of our words, deeds, and overall demeanor, we are to be "the light of the world" (Matthew 5:14) and must "take care that the light in [us] may not be darkness" (Luke 11:35). For "if the light in you be darkness, how great is the darkness!" (Matthew 6:23) At the Easter Vigil, the Paschal Candle gradually dispels the darkness of the chapel as its flame is extended to light the tapers held by all the members of the congregation—"a fire never diminished by sharing its light." And it burns brightly still. "Once you were darkness, but now you are light in the world" (Ephesians 5:8).

"The Lord Christ, in coming into this mortal life, did not manifest his glory, but veiled it in mortal flesh. He appeared like the pillar of cloud in the desert. But when he comes at the end of the world, when all visible joys shall be taken away, then the Lord, no longer hidden under a human form, will shine in his glory and splendor like a pillar of fire. The pillar of fire burns and gives light. To burn is its power, to give light is its glory. To burn is to judge, to give light is to make clear. To burn is the punishment of the wicked, to give light is the happiness of the just."

Our Blessed Lady never in her lifetime walked in darkness. Preserved from sin by the "foreseen" merits of her Son's passion, death, and resurrection, she is the first human being apart from him ever to have dwelt entirely and uninterruptedly in the light—she the radiant "Morning Star" (Litany of Loreto), the "woman clothed with the sun" (Revelation 12:1). She stands with us this Easter morning, united with the whole glorious company of heaven depicted above, as we see with our own eyes and become the witnesses that the light shines in the darkness, and the darkness has not overcome it.

❧ Sermon 25

The Empty Tomb

Dic nobis Maria, quid vidisti in via? "Tell us, Mary, what did you see on the way?" Mary replies to us with the fullness of Christian faith in the resurrection: *Sepulchrum Christi viventis, et gloriam vidi resurgentis.* "I saw the tomb of the living Christ and the glory of his rising." The tomb is empty because Christ is alive and risen. What else did she see? *Angelicos testes* (angelic witnesses), *sudarium* (the sweat cloth) *et vestes* (the burial linens).

These are the words that the great Easter Sequence gives to Mary. But her report to Simon Peter and the other disciple, as recorded in the Gospel of John, does not yet reflect the fullness of faith in the resurrection. At first she assumes that the body of Jesus has been stolen. "They have taken the Lord from the tomb, and we do not know where they put him" (John 20:2). The tomb is empty, to be sure, not because Christ is risen, it first seems, but because there has been a grave robbery—not an uncommon occurrence. When Peter later enters the tomb, he sees "the burial clothes there, and the cloth that had covered his head, not with the burial cloths but rolled up in a separate place."

In mentioning the sweat cloth or napkin (*sudarium*) that had covered the face of the entombed Christ, and burial linens (*vestes*) that had shrouded his body, the Easter Sequence draws our attention to what Peter first saw when he entered the tomb. For St. John Chrysostom, and for many before and after him, the state of the burial linens is key to grasping the full significance of the empty tomb: if the body had been stolen, when the thieves removed it, "they would not have stripped it first, nor...would they have taken the trouble to remove the napkin and roll it up and lay it in a place by itself apart from the linens. They would have taken the body as it was." The body was buried with myrrh, "which glues linen to the body no less firmly than lead. [John] tells us this so that when you hear that the napkin lay apart from the linens, you may not endure those who say that he was stolen. For a thief would not have been so foolish as to expend so much energy on a trifling detail."

The tomb is empty because, now that he is alive and risen, Christ no longer has need of it, and he is not to be found there. "Why search for the living among the dead?" the angels want to know. "He is not here, he is risen" (cf. Luke 24:5). Christ has departed from the tomb, having shed the burial linens and having laid aside the folded *sudarium* after wiping his face. Tell us, Mary, what did you see? She saw the tomb of the living Christ (*sepulchrum Christi viventis*) and the glory of his rising (*gloriam vidi resurgentis*), and later when she entered the tomb by herself, she saw the sweat cloth and the burial linens, and the angels.

These details are significant in the emerging realization on the part of these very first witnesses that Jesus has indeed risen from the dead. When Peter and John saw the burial linens arranged in an orderly fashion (which would most likely not have been the case had the body of Jesus been stolen), they believed with true faith that Christ had risen from the dead. John saw and believed: before he saw he did not know the meaning of the scriptures, but when he saw, he believed that Christ had risen from the dead. The first witnesses of the resurrection—Mary Magdalen, Peter and John—"did not yet understand that Scripture that he had to rise from the dead," that is, *until* they saw the empty tomb and the neatly arranged burial linens. Before they had encountered the risen Christ, wrote St. Cyril of Alexandria, "they inferred his resurrection from the bundle of linen cloths, and from that time believed that he had burst the bonds of death as holy Scripture had long ago proclaimed that he would do. When, therefore, they look on these events in the light of the prophecies that turn out to be true, their faith was from that time forward rooted on a firm foundation."

For Mary Magdalen, for Simon Peter, and for John—just as surely as for us—faith in the resurrection is a divine gift. But these first witnesses have a unique role to play in the infusion of theological faith in our souls. God raised Jesus on the third day and, Peter declares, "granted that he be visible, not to all people, but to us, the witnesses chosen by God in advance, who ate and drank with him after he rose from the dead." Not only are they the first witnesses, but they have been commissioned to preach and testify that Christ "is the one appointed by God as judge of the living and the dead." It is their witness *and* proclamation that provide the divinely ordained occasion for our faith in the resurrection.

The fullness of the Christian faith in the resurrection matured and blossomed in the hearts of these first witnesses. The layers in our own faith in the resurrection are mirrored in the sequence of discoveries and encounters in their experience of the risen Christ, as we hear them recounted in the resurrection narratives each Eastertide. For, just as he opened theirs, so also does God open our eyes to see and hearts to embrace "each and every event that happened to our Savior [as] an outward sign of the mystery of our redemption."

We understand, according to Pope Benedict XVI, that "the proclamation of the resurrection would have been impossible if anyone had been able to point to a body lying in the grave." But not just the empty tomb, there is also the orderly arrangement of the burial linens left behind. This was the experience of Mary, Peter and John, and now it is ours. For the faith in the resurrection to have a basis, the tomb certainly could not *not* have been empty. But not just the empty tomb, there also are the appearances. Neither alone are sufficient. Yet, then as now, it is not uncommon to believe that the spirits of the dead linger for a few days after death and can be encountered in some way. But Jesus does not appear as a ghost. Now risen from the dead, he is encountered as a truly embodied person who could be seen and touched, who could eat and drink. His risen body is transformed, but it is the same body that suffered and died; with the wounds and the pierced hands and feet still visible. And so on. Each separate experience and event, wrote St. Thomas Aquinas, "would not suffice by itself for showing perfectly Christ's resurrection, yet taken collectively establish it completely, especially owing to the testimonies of Scripture, the sayings of the angels, and even Christ's own assertions supported by miracles."

If Christ is truly risen from the dead, then sin and death are most surely vanquished. *Mors et vita duello / conflixere mirando* (death and life contended in a stunning battle): *Dux vitae mortuit regnat vivus* (the Prince of life who died reigns alive). He truly died and rose again. Otherwise how would we know that death is conquered? For Aquinas, the lapse of time between between his death and resurrection demonstrates this. "If he had risen immediately after death, it would have seemed that his death had not actually taken place, and so too his resurrection. To show that it was a genuine death, a prolongation of three days was sufficient, for during this period a man who [merely] appeared to be dead but was alive, would [inevitably] show signs of life." With Christ we have died to our sins and our lives are hidden with Christ in God. *Agnus redemit oves* (the lamb has redeemed the sheep): *Christus innocens Patri / reconciliavit peccatores* (the innocent Christ has reconciled sinners to the Father). Jesus is victorious over the sin to which he succumbed in death on the Cross. And so, dear friends in Christ, the fullness of our faith in the resurrection makes it possible for us to say with Peter and John and Mary Magdalen and all the Christian faithful: *Scimus Christum surrexisse / A mortuis vere* (we know that Christ is truly risen from the dead): *Tu nobis, victor Rex, miserere* (victorious King, have mercy on us). Amen. Alleluia.

❧ SERMON 26

The Sacrament of Divine Mercy

At the very first Sunday Angelus of his pontificate, Pope Francis spoke of the divine mercy: "God's face is the face of a merciful Father who is always patient," he said. "God never ever tires of forgiving us! ... The problem is that we ourselves tire, we do not want to ask, we grow weary of asking for forgiveness. He never tires of forgiving, but at times we get tired of asking for forgiveness. Let us never tire, let us never tire! He is the loving Father who always pardons, who has that heart of mercy for us all."

The Holy Father's description of the divine mercy is very concrete. God is merciful and patient, waiting for us to approach him and ask for pardon. This waiting on his part is tireless, but our approach can be delayed, hesitant, or even reluctant. We weary of asking but, fortunately for us, God never tires of waiting.

Now, to be sure, we can turn to God at any moment of our lives to ask for his pardon with the assurance that he will hear us. Still, with respect to his mercy, God has not left the burden solely on us. He has taken the initiative here in a striking manner to give a sacramental form to his mercy, putting it at our disposal in a tangible way. This point is of the greatest importance. As the Holy Father implies, God patiently waits for us in a concrete way in the Sacrament of Penance, a sacrament that might well and truly be called the "Sacrament of Divine Mercy." In faith, we can affirm with all seriousness that he patiently waits for us in the confessional where we can outwardly express our need for his forgiveness and, what is more, where he can address his words of mercy directly to us through the priest who speaks in the power of his only-begotten Son.

To understand better why this is so important, consider the encounter between Christ and Thomas in today's gospel. Having been absent when Jesus first appeared to the apostles, Thomas refused to believe their report of this visit. But the following week, when "Jesus came, although the doors were locked, and stood in their midst and said, 'Peace be with you,'" he immediately turned to Thomas and said, "'Put your finger here and see my hands, and bring your hand and put it into my side, and do not be unbelieving, but believe.' Thomas answered and said to him, 'My Lord and my God!'" Our Lord confronted Thomas's reluctance to believe very directly. He presented himself, indeed his very body—the nail marks in his hands and the wound in his side—so that Thomas could actually touch them.

We might well compare Thomas's unbelief with our reluctance and hesitation to ask for God's mercy when we need it. Christ meets Thomas's unbelief head-on by presenting himself in person. In the Sacrament of Penance Christ presents himself sacramentally to us in the person of the priest confessor who speaks and acts, as the Church declares, *in persona Christi*. It is to Christ that we confess our sins, and it is from Christ that we receive mercy and pardon. Just as the gift of faith is imparted to Thomas in the context of a direct personal encounter with Christ, so is the gift of divine mercy granted to us in a sacramental encounter with Christ who, hearing our sins, our sorrow for them, and our firm purpose of amendment, forgives and fortifies us in his grace.

In what is itself an act of mercy, accommodated to our human nature, God has given a sacramental and thus tangible form to the bestowal of his mercy. Not only can we express our need for divine mercy in private prayer—hoping that it will be heard—but God has instituted a sacramental form through which to impart his mercy so that, by a sacred ritual comprised of words and gestures, we may speak to him with unqualified assurance *and*, very importantly, he can speak to us.

There are thus two sides to the encounter of the Sacrament of Mercy. Pope John Paul II writes: "In faithfully observing the centuries-old practice of the Sacrament of Penance—the practice of individual confession, with a personal act of sorrow and the intention to amend and make satisfaction—the Church is...defending the human soul's individual right: man's right to a more personal encounter with the crucified forgiving Christ, with Christ saying, through the minister of the sacrament of Reconciliation: 'Your sins are forgiven'; 'Go, and do not sin again.'" Not only has the penitent the right to encounter Christ and receive the divine mercy directly from him. But, John Paul II continues, "this is also a right on Christ's part with regard to every human being redeemed by him: his right to meet each one of us in that key moment in the soul's life constituted by the moment of conversion and forgiveness."

The penitent's right to this personal encounter with Christ in the Sacrament of Divine Mercy cannot be compromised by reducing the reception of this sacrament to the occasions of communal penance services twice a year at Advent and Lent when there is little time for a proper examination of conscience or for anything more than a hasty confession of a few sins. As John Paul II writes: "Although participation by the fraternal community of the faithful in the penitential celebration is a great help for the act of personal conversion, nevertheless, in the final analysis, it is necessary that in this act there should be a pronouncement by the individual himself with the whole depth of his conscience and with the whole of his sense of guilt and of trust in God..." The full experience of the divine mercy in its sacramental form demands a discipline of frequent and regular confession in which one can reflect with a recollected heart on one's failings and the need for true conversion. How can one fully relish the richness of the divine mercy on the run?

But the Sacrament of Divine Mercy is a two-sided encounter. We tend to think of this sacrament mostly from our point of view. Mary

Gauthier's wonderful song "Mercy Now" expresses this well: "We could all use a little mercy now / I know we don't deserve it / But we need it anyhow / We hang in the balance / Dangle 'tween hell and hallowed ground / Every single one of us could use a little mercy now."

We all *do* need some mercy now, but—and do not ever forget this—God wants to give us some mercy now, if only we would ask. In a real sense, as John Paul II suggests, God "needs" us to ask. Our experience tells us why this must be so. If someone insults you, or offends you in some way, you may want to forgive the person in question, but that is very hard to do if they do not apologize and ask for your forgiveness. The situation in the Sacrament of Divine Mercy is not so different. As Pope Francis put it so aptly, "God's face is the face of a merciful Father who is always patient.... The problem is that we ourselves tire, we do not want to ask, we grow weary of asking for forgiveness." God is patiently waiting in the confessional to make us a gift of his mercy. We must not keep him waiting any longer.

The Sacrament of Divine Mercy—won for us by Christ in the events of the passion, death, and resurrection that we have celebrated in this Easter Season—is the concrete expression in space and time of the condescension and forbearance by which God looks with merciful forgiveness on our sins and the sins of the whole world. On this Divine Mercy Sunday, we must resolve to take advantage of this great sacrament, giving thanks "to the Lord for he is good, for his mercy endures forever." Amen.

❧ SERMON 27

The Triumph of Paschal Grace and Divine Mercy

T ODAY WE HAVE TWO NEW SAINTS: Pope St. John XXIII and Pope St. John Paul II. Their canonization has fittingly taken place on the Octave Day of Easter on which we celebrate Divine Mercy Sunday: their holy lives manifest the triumph of the divine mercy over sin and death, as does all holiness in human beings—not to mention the heroic virtue of canonized saints. We see at work in the lives of these two new saints the particular paschal grace, won for us by the passion, death, and resurrection of Christ, by which we are reconciled with the Father and made partakers of the divine life of the Blessed Trinity. We see as well the pouring forth of the divine mercy by which the sins of those who truly repent are forgiven and a share in the divine holiness is bestowed on us. Without this paschal grace and the abundant divine mercy it unlocks, there would be no saints, canonized or otherwise.

The holiness of these two great saints is manifest to the whole world—Pope John XXIII whom the Italians called "*il Papa Buono*" and Pope John Paul II at whose funeral Mass the crowd shouted "*santo subito!*" This is not the time or the place to recount the details of their lives, the rough lines of which we are all in any case more or less familiar with. Rather at this Holy Mass we want to give fervent thanks to God for granting us the example and teaching of these extraordinary popes whose heroic virtue was today recognized and proclaimed by the

Church, calling us, as Pope Benedict XVI said, "to rejoice with the entire community of believers in the certainty that thanks to the solemn Pontifical proclamation...[they have] attained God's glory."

To be sure, we want to honor Pope St. John and Pope St. John Paul today. But if either of them were standing in this pulpit this noonday, without question, they would entreat us rather to give glory to God who caused his Easter grace and his divine mercy to blossom in such a stunning way in their lives of perfect love. What is more, they would remind us that this grace and mercy are at work in our lives as well. "Blessed be the God and Father of our Lord Jesus Christ, who in his great mercy gave us a new birth to a living hope through the resurrection of Jesus Christ from the dead, to an inheritance that is imperishable, undefiled, and unfading, kept in heaven for you who by the power of God are safeguarded through faith, to a salvation that is ready to be revealed in the final time."

Our new saints would want me to remind ourselves of this today. In one of his greatest encyclicals, *Veritatis Splendor*, St. John Paul wrote that the "vocation to perfect love is not restricted to a small group of individuals" but to all the followers of Christ. The heroic virtue and outstanding holiness of these and other saints—our admiration of their goodness, our desire to venerate them properly, our dependence on their intercession and help, our reliance on their wise teachings—must never deflect our attention from the universal call to holiness. We make statues of the saints, and build niches for them in our churches and set aside shelves for them in our homes. All well and good. But we must avoid the temptation to, as it were, "shelve" our vocation to holiness at the same time, as if holiness were beyond us. The saints are given to us not only for our veneration but also and all the more so for our imitation. While most of us feel that our virtue is far from heroic and our holiness anything but outstanding, we must remember that God wants us all to be saints. His Easter grace and his abundant mercy are at work in the souls of each one of us here, drawing us to that "single and indivisible charity, which spontaneously tends towards that perfection whose measure is God alone."

If we dare to look at our lives as God sees them, we must acknowledge that we can discern many instances of his grace and mercy at work within us. When we avoid the pull of a powerful temptation, when we resist the urge to utter a harsh word, when we contain the anger that wells up in us from time to time, when we share our bounty with the poor or needy, when we inconvenience ourselves to help a friend, when we repent sincerely and confess our sins in the Sacrament of Penance—in these and countless other moments of our lives, the Easter grace and the divine mercy that flows from it are at work moving us steadily on the path to holiness and the perfection of charity.

The vocation to perfect charity—"to be perfect as your heavenly Father is perfect" (Matthew 5:48)—is that to which God calls each one of us, not just the canonized saints but every follower of Christ. No matter how imperfect we may seem to be in our own judgment, God sees us on the way to perfect union with him and with one another in him.

This is what God wants for all of us. It is no exaggeration to say that no one has ever wanted anything as much as God desires to share with us the perfect love of his own Trinitarian life. To be sure, God does not need our company. The Father, the Son, and the Holy Spirit are supremely content, we might say, with their own company. Their divine personal communion is complete, perfect, and happy. In more than one passage of his great work *Against Heresies*, St. Irenaeus makes this point very clearly: "God has no need of man." And again: "God who has no need of anyone gives communion with himself to those who need him."

This is a great mystery: The Father, the Son, and the Holy Spirit—despite being perfectly content with their own company—in their superabundant mercy, want to create a space in their communion for us, for creaturely persons. Listen again to St. Irenaeus: "These gifts make man glorious, giving him what he lacks: friendship with God."

This "imperishable, undefiled, and unfading" destiny Christ has revealed to us, and we believe him. As he says to Thomas, "Blessed are those who have not seen and have believed" (John 20:29). But not only has he revealed it to us, he makes it possible for us to attain this destiny.

Only he, the only-begotten Son, participates in this communion of Trinitarian life "by nature." Already, by Baptism, he draws us into the divine life by adoption: through our transformation in his image, Christ makes us capable of sharing in the divine life of the Trinity. "See what love the Father has bestowed on us that we may be called children of God" (1 John 3:1). With his own body and blood as our food and drink in the Eucharist, he shares the communion of his life with us, and makes us one with the Father and the Holy Spirit. Not for nothing does the Church call this sacramental participation in the Body and Blood of Christ "holy communion."

But this is not all. "The heralds of the truth and ministers of divine grace, who have explained to us from the beginning right down to our own time each in his own day the saving will of God, say that nothing is so dear and loved by him as when men turn to him with true repentance." Through the obedience and sacrificial death of his only-begotten Son, God in his great mercy overcame the disobedience and corruption that would have prevented us from enjoying the holy life of the Blessed Trinity. In Penance and the Holy Eucharist, our repentance makes us partakers in the sacrificial offering that redeems us from our sins and reconciles us to God.

My dear friends in Christ, the Easter grace and divine mercy that triumphed in the lives of St. John XXIII and St. John Paul will be victorious in us as well and will make us saints. Unbelievable? I don't think so. "Although you have not seen him you love him; even though you do not see him now yet believe in him, you rejoice with an indescribable and glorious joy, as you attain the goal of your faith, the salvation of your souls."

❧ SERMON 28

Divine Mercy: An Easter Gift to the Church

THIS YEAR MARKS THE FIFTEENTH ANNIVERSARY of the first universal celebration of Divine Mercy Sunday by Pope St. John Paul II in 2001. "Divine Mercy!" he exclaimed that morning in St. Peter's Square, "Divine Mercy! This is the Easter gift that the Church receives from the risen Christ and offers to humanity at the dawn of the third millennium."

In these years, we have come to experience the final day of the Octave of Easter—the Second Sunday of Easter—as a day particularly well-suited to the solemn celebration of gift of divine mercy. For, as Pope John Paul declared, divine mercy is truly an Easter gift to the Church. What happens on the very day when Christ rose from the dead, in his very first appearance to the disciples: what are his first words to them? "Peace be with you," he says twice. And then? "As the Father has sent me, so I send you. When he had said this, he breathed on them and said to them, 'Receive the Holy Spirit. Whose sins you forgive are forgiven them, and whose sins you retain are retained.'" Pope John Paul could say that divine mercy is an Easter gift because the risen Christ's first concrete action is to establish the holy Sacrament of Mercy. Christ gives to his disciples the power to forgive sins.

This first gift of Easter is itself an act of mercy. God has given a sacramental and thus tangible form to the bestowal of his mercy. He fits his gift of mercy to our human nature. Not only can we express our need for divine mercy in private prayer—hoping that it will be heard—but God has instituted a sacramental form through which to impart his mercy so that, by a sacred ritual comprised of words and gestures, we may speak to him with unqualified assurance *and*, very importantly, he can speak to us.

In the Sacrament of Penance Christ presents himself sacramentally to us in the person of the priest confessor who speaks and acts, as the Church declares, *in persona Christi*. It is to Christ that we confess our sins, and it is from Christ that we receive mercy and pardon. Just as the gift of faith is imparted to Thomas in the context of a direct personal encounter with Christ, so is the gift of divine mercy granted to us in a sacramental encounter with Christ who, hearing our sins, our sorrow for them, and our firm purpose of amendment, forgives and fortifies us in his grace. Recall that Thomas was absent when Jesus first appeared to the apostles, and he refused to believe their report of this visit. But the following week, when Christ again appears to the disciples, he speaks directly to Thomas: "'Put your finger here and see my hands, and bring your hand and put it into my side, and do not be unbelieving, but believe.' Thomas answered and said to him, 'My Lord and my God!'" Our Lord confronted Thomas's reluctance to believe very directly. He presented himself, indeed his very body—the nail marks in his hands and the wound in his side—so that Thomas could actually touch them.

Confession is just like this. As Christ meets Thomas's unbelief head-on by presenting himself to him in person, so he wants to encounter us directly when we seek his mercy. Pope St. John Paul wrote that in "the practice of individual confession, with a personal act of sorrow and the intention to amend and make satisfaction, the Church is... defending...man's right to a more personal encounter with the crucified forgiving Christ, with Christ saying, through the minister of the sacrament of Reconciliation: 'Your sins are forgiven'; 'Go, and do not sin again'." Not only has the penitent the right to encounter Christ and receive the divine mercy directly from him. But, Pope John Paul continued, it is also Christ's right "to meet each one of us in that key moment in the soul's life constituted by the moment of conversion and forgiveness." Just as Christ desires to address Thomas's unbelief directly to bestow upon him the gift of faith, so he desires to meet us to grant the great gift of his forgiveness and mercy in the Sacrament of Penance.

Sometimes, though, rather than seek out the grace of the Sacrament of Mercy, we may prefer to remain behind locked doors. As Pope Francis said in his homily on Ash Wednesday this year: "There may be a few obstacles, which close the door of the heart. There is the temptation to lock the doors, or to live with our sin, minimizing it, always justifying it, thinking we are no worse than others; this, however, is how the locks of the soul are closed and we remain shut inside, prisoners of evil. Another obstacle is the *shame of opening* the secret door of the heart.... There is a third pitfall, that of *distancing ourselves from the door*: it happens when we hide in our misery, when we ruminate constantly, connecting it to negative things, until sinking into the darkest repositories of the soul." But locked doors do not restrict Christ's entry into our hearts. "Jesus came, although the doors were locked, and stood in their midst and said, 'Peace be with you.'" To quote Pope Francis again: "The Lord's grace alone frees us. Therefore let us be reconciled, let us listen to Jesus who says to those who are weary and oppressed: 'Come to me' (Matthew 11:28). Not to dwell within themselves, but to go to him! Comfort and peace are there."

The Sacrament of Divine Mercy—won for us by the passion, death, and resurrection of Christ that we have celebrated in this Easter Season—is the concrete expression in space and time of the condescension and forbearance by which God looks with merciful forgiveness on our sins and the sins of the whole world. The fifteenth anniversary of the universal celebration of Divine Mercy Sunday falls this year during the Jubilee of Mercy. We must resolve to take advantage of the great Sacrament of Mercy during this year of grace, giving thanks "to the Lord for he is good, for his mercy endures forever." Amen.

❧ SERMON 29

The Saga of Divine Mercy

As THE EASTER OCTAVE DRAWS TO A CLOSE TODAY, it is fitting that the sacred liturgy should focus explicitly on the theme of the divine mercy that runs through the whole season of Lent and especially Holy Week and Easter. The great saga of divine mercy—the mercy poured out for us in the passion, death, and resurrection of Christ—is at the heart of the Pascal Mystery. Rightly does the Lord Jesus gently reproach us on Good Friday: "My people, what have I done to you? Or how have I grieved you? Answer me.... What more should I have done for you and have not done?" Of course, the answer is that nothing more could be done for us than that the Father has sent his only-begotten Son to die for our sake. This is the greatest act of divine mercy absolutely speaking. By God's grace then, my brothers and sisters, grasp and understand in what font you have been baptized, by whose Spirit you have been reborn, and by whose blood you have been redeemed. "What more should I have done for you and have not done?"

Yet, amazingly, he does do more: His mercy is without end, mercy upon mercy. Just consider the two appearances of Christ to his disciples after the resurrection recounted in today's Gospel. These appearances are replete with gestures of divine mercy in our regard. "Jesus did not let a single day pass," before he hastened to join them in the locked room to strengthen their faith. He came on the evening of the first day. "He showed them his hands and his side. The disciples rejoiced when they saw the Lord." In his mercy Christ "resolved...to appear once more as he had been in the past so that they might realize he was wearing no other form than the one in which he had suffered crucifixion." "For the healing of doubting hearts, the marks of the wounds were still preserved."

Our Lord shows yet more mercy, for in his providence, he wants to fortify the faith of those who would come after the disciples—you and me. "Although you have not seen him you love him; even though you do not see him now yet believe in him, you rejoice with an indescribable and glorious joy, as you attain the goal of your faith, the salvation of your souls." As Pope St Gregory the Great said in an Easter sermon: "It was not an accident that [Thomas] was not present [when our Lord first appeared to his apostles]. The divine mercy ordained that the doubting disciple should, by feeling in his Master the wounds of the flesh, heal in us the wounds of unbelief. The unbelief of Thomas is more profitable to our faith than the belief of the other apostles." "Thomas doesn't simply desire to see the Lord, but looks for the marks of the nails, that is, the wounds in his body. Then he would agree to believe with the rest that Christ had indeed risen again, and risen in the flesh." Christ "offers to the doubters' eyes the marks of the Cross that remained in his hands and feet, and invites them to handle him with careful scrutiny. He does this because the traces of the nails and spear had been retained to heal the wounds of unbelieving hearts, so that not with wavering faith but with the most certain conviction they might comprehend that the nature that had been laid in the sepulcher was to sit on the throne of God the Father." As if to confirm his merciful purpose to ensure and strengthen the faith of those who would come after the disciples, Christ declares to Thomas: "Have you come to believe because you have seen me? Blessed are those who have not seen and have believed."

And then, words of mercy are the first words that Jesus addresses to the gathered disciples. When he came and stood in their midst, twice on the very day of his resurrection and then again eight days later he says: "Peace be with you." Before he gives them the power of releasing others from their bonds, he desires in his mercy to give them peace of mind concerning themselves.

The disciples would surely have been troubled by the memory of their failures during the passion and crucifixion of their Master. One denied him, others fled, Thomas doubted, all forsake him. By his gift of peace Christ grants them forgiveness for these transgressions. Thus the divine mercy is first directed to the apostles themselves. "'Peace be with you,'" he said, "'As the Father has sent me, so I send you.' And when he had said this he breathed on them and said to them, 'Receive the Holy Spirit.'" In his Commentary on the Gospel of John, St. Cyril of Alexandria wrote: "By promising his Spirit to them through the outward sign of his breath, [he wants to show] that the Holy Spirit is not alien to the Son but consubstantial with him and through him proceeding from the Father." What is more, continues Cyril, "he shows that the gift of the Holy Spirit necessarily attends those who are ordained by him to be apostles of God.... Transforming them into something other than they were before, Jesus consecrates them by actual sanctification, making them partakers in his nature, through participation in the Spirit and in a sort of strengthening of the nature of humanity into a power and glory that is superhuman."

But there is yet more mercy to be shown to us. Consider this: Christ provides for all those who would come after the apostles, through them and through their successors, the supreme sacrament of divine mercy: "Peace be with you.... Receive the Holy Spirit. Whose sins you forgive are forgiven them, and whose sins you retain are retained." Thus, into the repentant hearts of those who confess their sins and ask for forgiveness in the Sacrament of Penance, there comes the peace and comfort of Christ's mercy.

He gently asks us today "My people: What more should I have done for you and have not done?" In reply, we want to say: Yes, dear Lord, you have indeed done enough, but continue to do more. "Blessed be the God and Father of our Lord Jesus Christ, who in his great mercy gave us a new birth to a living hope through the resurrection of Jesus

Christ from the dead, to an inheritance that is imperishable, undefiled, and unfading."

❧ SERMON 30

The Fountain of Divine Mercy

For NEARLY TWENTY YEARS NOW, the Church has celebrated Divine Mercy Sunday on the Second Sunday of Easter. Few people realize that it was our Lord himself who desired that this should be so. St. Faustina records these words in her diary: "My daughter, tell the whole world about My inconceivable mercy. I desire that the Feast of Mercy be a refuge and shelter for all souls, and especially for poor sinners. On that day the very depths of My tender mercy are open. I pour out a whole ocean of graces upon those souls who approach the fount of My mercy. The soul that will go to Confession and receive Holy Communion shall obtain complete forgiveness of sins and punishment. On that day all the divine floodgates through which grace flow are opened. Let no soul fear to draw near to Me, even though its sins be as scarlet. My mercy is so great that no mind, be it of man or of angel, will be able to fathom it throughout all eternity. Everything that exists has come forth from the very depths of My most tender mercy. Every soul in its relation to Me will contemplate My love and mercy throughout eternity. The Feast of Mercy emerged from My very depths of tenderness. It is My desire that it be solemnly celebrated on the first Sunday after Easter. Humanity will not have peace until it turns to the Fount of My Mercy."

In his homily on Divine Mercy Sunday in 2001, Pope St. John Paul II exclaimed: "Divine Mercy! This is the Easter gift that the Church receives from the risen Christ and offers to humanity." The image of the Divine Mercy is itself in real sense an Easter image. The two rays of light that extend brightly from the heart of Christ, as St. Faustina's diary explains, "denote Blood and Water. The pale ray stands for the Water which makes souls righteous. The red ray stands for the Blood which is the life of souls... These two rays issued forth from the very depths of My tender mercy when My Agonized Heart was opened by a lance on the Cross."

On Good Friday, after Christ's side was pierced with a lance, "there came forth water and blood" (John 19:34). According to St. John Chrysostom: "Not without purpose or by chance did these fountains spring forth. Rather, it is because the church consists of these two together. And those who have been initiated know this, being regenerated indeed by water and nourished by blood and flesh. And so, the mysteries take their beginning." And Pope Benedict XVI writes: "From the Lord's pierced Heart proceeds the life-giving stream of the sacraments; the grain of wheat, dying, becomes the new ear, carrying the fruit of the Church forward through the ages." "This is the one who came through water and blood, Jesus Christ, not by water only" (1 John 5:6).

Given the enormous power of the flow of blood and water from the pierced side of Christ, it is even more remarkable that our Lord should invite Thomas the Apostle to place his hand precisely there: "Bring your hand and put it into my side." An ancient Christian poet marvels at this: "Who protected the hand of the disciple which was not melted / At the time that he approached the fiery side of the Lord? How could a right hand of clay have touched / Sufferings which had shaken Heaven and earth? ... For, though his hand was perishable...it was not burned / When it touched the side which was like burning flame." But it was precisely here that Thomas had to put his hand so that he might believe. It was precisely in this way that the infinite love and mercy of Christ would touch Thomas in the depths of his being. "Doubting Thomas, who needs to be able to see and touch before he can believe, puts his hand into the Lord's open side; in touching, he recognizes what is beyond touch and yet does actually touch it; he beholds the invisible and yet really sees it: 'My Lord and my God.'"

The sacramental grace that flows from the heart of Christ is a gift of the Divine Mercy that comes to us at Easter. "All of us are Thomas unbelieving; but, like him, all of us can touch the exposed Heart of Jesus and thus touch and behold the Logos himself. So, with our hands and eyes fixed upon this Heart, we can attain to the confession of faith. 'My Lord and My God.'" This happens to us through the sacraments. "The blood and water that flowed from the pierced side of Jesus are types of Baptism and the Eucharist, the sacraments of new life." "So where were you baptized, see where Baptism comes from, if not from the Cross of Christ, from his death. There is the whole mystery; he died for you. In him you are redeemed, in him you are saved." The Easter grace has come into our hearts as well. And just as he appeared to the apostles, "Christ visits us and appears to us all, both invisibly as God and visibly in the body. He allows us to touch his holy flesh and gives it to us. For through the grace of God we are admitted to partake of the blessed Eucharist, receiving Christ into our hands, to the intent that we may firmly believe that he did in truth raise up the temple of his body."

The fountain of mercy that flows from the heart of Christ touches every one of us, just as it touched the apostle Thomas and caused him to believe. We must understand that all of us are invited to touch the side of Christ and in turn to be touched in the depths of our being by his grace, just as Thomas was. Christ's mercy washes us clean, forgives us, feeds us, heals us and restores us. On this feast of the Divine Mercy, we give glory and praise to him. "At the Lamb's high feast, we sing / Praise to our victorious King / Who has washed us in the tide / Flowing from his pierced side ... Where the Paschal blood is poured / Death's dark angel sheathes his sword... Mighty victim from the sky, / Powers of hell beneath you lie; / Death is conquered in the fight, / You have brought us light and life."

❧ SERMON 31

The Wounds of Jesus Are Wounds of Mercy

OUR LORD ROSE IN HIS TRUE HUMAN BODY, bearing the wounds of his passion. When, in his great mercy, he shows us these wounds, it is to heal our unbelief and strengthen our faith in his resurrection. As Pope Francis has said, these wounds are truly wounds of mercy.

When the Apostle Thomas hears the report that the other disciples have seen the Lord, he does not believe it: "Unless I see the mark of the nails in his hands and put my finger into the nailmarks and put my hand into his side, I will not believe." What does Christ do to dispel these doubts? He shows Thomas his wounds.

Thus, when in the following week Christ appears again to the disciples, he does not wait for Thomas to speak but turns to him immediately and, employing the very terms that Thomas had used to express his unbelief, Jesus says to him: "Put your finger here and see my hands, and bring your hand and put it into my side, and do not be unbelieving, but believe." Thomas is moved by grace to confess his faith in his risen Lord: my Lord and my God. Having seen and touched the man whom he knew as teacher and master, he now confesses the God whom he neither saw nor touched.

Christ never appears to his disciples after his resurrection without his wounds. He appears, not as a ghost or a phantom, not in the camouflage of a generic human body, but in the body that has always been his, at once son of God and son of Mary, who was crucified for our sake under Pontius Pilate, who suffered death and was buried, and who rose again on the third day in accordance with the Scriptures. His body is transformed and glorified but is really his own, for it bears the very wounds of his passion.

If his risen body were an imaginary one, there would not have been a genuine resurrection but only an apparent one. It is in that very same body, bearing the marks of his passion and death, that Christ, truly risen from the dead, appears to his disciples.

"Jesus Christ does not appear to his disciples without his wounds," says Pope Francis, and "those very wounds enabled Thomas to profess his faith." The wounds of Jesus are wounds of mercy. Because Christ has risen from the dead still bearing his wounds, we can know for certain that he did not succumb to the forces of sin and death that conspired to destroy him and that conspire to destroy us as well. "Do not be afraid," he declares to us. "I am the first and the last, the one who lives. Once I was dead, but now I am alive forever and ever." In this great drama of divine mercy, Christ shares his victory over sin and death with us. The fullness of our faith in the resurrection lies in the profound conviction that, having died with Christ, we will rise with him in glory.

Pondering these glorious wounds, says Pope Francis, "we can see the entire mystery of Christ and of God…and we can retrace the whole history of salvation." It is for the sake of his own glory that, after rising from the dead, Christ did not allow these wounds to be concealed or effaced. For the wounds are, in effect, the trophies of his victory. They are not marks of ignominy but, as St. Augustine said, they are "marks of honor." Bearing these wounds, the body of Christ is not less perfect, but more perfect, even beautiful because of them, St. Thomas Aquinas wrote, and so "the scars which Christ manifested after the resurrection never left his body afterwards." Christ carries the signs of these wounds with him into eternity. Hear Pope Francis again: "The wounds of Jesus are wounds of mercy.… Jesus invites us to behold these wounds…to enter into the mystery of these wounds which is the mystery of his merciful love."

The experience of the Apostle Thomas is in an important sense exemplary for us. "Rest in Christ's passion and live willingly in his holy wounds. Had we but with Thomas put our fingers into the print of his nails and thrust our hands into his side...the joys and miseries of life would soon become indifferent to us." The wounds of Jesus are wounds of mercy. Where is there safety and sure rest for us except in the Savior's wounds? "There the security of my dwelling depends on the greatness of his saving power.... I have sinned gravely, my conscience is disturbed but not confounded, because I shall remember the wounds of the Lord." The wounds of Christ are a refuge for us, as they were to Thomas. "When it seems to you that your suffering exceeds your strength, contemplate my wounds." Thus in the *Anima Christi* we pray, "Within Thy wounds hide me."

Picture this if you dare: Christ standing before his heavenly Father and pleading for us, *still bearing his wounds.* "He preferred to bring into heaven the wounds borne for us. He did not wish to erase them so that he might show God the Father the price of our liberty." Through Christ, our undefeated royal champion, flow the inexhaustible riches of divine mercy from the Father in the Holy Spirit. This is what Pope Francis means when he says, "The Lord's wounds, the Lord's Stigmata, are the very door through which mercy comes."

We ourselves will become witnesses of this marvelous truth: the wounds of Jesus are wounds of mercy. For "the blessed in heaven, seeing these wounds, will know the Lord's great love for them." Dear friends in Christ, already in Advent we anticipated this future vision of our Savior's wounds: "Lo he comes with clouds descending: The dear tokens of his passion / Still his dazzling body bears / Cause of endless exultation / To his ransomed worshippers / With what rapture, with what rapture, with what rapture / Gaze we on those glorious scars." Amen. Alleluia.

❧ PART III ❦

Seasonal Sermons

❧ Sermon 32

The Massacre of Innocents

A WEEK AGO TODAY, in St. Rose of Lima Church in Newtown, Connecticut, the Dominican Fr. Peter John Cameron opened his homily with the startling words: "Never before has the Massacre of the Holy Innocents taken place before the Birth of Christ. But that is what has happened in Newtown." At another point in his homily he mentioned that he had run into a man that morning who reported that someone had said to him that Christmas should be canceled this year. "No," Fr. Cameron declared, "Christmas *will not* be canceled! We need Christmas more than ever! Because the *only way* that we can make sense of this horror is if God himself becomes flesh and comes to dwell among us as our friend. We need the presence of Jesus Christ in our midst to rescue us from this misery."

All of us are stunned by the horror of Newtown and weighed down with the misery of it. When I visited my optometrist this week, he was so overcome with emotion that he could hardly speak. So many people feel this way. An overwhelming sorrow fills all our hearts. The massacre of the Holy Innocents has happened *before* Christmas this year, but only the mystery of Christmas makes it possible to cope with it. How can that be possible?

Micah speaks to us today of the one whose "greatness shall reach to the ends of the earth." These words of prophecy are echoed in the rarely sung third verse of "Joy to the World": "No more let sins and sorrows grow, / Nor thorns infest the ground; / He comes to make his blessings flow / Far as the curse is found, / Far as the curse is found."

Far as the curse is found. Now there is a flash of biblical Christian realism with which to face the horror and misery we feel. Looking at things with the eyes of faith, terrible tragedies, like Newtown and Columbine and Stockholm, remind us of the radical peril that surrounds human existence. There was mental illness involved in these acts of horrific violence. But there was also cunning and malice. In Newtown perhaps this disturbed and hurting young man was jealous of the affection that his mother had shown for her students. We do not know. An extreme and mentally unbalanced response, but also an appallingly evil act. We want to throw medicines, and programs, and therapies, and gun control at these horrors. And, naturally, these measures are indispensable. But the curse finds a way to dodge our feeble remedies, and comes out shooting with semi-automatic weapons.

Like the sacrifices and offerings, holocausts and sin offerings of which the Letter to the Hebrews speaks today, our remedies cannot get at the root of the problem. By God's will, "we have been consecrated through the offering of the body of Jesus Christ once for all"—the divine remedy for the evils that threaten us. For he has come to make his blessings flow far as the curse is found.

For this child, whose coming we will soon celebrate, the road that begins in Bethlehem continues on to Golgotha, and beyond to glory. The feast of the Nativity of Our Lord in the flesh celebrates the glory of the champion of our salvation. But between the Nativity and the glory there was the Cross, the passion and the death of our precious Savior. With Mary on Christmas night we will joyfully gaze on the child over whose ruined body we shall later shed bitter tears. The Father of heaven and earth did not hesitate to allow his only-begotten Son to become the Son of Mary in order to make his blessings flow far as the curse is found.

We find ourselves at the absolute center of the Christmas mystery. What Mary and Joseph, the angels and archangels, the shepherds and now, brothers and sisters in Christ, all of us—what they and we behold with nearly breathless wonder is the birth of the one who, taking on our humanity, will lay down his life for us in the Sacrifice of the Cross so that we can become sharers in his divinity. This wonderful exchange restores us to life, making possible things otherwise completely beyond our reach and imagination: namely, participation in the divine life, and forgiveness and healing of our sins.

Born into our human nature, Christ makes it possible for us to be *reborn* as his brothers and sisters in the communion of Trinitarian love. By assuming our human frailty, the sinless One is victorious within the very arena of earthly existence where we lay under the curse, condemned to sin and death. Not from outside, but from within the arena of human existence, he comes to make his blessings flow. Like a flowing river, the uncontainable surge of his grace streams into every crevice and corner of our lives sweeping away our sins and sorrows, and all the thorns that infect the ground. How far? Far as the curse is found, deep into the dark fissures of our hearts where the thorns of envy and malice, pride and lust, greed, hatred and despair would find a niche and thrive. How far then do his blessings flow? As far as the curse is found.

But we must embrace these blessings and shake off the attachments to sin that keep us mired in the realm of the curse. We must strive to keep our hearts pure, to confess our sins regularly, not just twice a year in Advent and Lent, so that we allow the devil no point of entry into our hearts and minds. We cannot change the world. We cannot prevent tragedies like Newtown from recurring. But we can open our hearts to the Christmas grace.

❧ SERMON 33

Surprised by Death

JUST ABOUT A WEEK AGO the strongest tropical cyclone on record made landfall over Fiji in the South Pacific doing $500 million damage and killing 44 people. Were these 44 greater sinners than the thousands of islanders who survived?

The tragedies mentioned by our Lord in today's Gospel are like this one—things in the news, so to speak. Is there a lesson to be drawn from stories like this? That the people who perished in them were greater sinners than others? "I tell you, no," says Jesus; those who perished were not greater sinners than those who survived. The lesson lies elsewhere: Like the Galileans killed by Pilate and the eighteen souls crushed by the tower in Siloam, the people whose lives were taken by cyclone Winston were surprised by death. If the end of life can be so unexpected, then there is nothing to be gained by postponing repentance for our sins.

If you knew that your life was going to end on such and such a day five years from now, then you could delay repentance until a safe interval before that date. But we do not know this—and for the most part, we do not want to know. "These things are warnings for us," writes St. Paul. What our Lord wants us to think about is that the moment of death will be as unexpected for us as for the people who perished in these various catastrophes. "Unless you repent," he warns, "you will all likewise perish."

Our Lord introduces a parable to amplify this point. "Lo, these three years I have come seeking fruit on this fig tree and I find none," says the owner of the vineyard. "Cut it down: why should it use up the ground?" God has been patient with our procrastination, with our failure to bear the fruit of repentance: the owner of the vineyard has come no less than three times to check on the fig tree. But he is encouraged to be even more patient. "Let it alone, sir, this year also," says the kindly vinedresser, "till I dig about it and put on manure. And if it bears fruit next year, well and good; but if not, you can cut it down."

Thus the parable underscores Christ's point. Although God is patient with our procrastination, he is not indefinitely so. The point is clear: We should not put off repentance until it is too late or until God's patience runs out. Now is the time to repent.

The wonderful thing is that God's patience extends over the whole history of salvation. For St. Gregory the Great, the three times that the owner of the vineyard has come to the fig tree signify the three great ages of the economy of salvation: the first, *the time before the law* when our very natures formed in the image of God directed us to him; then, the second, *the time under the law*, begun when Moses heard the voice of the Lord from the burning bush saying "I have seen the affliction of my people who are in Egypt, and have heard their cry.... I know their sufferings and I have come to deliver them."; and, finally, now, our time, "the last times," *the time under grace* when he comes to us in the person of his only-begotten Son who did not hesitate to give his life for the sake of our salvation.

Justly does God complain, declares St. Gregory, "that for three years he found no fruit, for there are some wicked men whose hearts are neither corrected by the law of nature breathed into them, nor instructed by precepts, nor converted by the miracles of his incarnation."

On Good Friday, Christ will address us with the reproaches: "O my people, what more could I have done for you?" So much love and compassion have been poured into the work of our salvation that our hearts cannot fail to be moved as we hear Christ's words to us today:

Delay no more. Do not wait to be surprised by death. Do not try God's patience a moment longer.

Let us throw ourselves on the mercy of God, and fly to the Sacrament of Penance, confess our sins and to hear Christ's words of forgiveness and healing, receiving his absolution and blessing from the priest through whom he speaks to us, in the name of the Father, and the Son, and the Holy Spirit. Amen.

❧ SERMON 34

Judge Not and You Shall Not Be Judged

JUDGING OTHERS. "You will not easily find any one, whether a father of a family or an inhabitant of the cloister, free from this error," says St. John Chrysostom. And, also commenting on this gospel passage, St. Cyril says: "Here [Christ] expresses the worst inclination of our thoughts and hearts, which is the beginning and origin of a proud disdain. For although it becomes men to look into themselves and walk after God, this they do not, but rather look into the affairs of others... and make them a subject of reproach."

Indeed, we hardly need these great Fathers of the Church to tell us what we already know too well. Judging the faults and weaknesses of others is one of our favorite pastimes, one which not only keeps our minds busy, but also our tongues wagging. How difficult it is for us to heed our Lord's injunction: "Judge not, and you shall not be judged. Condemn not, and you shall not be condemned. Forgive, and you shall be forgiven."

Let us be clear at the outset: There certainly are circumstances in which we are not only permitted to judge, but *required* to do so. Parents, confessors, teachers, superiors, court justices, and so on, have the responsibility to judge those in their charge, and to act upon their judgments. We should not imagine that our Lord is encouraging us to shirk our duties in these areas. On the contrary, we have a solemn responsibility before God and before others to judge prudently and justly when we are called upon to do so.

No, Christ has a different set of circumstances in view when he warns us against judging others. He is thinking of the ordinary, day-to-day circumstances of life—circumstances with which we are entirely familiar—in which we expend a great deal of time and energy observing, evaluating, criticizing, and judging other people, not because we have a particular responsibility which makes it necessary to do so, but because we find doing so practically irresistible.

We have become so accustomed to doing all this judging that our sense of the sinfulness of this behavior has been dulled. We should ask ourselves honestly: What is wrong with judging others, and why does our Lord warn us to avoid doing so?

There are at least two reasons why judging others is bad for us. The first reason is in part quite obvious, but we hate to admit it. Our own judgment always leads us to pronounce ourselves innocent and to pronounce others guilty. The problem here is not a simple one. It is not just that, by judging others, we neglect our own guilt and fail to correct our own weaknesses and failings. This is a real problem: We become experts where we could do well to remain ignorant—other people's faults—and ignorant where we are urgently in need of expertise—our own sins and weaknesses. But there is an even more serious problem. When we judge others guilty and, in effect, pronounce ourselves innocent, we remove ourselves from the gaze of the divine Judge, the one who gave his life on the Cross for our sins as well as for those of our neighbor, and who judges us with mercy and forgiveness—but only when we have accused ourselves and begged for his mercy. In the end, the great danger in judging others is that we will find ourselves excluded from the merciful and saving judgment of Christ, especially in the Sacrament of Penance where we first accuse ourselves of our sins in order then to hear the words of absolution which the priest pronounces upon us *in persona Christi*.

This reflection leads us to the second reason why judging others is bad for us and thus why our Lord warns us to avoid doing so. For in these areas so intimate to the soul of every human being—indeed, even our very own souls—only the divine Judge who died for our sake is competent to issue judgment. We are not even competent to judge ourselves, much less to judge others. Recall the encounter between Christ and the woman caught in adultery. What happens when our Lord says to her accusers: "Let him who is without sin cast the first stone"? Of course: her accusers depart one by one, leaving behind only Christ and the woman. How can we understand this event if we do not see that all the human judges have been declared incompetent—thrown out of office, as it were—and only the divine Judge remains?

We are accustomed to thinking of the image of Christ as Judge as a terrifying one: we tremble at the thought of facing the divine Judge. But just the opposite is the case. We should not be terrified; we should rather be relieved. To know and to acknowledge that Christ is the only true Judge of our souls and the souls of our neighbors is a tremendous liberation. Far from being something frightening, it should be a source of rejoicing and delight. We can give up all this judging that we are always engaged in, and leave it to the Judge who suffered and died so that our sins could never finally be the cause of our condemnation. Whenever we find ourselves judging others, we should remember this: we have been deposed from office and declared incompetent, and we must leave the judgment to Christ who says to us: "Judge not, and you shall not be judged. Condemn not, and you shall not be condemned. Forgive, and you shall be forgiven."

❧ SERMON 35

The Merciful Judge Who Saves Us

MUCH EXEGETICAL INK has been spilt on speculation about the words that Jesus might have traced in the sand during the incident recorded in today's Gospel reading, but the real significance of this extraordinary moment surely lies elsewhere. Two things are noteworthy.

In the first place, of course, the most important thing about this incident is that, whereas the crowd would have condemned and stoned her, Christ forgives the woman caught in adultery. We need to know and be convinced that this forgiveness is always ours when we confess our sins—as we should do regularly in the precious Sacrament of Penance—and strive to live in and with Christ, the unquenchable font of divine mercy. But there is a second element in this incident that is of enormous significance. With the departure of all these self-deputed judges, Christ alone stands as the judge.

We sometimes read that a judge has been dismissed from the bench for having taken a bribe or otherwise compromising his or her office. It is a rare thing, thank God, and the news always unsettles us. But imagine with me for a moment that all the judges were declared to be culpable and unworthy of office. To my mind, the departure of the crowd signifies something like this: all the judges—like Susannah's accusers and the crowd in today's Gospel—have been declared incompetent and thrown out of office.

Understand that I am not referring to the judges who serve us in all the levels of the judicial system. No, the departure of the crowd one by one signifies that *we* are the judges who have now been relieved of office—naturally, *not* in the circumstances where our professions or positions require that we make judgments (about performance, or qualifications and abilities, or culpability in defined circumstances, and so on), but in the deeper and more pervasive sense that we have appointed ourselves judges and make it our business to be experts in the faults and shortcomings of everyone around us, and in the knowledge of our own guilt or innocence.

In a remarkable discussion of the "Judge Judged in Our Place," the Reformed theologian Karl Barth wrote: "For where does our judgment always lead? To the place where we pronounce ourselves innocent, and where, on account of their...sins, and with more or less indulgence and understanding or severity and inflexibility, we pronounce others as guilty." But our judgment can lead in another way as well, to scrupulosity and despair when we declare our sins innumerable or unforgivable. "The fruit of [the] tree [of good and evil] which was eaten with such relish is still rumbling in all of us." More often than not, it is upon others that our judgment falls. "It is...an affliction always to have to make it clear to ourselves [that we are in the right] so that we can cling to it that others are in one way or another in the wrong, and to have to wrack our brains how we can make it clear to them, and either bring them to an amendment of their ways or give them up as hopeless.... It is a terrible thing to know good and evil if only in this ostensible and ineffective way."

"We are all in process of dying from this office of judge which we have arrogated to ourselves. It is, therefore, a liberation that it has come to pass in Jesus Christ that we are deposed and dismissed from this office because he has come to exercise it in our place." In addition to Christ's power to forgive, this also is what is revealed to us in the incident of the woman caught in adultery. No one is without sin, and thus no one can be a judge either of the hearts of others, or even of his own heart. Only the absolutely sinless one who took upon himself the sins of the whole world, and thus ours as well, can be the true Judge upon whose righteousness and mercy we can confidently rely. In his Cross and Resurrection, Christ won the right to be the only Judge of the good and evil in the human heart.

And what a relief it is! It is a mistake to regard the figure of Christ the Judge as a forbidding or fearsome one. On the contrary, it is liberating. "I am not the Judge. Jesus Christ is the Judge. The matter is taken out of my hands. And that means liberation. A great anxiety is lifted, the greatest of all." "[T]he fact that Jesus Christ judges in our place means an immeasurable liberation and hope."

When we find our minds full of critical judgments about others—as we so frequently do—we should remind ourselves that this activity is, if you will, above our pay scale, that Christ alone can fill the office of judge. When we find ourselves anxious about our own sins, even after having sought forgiveness and performed the required penance, we should remember that we stand before the Judge upon whose good and redemptive will we can count absolutely.

In either situation, each of us must think: "He who knows about myself and others as I never could or should do, will judge concerning me and them in a way which is again infinitely more just than I could ever do...."

Recall the historical context of the incident recounted in today's Gospel. Possibly around the year 30 A.D., the Roman authorities in Palestine prohibited the execution of sentences of capital punishment by the Jewish leadership in Jerusalem. This ruling would have created considerable difficulties for the Jewish authorities since the Mosaic law prescribed the death penalty for a variety of offenses, including adultery, as in the case recounted in today's Gospel.

Hence the challenge posed by the scribes and Pharisees in this situation. If Jesus were to have encouraged the crowd to carry out the sentence prescribed by the Mosaic law, he would have appeared to contravene Roman authority. If, on the other hand, he were to have prevented the stoning, he would have appeared to discount the seriousness both of the offense and of the injunctions of the Mosaic law itself. In one of the "coolest"—if you will permit me the expression—actions recorded in the Gospels, in the face of this dilemma, Jesus bends to the ground and begins writing in the sand. When the crowd fails to disperse, he rises and says, "Let the one among you who is without sin be the first to throw a stone at her." At last, when he again bends to the ground, the crowd gradually departs, one by one, and Christ alone stands as the Judge. What a relief!

❧ SERMON 36

Let Go the Demons

"WHAT HAVE YOU TO DO WITH US, Jesus of Nazareth? Have you come to destroy us? I know who you are—the Holy One of God!" Who speaks these chilling words? We can be sure, in the first place, that these are the words of the unclean spirit who possesses the man in the synagogue at Capernaum. The spirit speaks in the first person plural and in the first person singular—signifying the general knowledge among his fellow spirits that Jesus of Nazareth is the holy one of God. St. Augustine points out that the spirit's words "show clearly that the demons had much knowledge, but entirely lacked love." And elsewhere, "Faith is mighty, but without love it profits nothing.... They confessed a sort of faith, but without love. Hence they were devils"—and they are quite right to fear that Christ has come to destroy them. That he now casts this unclean spirit out of the man is but a sign of things to come. This moment is just one in the long battle against Satan and his principalities in which Christ will be victorious.

There is a temptation to pursue the peculiar fascination and dalliance of our age with the spiritual powers, and to confirm us in our faith in their absolute subordination to the power of Christ's Cross and resurrection. But there is something else to consider here. These words—"What have you to do with us, Jesus of Nazareth? Have you come to destroy us? I know who you are—the Holy One of God!"—while, certainly those of the unclean spirit, are also on the lips of the man possessed. He speaks them. And thus the possibility arises; *These could be our words too, and sometimes they indeed are.* This is a possibility that we would rather not contemplate. But we recognize immediately that it is a real possibility. We know that we can and do say these words. We are attached to our particular set of "demons," so to speak, and we would rather not let go of them. They provide us with enjoyments of one sort or another to which we have become accustomed and which we are disinclined to relinquish. They are too delicious. We each have our list—I shall not rehearse the possibilities here. Some come to mind: grudges, lusts, vanities and jealousies, along with yearnings, hatreds, and hungers which we just do not want to let go of.

And Christ appears before us with authority and power, and also mercy and love. We cry out nervously: What have you to do with me, Jesus of Nazareth? Have you come to destroy my precious demons? Can I not enjoy them for the time being? For a little while longer, surely? I know that you are the Holy One of God, and that you want to make me holy too. That would be nice, of course, and it's really something that I would rather like, but perhaps not just yet.

At the synagogue of Capernaum, Christ ignores the protests of the unclean spirit. "Quiet," he says, and with that drives the spirit away.

He will do the same for us if we let him, but generally not if we are determined to hold our demons close to our hearts. In his name, I beg you and I exhort myself as well: Let go of them so that the Holy One of God will make us free to live in the holiness which he won for us by the victory of the Cross.

❧ SERMON 37

Christ Brings True Peace to Our Hearts

OUR EXPERIENCE SUGGESTS that we did not need the coming of Christ to set mothers-in-law and daughters-in-law at odds. It happens all the time already! But, of course, we know that our Lord is not referring to everyday family conflicts, but to those that could arise in reaction to his message. He wants to bring us peace, but his message can and has divided people who accept it from those that do not. Thus, there is no contradiction here between his promise to bring us his peace and his warning against the division that can inevitably follow upon his proclamation of the message of salvation. Many commentators have noted this. Aquinas says somewhere that it would not be an act of piety towards one's parents if one in this way neglected to worship God. In the same way, the Fathers have understood that the fire Christ brings is not the fire of destruction but the fire of purification, warmth, and life. When Christ says "I have come to set the world on fire," his hearers would have understood, as we must, that he is evoking this common biblical meaning of fire. As gold and silver are purified by fire, so our Savior in the power of the Holy Spirit cleanses the minds of those who believe in him.

Since we are clandestinely celebrating the feast of St. John Eudes today, in honor of one of our number whose patron he is, I asked myself what he would have to say about this Gospel this morning. He was quite a great preacher, as you know, having preached over one hundred missions in his life. In fact, after a long life spanning practically the whole of the seventeenth century (1601–1680), he died after preaching a mission in the cold outdoors. Not just a great preacher, though, one of his famous remarks was: "The preacher beats the bushes, but the confessor captures the birds." He was associated with the other leaders of seventeenth-century spirituality, especially Cardinal Bérulle (founder of the French Oratory of which John Eudes was a member for a good part of his life) and Jean-Jacques Olier (founder of the Sulpicians). John Eudes himself founded two congregations, one for the education of seminarians (Congregation of the Hearts of Jesus and Mary) and another, with Madeleine Lamy, for women converted from an immoral life (Congregation of Charity of Our Lady of Refuge). Perhaps he is best known for promotion of devotion to the Hearts of Jesus and Mary.

What might he have said this morning? I think John Eudes would have been struck by the observations of St. Ambrose on today's Gospel. After a fairly straightforward treatment of the passage along the lines already indicated, St. Ambrose launches into what he calls a "mystical" reading of the house divided according to which it stands for a single person, made up of body and soul, and contending emotions and desires. "As long as there remained in one house the vices conspiring together with one consent, there seemed to be no division; but when Christ sent fire upon the earth which should burn out the offenses of the heart, or the sword which should pierce the very secrets of the heart, then the flesh and the soul renewed by the mysteries of regeneration cast off the bond of connection with their offspring." We can see in this passage the germ of a whole theology of the spiritual life. Everything is "peaceful" until we begin to hear the voice of Christ and feel the purifying power of his grace, won for us by the "baptism" which he so ardently willed to embrace for our sake, his crucifixion and death. We are made sad by the prospect of our sins—by the struggle and division caused within us by our contending passions and attachments. But in this struggle Christ has gone well beyond us: he has gone so far as to shed his blood for our sins (cf. Hebrews). And it will be because of him that true peace will reign in our hearts. Let St. John Eudes have the last word in "his" homily today: "You belong to the Son of God...you ought to be in him as members of the head. All that is in you must be incorporated into him. You must receive life from him and be *ruled* by him." He is the King whose purifying fire and piercing sword will bring true peace to our hearts.

❧ SERMON 38

Two Shall Become One Flesh

GOD CAUSED ADAM TO FALL INTO A DEEP SLEEP, and from his side God took a rib which he formed into Eve. "Adam's sleep," writes St. Augustine, "was a mystical foreshadowing of Christ's death. God allowed his only-begotten Son to fall into the deep sleep of death, and from his side flows the blood and water from which the Church is formed. But, not only is the *creation* of the Church foreshadowed here. For the woman who is formed from Adam's rib becomes his spouse. Thus we read: "A man shall leave his father and mother and be joined to his wife and the two shall become one flesh." Here the *union* of Christ and his Church is also prefigured.

The common patristic reading of this passage is well expressed in the homily of the sixth-century Syrian Mar Jacob of Sarug: "In his mysterious plans, the Father destined a bride for his only Son and presented her to him under prophetic images.... [Genesis speaks] of man and woman in this way in order to foretell Christ and his Church..., Christ becoming one with the Church through the mystery of water [in baptism]... bridegroom and bride...wholly united in a mystical manner." Indeed, Mar Jacob concludes: "Wives are not united to their husbands as closely as the Church is to the Son of God."

Little wonder that, in his letter to the Ephesians (5:32), St. Paul called this "a great mystery"—stirred to awe, we sense, at this amazing dispensation of divine love and grace. In the letter to the Hebrews today, we hear to what length this love would reach: "He 'for a little while' was made 'lower than the angels' that by the grace of God he might taste death for everyone."

"What husband but our Lord ever died for his wife," asks Mar Jacob, "and what bride ever chose a crucified man as her husband? Who ever gave his blood as a gift to his wife except the one who died on the Cross and sealed the marriage bond with his wounds? ... Death separates wives from their husbands, but in this case it is death that unites the bride to her beloved."

With exquisite delicacy, divine providence has woven these deep patterns of figuration and typology into the fabric of the Sacred Scriptures in order to excite in us a readiness to be taught that corresponds to God's desire to teach. In a sermon on today's Gospel, St. Augustine invites us to pray for this very grace: "O God, make us hungry to learn what your love makes you so ardent to teach." The Church has understood that what God wants to teach us in these remarkable texts is that the entire economy of salvation unfolds when we ponder this sacrament.

Thus, our attention is drawn to a fundamental truth about human nature. God formed Eve out of Adam's rib. Men and women share the same nature, just as Christ gives a participation in the divine nature to the members of his holy Church.

What is more, we learn that God implanted a powerful natural inclination in men and women that draws them together for intimacy and procreation. In a similar way, Christ shares with the members of the Church an intimate and profound communion with the Holy Trinity—thus "bringing many children to glory" and not ashamed to call them brothers and sisters, as Hebrews affirms.

As with the other sacraments—and perhaps even more so in matrimony—the natural signification underlying the sacramental reality is, as it were, permanently transformed by its being taken up into the sacramental economy. Having been employed in the sacraments, water, bread, wine, and oil never seem quite the same to us: an aura attaches to them, suggesting their special place in the sacramental economy. All the more striking is the sacramental transformation of the natural significations embedded in the spousal union of man and woman—at least once we have grasped what God in his love desires to teach us.

Christ's teaching on the indissolubility of marriage fits into a rich biblical faith about the sacrament of matrimony: Husband and wife can no more be separated from one another than Christ can be separated from the Church. All the other arguments in support of this teaching— moral, canonical, psychological—must be framed with a view to this high sacramental vision of matrimony.

The *Catechism of the Catholic Church* states: "Although the dignity of this institution is not transparent everywhere with the same clarity, some sense of the greatness of the matrimonial union exists in all cultures." But it will not be news to any of you that, in present circumstances, the Catholic teaching about marriage—derided as "socially conservative"—typically meets with indifference and even hostility.

The Church's pastors have sought to face this challenge. Marriage was certainly one of the things on Pope Benedict's mind when he said in the Czech Republic last week: "Your country, like other nations, is experiencing cultural conditions that often present a radical challenge to faith and therefore also to hope." It is hardly surprising that the sanctity of marriage turned out to be perhaps the overarching pastoral concern of the entire teaching pontificate of his venerable predecessor, Pope John Paul II. Indeed, when they come to Rome for their *ad limina* visits, bishops from every corner of the globe, almost without exception, mention marriage and divorce as among the biggest challenges they face.

And the challenges are indeed formidable. In place of the demand for fidelity and commitment fundamental to the Catholic vision of matrimony, the ambient culture—with the strong support of the media and social advocacy elites—favors relationships that are thought of as in principle tentative and provisional. The sexual revolution encourages multiple temporary relationships. Somewhat unexpectedly, perhaps, the problem has become not so much the prevalence of divorce but the eclipse of marriage itself, in favor of partnerships of varying degrees of durability and commitment. "Sex in the city" does not seem to have made people happier, however. On the contrary, with its empty promise of liberation and personal autonomy, it seems able to deliver only increased levels of loneliness and alienation.

This is not the place to analyze these conditions or to offer detailed strategies for addressing them. But recall that the Pharisees posed the issue to Christ as a test, and, as Origen remarks, "If our glorious Savior was tested in this way, should any of his disciples called to teach be annoyed when questioned by some who probe, not from the desire to know, but from the intent to trip up?"

But our overall strategy must be to aim high—to frame the moral issues in terms of the mysteries of our faith. In the sacrament of matrimony, nothing less than the union of Christ with his Church is signified. This is a great mystery, as St. Paul reminds us, and perhaps only a childlike faith—always ready to embrace the wonders of God's loving plan with amazement and love—will be prepared to grasp it.

PART IV

Feasts and Solemnities

❧ SERMON 39

Consumed by the Holy Mysteries

IN HIS PREMIERE BIOGRAPHY OF ST. THOMAS, Gugliemo di Tocco wrote of the saint that "he celebrated Mass every day, his health permitting, and afterward attended a second Mass celebrated by one of the friars or some other priest, and very often served at the altar. Frequently during the Mass, he was literally overcome by an emotion so powerful that he was reduced to tears, for he was consumed by the holy mysteries of this great sacrament and strengthened by their offering."

"Consumed by the holy mysteries of this great sacrament." The Italian term here is *divorato*—devoured, eaten up, consumed—by the mysteries.

Surely Tocco's vivid description of Aquinas's devotion at Mass stops us dead in our tracks—we, whose celebration of or participation in the Holy Mass are frequently distracted or routinized or just bored. We are tempted to excuse ourselves with observations like "well, of course, Aquinas was a saint, and this is typically saintly behavior," or "as a very smart theologian, Aquinas had a more penetrating grasp of things than we do." But instead of these evasions, what we should do is ask ourselves: What I am missing?

Rare indeed are there mysteries that consume or devour our jaded sensibilities. Perhaps a really good thriller might do so on occasion. But we assume that holy mysteries will be something very different from murder mysteries or natural mysteries.

But we should not exaggerate the contrast between holy mysteries and other sorts of mysteries. In ordinary usage, the word "mystery" refers to something that remains as yet unexplained or something that is simply inexplicable. We expect the mystery to be resolved in the final pages of a thriller, but at the same time scientists speak of the enduring mysteries of the universe. These kinds of mysteries are not unlike holy mysteries in that, in both cases, our capacity to understand or penetrate a particular reality is challenged in a significant way.

The crucial difference between the Catholic and common uses of the word "mystery" lies here. When the term is applied to divine realities, the mystery involved is by definition without end. This is not to say (as nominalists, in contrast to Aquinas, seemed to want to say) that the things of God are permanently or radically incomprehensible and ineffable, but that they are endlessly comprehensible and expressible. Not darkness, but too much light is what we encounter here. That irritating conversation stopper, "it's a mystery," does not mean that we have nothing further to say *but that we cannot say enough* about the matter in hand. The mysteries of faith are so far-reaching in their meaning and so breathtaking in their beauty that they possess a limitless—that is to say, literally an unending and inexhaustible—power to attract and transform the minds and hearts, the individual and communal lives, in which they are pondered, digested, and, ultimately, loved and adored.

Not for nothing can we use the word in the singular and in the plural, mystery *and* mysteries. The all-encompassing mystery—*in the singular*—is nothing less than and nothing else but God himself, and the mysteries—*plural*—are its many facets as we come to know them.

St. Thomas insistently taught that the mystery of faith is radically singular because the triune God who is at its center is one in being and in activity, and comprehends in one act of omniscience the fullness of his truth and wisdom. Through the infused gift of faith—thus called a theological virtue—the believer is rendered capable of a participation in this divine wisdom, but always and only according to human ways of knowing. We truly know God, but not in the way that he knows himself. According to Aquinas, the human comprehension of the singular mystery of divine truth is necessarily plural in its structure.

In this sense, we can speak both of the mystery of faith—referring to the reality of the one triune God who is known through the act of faith—*and* of the mysteries of faith—referring to our way of knowing in the Church the various elements of the singular mystery of God. All the mysteries of our faith point us to the single mystery at their center, nothing else but God himself, one and three.

Coming to the center of this mystery, we affirm with astonished delight the divine desire to share the communion of Trinitarian life with human beings, with us. No one has ever desired anything more. God himself has revealed to us (how else could we have known it?) that this divine desire—properly speaking, intention and plan—is at the basis of everything else: creation itself, the incarnation of the Word, our redemption through the passion, death, and resurrection of Christ, our sanctification and glory through the power of the Holy Spirit. Thus St. Paul speaks to us today of the grace he received precisely "to bring to light for all what is the plan of the mystery hidden from ages past in God who created all things, so that the manifold wisdom of God might now be made known through the Church."

Amazingly, then, it turns out that the divine mystery is the key to all other mysteries. Far from being opaque, it throws light on everything else. To see everything with the eyes of faith—to adopt, as it were, a "God's eye view"—is to see and to understand everything in the light of this divine plan, "to bring to light for all what is the plan of the mystery."

Glory, bliss, beatitude—these wonderful terms refer to the consummation of our participation in the communion of Trinitarian life already begun in Baptism, nothing less than seeing God face to face. At the heart of the mystery and the mysteries, finally, is the mystery of divine love. The Catholic tradition has not hesitated to call this participation in the divine life a true friendship with God.

Given all this, was it not fitting that God should be moved to send his own Son into the world and, in the exquisite divine condescension of the Incarnation, to take on a human nature so that he could be known and loved by us as Jesus of Nazareth, Christ and Lord? Was it not fitting that the Son of Man should offer his life to the Father on the Cross in a sacrifice of love for our reconciliation? Was it not fitting that Christ should remain with us in the Eucharist?

Aquinas teaches us to regard these mysteries in the light of the overarching mystery of the divine love. This is very clear in what he wrote about the final question: "It is a law of friendship that friends should want to be together.... Christ does not leave us without his physical presence on our pilgrimage, but he unites us to himself in the sacrament in the reality of his body and his blood."

At the start we asked ourselves: What are we missing? What does it mean to be "consumed by the holy mysteries of this great sacrament"? The answer is really very simple. It means to be consumed by the love they embody and reveal. Is it any wonder that Aquinas wept in the contemplation of these holy mysteries?

May this great saint, who experienced such rapture whenever he celebrated the Eucharist, help us not to miss being consumed by the love of our divine friends who give themselves to us in this great sacrament, to their eternal glory and to our unending benefit, the Father, the Son, and the Holy Spirit. Amen.

❧ SERMON 40

Divine Wisdom in Teaching and Learning

W HO OF US—whether student or professor—has not marveled at the fact that St. Thomas intends his *Summa Theologiae* as a work for beginners in theology—*ad eruditionem incipientium?* To be sure, St. Thomas is not thinking of beginners simply speaking, for he would have presupposed in his readers a grounding in the humanities and in Sacred Scripture. But he wants to exclude useless questions and needless repetition in favor of a disciplined ordering of topics that arises from the inner logic of the subject matter itself and the sequence in which the truths of the Christian faith can best be absorbed by students at the beginning of their study of theology or *sacra doctrina.*

The confidence on St. Thomas's part that this complex and learned work could function as a text for beginners rests on a conviction about the profound intelligibility of truths of the faith. "I prayed and prudence was given me; I pleaded and the spirit of Wisdom came to me." Divine wisdom comes to us only as a gift. As granted to us in Baptism, it is radically unitary because the triune God who is at its center is one in being and in activity, and comprehends in one act of omniscience the fullness of his truth and wisdom. Through the infused gift of faith— thus called a theological virtue—the believer is rendered capable of a participation in this divine wisdom, but always and only according to human ways of knowing. We truly know God, but not in the way that he knows himself. According to Aquinas, the human form that divine wisdom takes in our knowledge and understanding is necessarily plural and in a true sense scientific in its structure.

When expounded in an orderly manner by a qualified teacher, the doctrines of the Christian faith can be seen and to a certain extent understood both in their intelligibility and communicability even by the beginning student.

St. Thomas explains this relationship between the teacher and student of divine wisdom in his Inaugural Lecture at the University of Paris in 1256. He draws upon a verse from Psalm 104: "You water the mountains from your chambers; from the fruit of your labor the earth abounds" (Psalm 104:13)—*rigans montes de superioribus suis de fructu operum tuorum satiabitur terra,* (Psalm 103:13 [Vulgate]). Accordingly, he states in the opening words of his address, "The king of the heavens, the Lord, established this law from all eternity, that the gifts of his providence should reach what is lowest by way of things that are in between."

Thus, Aquinas says, the minds of teachers can be likened to the mountains upon which the rain falls. Like the mountains, they are watered by the wisdom of God that is above and it is by their ministry that the light of divine wisdom flows down into the minds of the students who are likened to the fertile earth. In order for this transmission of divine wisdom to be effective, the teachers must be innocent, intelligent, fervent, and obedient, while the students must be docile, able to assess what they hear, and have the capacity to discover things. Because the fruit of the mountains is not ascribed to teachers but to God, they can communicate divine wisdom only in a ministerial or instrumental role. Although no one is equal to this ministry by himself and from his own resources, he can hope that God will grant him the proficiency needed to communicate to others the divine wisdom he has received from God.

St. Thomas maintained this profoundly contemplative understanding of nature of theological teaching and learning throughout his life. In the inaugural address, theology involves a participation in the divine wisdom, and it is the mission of the theologian to transmit this wisdom to others. Ten years later, as he begins working on the *Summa Theologiae*, he describes *sacra doctrina* as "an imprint on us of God's own knowledge"—*velut quaedam impressio divinae scientiae*—and later in the *Summa* describes his work as *contemplata aliis tradere*, deriving preaching and teaching from "the fullness of contemplation."

But what is truly remarkable about this contemplative understanding of theology are its underlying convictions about the intelligibility and communicability of the divine wisdom that is it object. Notwithstanding the radical transcendence of divine wisdom—its essential incomprehensibility and ineffability—with respect to human cognitive capacities, it can be taught and learned. The limits here are on the human side: the problem is not that divine wisdom is opaque but that it is too dazzlingly bright for the human mind. In his astonishing love for us, God grants us a participation in the divine wisdom by the grace of faith. But because this faith cannot fail to plumb the mysteries of divine wisdom, as *fides quaerens intellectum* it devotes itself diligently to understanding what is endlessly intelligible but not beyond its ken. "I preferred [wisdom] to scepter and throne, and deemed riches nothing in comparison to her.... Beyond health and beauty I loved her, and chose to have her rather than the light, because her radiance never ceases."

Furthermore, although before the depths of divine wisdom, silence is sometimes the only appropriate response, there are also times when we must speak. "Now God grant I speak suitably and value these endowments at their worth: for he is the guide of wisdom and the director of the wise." As we have seen, according to Aquinas, this is the teacher's basic prayer. About what he has learned of the divine wisdom, he cannot remain silent.

Surely this applies not only to the masters of theology, but also to the preaching friars who are commissioned to preach the Gospel. Among the students of Aquinas throughout his lifetime of teaching, there would have been many preaching friars. In his inaugural address, St. Thomas says that an indication that someone has truly learned what a master has to teach is that the knowledge he has newly acquired becomes fruitful. Because it is infinitely intelligible, the divine wisdom can be understood by the student—whether as a future teacher or as a future preacher—who therefore must be enabled to communicate it to others. This involves not simply understanding that what the teacher says is true but understanding *why it is true*. It is for this reason above all that Aquinas insists that *sacra doctrina* is a proper form of *scientia*. In this way, both the intelligibility and the communicability of the divine wisdom can be insured. The more *sacra doctrina* approaches *scientia*, the more firmly and fruitfully does it implant itself in the student's mind, and the more surely can he bring the Christian faith to life in hearts and minds of his hearers, whether his audience be a classroom full of students or a church full of the faithful.

St. Thomas's insistence on the scientific character of *sacra doctrina* does not reflect a concession to philosophical or secular standards of rationality but arises from the logical coherence and inner intelligibility of divine wisdom itself. The body of Christian doctrines—that is, the formulation of divine wisdom according to human ways of knowing—thus demands and sustains a scientific exposition grounded in reasoning and argument. What is at stake is the very possibility of the assimilation and communication of truth of the Gospel. "Consecrate them in the truth," our Lord prays, "Your word is truth. As you sent them into the world, so I sent them into the world. And I consecrate myself for them, so that they also may be consecrated in truth." In this light, St. Thomas's concern to demonstrate the scientific character of *sacra doctrina* reveals itself as pastoral and evangelical, not simply scholarly and academic. In the end, the solicitude of this saintly teacher for the advanced scholar no less than for the beginning student of theology is a passionate solicitude for the divine wisdom. "Beyond health and beauty I loved her, and chose to have her rather than the light, because her radiance never ceases."

❧ Sermon 41

Munus Petrinum

ACCORDING TO TRADITION, the feast of the Chair of St. Peter marks the anniversary of the day when St. Peter, having borne witness to the divinity of Christ, was appointed by our Lord to be the rock of his Church—*quo electus est primus Petrus papa*, as the very ancient Western liturgies have it. Peter is thus the first to be seated in the chair that then comes to symbolize the episcopal office of the pope as bishop of Rome.

The history of this feast—which dates from at least the fourth century—is both long and complex. Sparing you all the fascinating details, I will comment only on two things about it that shed light on the profound theological and spiritual significance of the role of St. Peter and his successors in the economy of salvation.

Note, first of all, that there were at one time two feasts of the chair of St. Peter. In the calendar in force until the reform of the liturgy after the Second Vatican Council, January 18 marked the feast of the Chair of St. Peter in Rome while February 22 that of the Chair of St. Peter in Antioch. The second thing to notice is that there is actually a chair in the picture. The chair in question is associated with St. Peter's sojourn in Rome, and, in particular, with a chair venerated since ancient times as the *cathedra Petri*. Since the seventeenth century this wooden chair has been enclosed in the bronze of Bernini's magnificent sculpture, enthroned above the Altar of the Chair in St. Peter's Basilica and held aloft by the four Doctors of the Church (Ambrose, Augustine, Athanasius, and Chrysostom).

The fact that there were at one time two feasts of the Chair of Peter reminds us that Christ consigned to Peter a *munus*, a ministry, that he exercised first in Jerusalem, and then at Antioch, and only ultimately at Rome. This recognition offsets the danger that the theology of the papal ministry can become, in effect, a theology of the primatial character of the see of Rome. Then we are tempted to concentrate on the history of the exercise of papal ministry by successive bishops of Rome, on the relationship of the bishop of Rome to the college of bishops, on the canonical dynamics of the bishop of Rome's universal jurisdiction, on the relationship of the bishop of Rome to other patriarchal— and primatial—sees and implicitly to the leadership of other churches and ecclesial communities. Now don't get me wrong: these are indeed important issues.

But the *munus petrinum* entrusted by Christ to Simon Bar Jonah is in fact both temporally and logically prior to its location in or its identification with the see of Rome. Before there was a primatial see at Rome, there was the divinely instituted ministry of Peter within the "college" of the Apostles. The primacy of the see of Rome was immediately recognized because it was the see from which Peter and his successors—in the exquisitely apt design of divine providence—would come to exercise their ministry. It could have been Jerusalem where Christ suffered and died under Pontius Pilate, or Antioch where his followers were first called "Christians." The prominence of Rome—not only geopolitical and cultural, but specifically Christian as the place where the blood of the martyrs was shed and where the Apostles Peter and Paul sojourned and gave their lives for Christ—is naturally not to be overlooked. But the *munus petrinum*—the office of guiding and teaching and governing the Church—was bestowed upon Peter by Christ before ever he came to exercise it from the *cathedra* of the bishop of Rome.

And this brings us to the second fascinating thing about this feast: There is actually a chair in the picture, however obscure its history and provenance. An instance of the remarkable concreteness of Catholic sensibility, the association of an existing episcopal *cathedra* to be venerated spurs our faith and devotion as we contemplate the grace of the petrine ministry. Not for nothing is the chair of Peter considered a sacramental in Catholic theology and practice. Here we touch on the fundamental Catholic conviction that God uses the tangible and visible things of earthly existence both to signify and, uniquely in the sacraments, to bestow his spiritual gifts.

Above all, he uses consecrated persons as instruments of his grace. The Holy Father, the cardinals, the bishops, the priests, and the deacons of the Church: they are the instruments through whom God willed to pour out his grace on us in the Church through the preaching of the Word and the celebration of the Sacraments. In this way, God adapted himself to our human nature—by sending his only Son who in turn commissioned the Apostles and their successors—so that we might receive his word and his grace from other human beings. The hand of another human being blesses us, pours the water of Baptism on our foreheads, offers the body and blood of Christ to us in the Eucharist, and is raised in absolution unto the forgiveness of sins. Through these persons—St. Peter first among them—and through these actions and objects, God's grace is bestowed on us.

Dear friends in Christ, your pilgrimage to Rome during these days recalls your recent journey into full communion with Peter. May Our Lady of Mount Carmel—who is especially honored in this church and whose feast was first celebrated by the Whitefriars (as the Carmelites were known) of Cambridge in 1374—lead us into that spirit of prayer, contemplation, and thanksgiving that has given so many great saints to the Church. Amen.

❧ SERMON 42

Bound to the See of Peter

IMAGINE THE SCENE: A cold January day in 1566, one saint kneeling at the feet of another in the Sistine Chapel. St. Charles Boromeo begging Michele Ghislieri to accept election as the successor to Pope Pius IV. The normally strong and self-controlled Cardinal Alessandrino (as Ghislieri was known) had burst into tears when St. Charles commanded: "In the name of the Church, pronounce your acceptance, most Holy Father!" "I cannot! I am not worthy," he kept repeating. At last, Cardinal Boromeo's ear caught the barely audible words of acceptance, and the Dominican Cardinal Alessandrino became Pope Pius V.

Since arriving in Rome over a decade earlier, the saint had wanted nothing more than to return to the beloved Dominican friars with whom he had spent his life. At the suggestion of Cardinal Carlo Carafa, Pope Julius III had brought him to Rome to become Commissary General of the Inquisition. When a few years later, Carafa became Pope Paul IV, and Fr. Michele implored the new pope to allow him to return to his convent so that he could "live and die as a Dominican," Carafa responded by making him a bishop and then a cardinal, saying: "I will bind you with so strong a chain that, even after my death, you will never be free to return to your cloister." It is no surprise that, as a cardinal and even as pope, Michele Ghislieri strove to be faithful to the Dominican vocation he had first embraced when he was twelve years old.

The young Michele had startled two Dominican friars who were passing through Bosco (the town of his birth) by asking if he could become one of them. They were so impressed by his answers to their questions that, with the blessing of his parents, they allowed him to travel with them to the priory of Voghera in Lombardy where his vocation could be tested. From the start, the friars loved the boy. They called him a treasure, for his progress in the spiritual life outstripped his rapid advance in his studies. As a novice in Vegevano, his fellow novices looked upon him as one already far advanced on the road to sanctity— silent, recollected, prudent, yet docile, humble, reverent towards his superiors, and jealously observant of the Dominican rule.

There is no time this morning to recount his activities in his long life as a Dominican, most of it spent in studies, teaching, preaching, and governance. Ordained a priest in Genoa at the age of twenty-four, Father Michele was known by his brethren to be the first to kneel before the Blessed Sacrament in the morning, and the last to say farewell at night. As a young professor, he used to say to his students: "The most powerful aid we can bring to this study is the practice of earnest prayer. The more closely the mind is united to God, the richer the stores of light and wisdom that will follow its researches." His brilliant defense of the faith during the Dominican provincial chapter at Parma in 1543 brought him to the attention of the College of Cardinals, and he was subsequently appointed to the difficult and thankless post of Inquisitor at Como. A few years later, he would be called to Rome to head the Inquisition, and here he remained for the rest of his life.

We cannot enter into the many achievements of his pontificate: his implementation of the reforms of the Council of Trent, especially in the liturgy; his promotion of devotion to the Rosary; and his successful efforts to mobilize the leaders of the nations against the threat of the Turks (of whom it was said that they feared the prayers of the Pope more than they feared all the armies of Europe).

Although St. Pius was never able to return to his Dominican cloister, the legacy of St. Dominic remained with him in at least one important respect that is also significant for us and for our work in the Congregation: love of the truth and zeal for souls. His intellectual formation as a Dominican, combined with his long experience as a champion of the faith, gave him a profound awareness of the power of error to contribute to unhappiness and disorder in human life, and thus of the authentically pastoral necessity of proclaiming the full truth of the Catholic faith without compromise. In imitation of this great saint, we must pray for the love and the zeal that form the deepest wellspring for the proclamation of the doctrine of the faith.

The election of Cardinal Alessandrino had not been greeted with much enthusiasm by the people of Rome on that cold January day in 1566 because he was regarded as too severe. At the time, he had prayed: "God grant me the grace to act so that they may grieve more for my death than for my election." Such was indeed the case when St. Pius V died peacefully in the early hours of the morning on May 1, 1572.

❧ SERMON 43

The Science of the Cross

"THIS IS THE TRUTH!" These were Edith Stein's words when she knew that she would become a Christian. Naturally, they are words that thrill a Dominican's heart. But it is no accident that they were the words Edith Stein uttered when she had finished reading a book by a great Carmelite mystic. For many years afterward, her spiritual home was a Benedictine abbey. Perhaps, with factors like these in mind, the Catholic philosopher Eric Przywara was led to say of Edith Stein that she was the product of three orders: the Dominican, the Benedictine, and the Carmelite. It turns out that her attraction for these great spiritual traditions illumines the great passions of her life—for truth, for contemplation, and for the Cross.

In the summer of 1921, Edith Stein had joined other members of the Göttingen Philosophy Circle for a long visit at the home of her good friend Hedwig Conrad Martius. Looking for something to read while home alone one evening, she chanced upon St. Teresa of Ávila's autobiography. She read through the night and in the morning when she had finished reading the book, she exclaimed, "This is the truth!" She promptly went out and bought herself a catechism and a daily missal. Within a few months, on January 1, 1922, she was baptized a Catholic at St. Martin's Church in Bergzabern.

Her exclamation "This is the truth!" climaxed a long search for the truth that had consumed Edith Stein throughout almost a decade of intense philosophical work and would continue to define her life of research and teaching during the following years before her entry into Carmel and right up to the weeks before her death.

The Dominican connection was clearly present, both in her study and translation of the works of Thomas Aquinas, and in her years of teaching the Dominican nuns at Speyer. The Dominican tradition struck a deep chord. At one point, Edith Stein termed God "The Great Educator." She was a great seeker after the truth who is God. By divine grace, her pursuit of truth led her to the Catholic faith. Her philosophical work is a permanent contribution in several areas of phenomenological reflection, not least of which on the ontology of woman, which influenced the teaching of Pope John Paul II on the place of women in the Church. In the end, only God could satisfy her insatiable thirst for truth. No surprise, then, that Edith Stein was drawn to a life focused on God alone.

Her love of prayer and silence had been nurtured by her mother throughout her Jewish childhood. During her teenage years, even though she confessed that she had become unable to pray to a personal God, she experienced an intense inner life. Little wonder that after her conversion from atheism, she almost immediately wanted to become a contemplative. During the decade between her conversion and her entry into Carmel in 1933, she was a frequent visitor at the Benedictine abbey of Beuron where she particularly relished the monastic environment of silence and dedication, and the solemn liturgical celebrations of Christmas and Paschal tide. Father Raphael Walzer, the abbot of Beuron, was her spiritual director. Her love for the Benedictine tradition is reflected in her choice of the name Teresa Benedicta of the Cross when she entered Carmel.

In the years when she taught at Speyer, Edith Stein became increasingly dissatisfied with secular life, and the conviction steadily grew that she had an authentic vocation to the contemplative life. After thirteen hours of prayer one day in St. Ludgeri's Church in Münster, she recognized that she was being called to the Carmelites. She was forty-two years old when, on October 4, 1933, she entered Mary Queen of Peace

Carmel in Cologne and was able to celebrate the feast of St. Teresa of Ávila there on the next day.

Many of the nuns who knew her there have attested to the intensity with which she embraced the life of prayer and contemplation, of silence and mortification—in short, the life of love—for which she had so long yearned. That Edith Stein was very happy about this was no secret. Indeed, her joy was evident. She said: "I have never laughed so much during my entire life as I have these two years as a novice." She devoted herself with characteristic energy to the life and observances of the Cologne Carmel, and even found time to complete one of her most important philosophical works, *Finite and Eternal Being*, but it would not be published until 1950. Because she was Jewish, she had lost her right to publish. It was 1935, the year of her first vows as a Carmelite and the year of the promulgation of the fateful Nuremberg Statutes which deprived Jewish people of all legal rights. Already, the shadow of the Cross loomed large on the horizon.

"I spoke to our Savior and told him that I knew it was his Cross which was now being laid on the Jewish people. Most of them did not understand it; but those who did understand must accept it willingly in the name of all." Edith Stein's words showed that she vicariously identified herself with her people. It was a matter of great significance for her—a conviction instilled in her by her mother—that she had been born on the feast of Yom Kippur, the Jewish Day of Atonement. At her entrance into Carmel, she wrote: "I am confident that the Lord has taken my life for all the Jews. I always have to think of Queen Esther who was taken away from her people for the express purpose of standing before the king for her people. I am the very poor, weak and small Esther, but the king who selected me is very great and merciful" (cf. Esther 8:3–6). She could not then have known how prophetic these words would turn out to have been. After her conversion, Edith Stein increasingly saw herself as providentially standing for and with her people against the terrible and mounting evil of Nazi hatred of the Jews which would culminate in the genocidal Holocaust. She was in no way isolated from this accumulating horror, either as a Catholic or later as a nun of Carmel.

Her identification with the Cross of Christ, and her love for it, had drawn her to Carmel in the first place. Sister Teresa Benedicta of the Cross wrote the following: "I am quite content in any case. One can only learn the 'Science of the Cross' if one feels the Cross in one's person. I was convinced of this from the very first and have said with all my heart 'Hail Cross, our only hope.'" On the night of December 31, 1938, she left Cologne for the Carmel of Echt in the Netherlands where her sister Rosa (who had also become a Catholic) joined her in 1940 and where she remained, wearing the mandated Jewish star on her Carmelite habit, until August 2, 1942, when Nazis came to arrest her.

The events of the last month of her life show clearly why this great saint is now venerated by the Church as a martyr. After July 26, 1942, when the Dutch bishops protested the deportation of Jews in a pastoral letter read in all the churches, the Nazis retaliated by arresting all Catholics (but not other Christians) of Jewish origin. On August 2 they came for Edith and her sister Rosa who, after passing through several other camps, arrived finally at Auschwitz on August 9 and died in the gas chambers there on that very day.

Thus it happened, in God's mysterious design, that Edith Stein went to her death, as a Jew embracing solidarity with her people and as a Christian bearing witness unto death in a Catholic protest against the evil of Nazi anti-Semitism. Only in the science of the Cross could such a death signify a victory. We learn this science from Christ who, in a definitive way, conquered the evil of sin and death through the Cross, and who leads each one of us, one by one, through the same passage—*passio*—so that sin will die in us and will yield to the newness of life. In declaring Edith Stein a saint and martyr, the Church expresses the faith that, in the end, it is God himself who blessed and enabled her to willingly embrace the Cross and with it her vicarious representation of her people. It is God who by this sign confirms our faith in Christ's victory over evil, even in the organized and seemingly superhuman form it assumed in Nazi anti-Semitism and the Holocaust.

The Dominican love of truth, the Benedictine love for a life focused on God alone, and the Carmelite love of the Cross converged in a remarkable way in the distinctive spirit of this great saint. For what she learned and embodied so stunningly in her own life is that the ultimate truth that God teaches us can only be summed up in the science of the Cross. Let Edith Stein have the last word about this: "The bridal union of the soul with God, for which it is created, is purchased through the Cross, perfected with the Cross, and sealed for all eternity with the Cross."

❧ SERMON 44

The Universal Call to Sanctity

WHAT DOES GOD WANT? What does he desire? Why did he create the world? Why did he send his only Son to become one of us, teaching us and dying for us? Why did he institute the Church and the sacraments? What is the meaning of all this? What does God really want?

What is the answer to these questions? Of course we must answer that God wants for nothing. Still it is no exaggeration to say that no one has ever wanted anything as much as God desires to share with us the communion of his own Trinitarian life.

We must admit that God does not need our company. The Father, the Son, and the Holy Spirit are supremely content, we might say, with their own company. Their divine personal communion is complete, perfect and happy. In more than one passage of his great work *Against Heresies*, St. Irenaeus makes this point very clearly: "God has no need of man" And again: "God who has no need of anyone gives communion with himself to those who need him."

Here we are confronted with a great mystery: The Father, the Son, and the Holy Spirit—despite being perfectly content with their own company—want to create a space there for the us, for creaturely persons. Listen again to St. Irenaeus: "These gifts make man glorious, giving him what he lacks: friendship with God. We give nothing to God, for God does not need our love."

Christ has revealed to us—for how else could we have known?—that everything that exists—the universe in its vastness, the stars and the planets, the earth and all it contains, the blue skies, the green fields and the ocean depths, the plants and the flowers, all creatures great and small—all these things exist because of the divine desire to share the communion of Trinitarian life with human persons—in short, with us. Only the Son participates in this communion of Trinitarian life "by nature." And he allows us to participate in it by the adoption: Through our transformation in his image, Christ makes us capable of sharing in the divine life of the Trinity. "See what love the Father has bestowed on us that we may be called children of God." With his own body and blood as our food and drink, he shares the communion of his life with us, and makes us one with the Father and the Holy Spirit. Not surprisingly, the Church calls this sacramental participation in the Body and Blood of Christ "holy communion." Though persons who are not God, we have in this way the ability to participate in the communion of the divine persons.

But this is not all. God in his great mercy found the remedy for the catastrophe of sin. The disobedience and corruption that make us enemies of God, and that would make it impossible to enjoy the supremely holy life of the divine persons, are overcome by the obedience and sacrificial death of his only-begotten Son. Our Eucharistic communion constitutes a participation in the sacrificial offering that redeems us from our sins, reconciling us to God. He who eats this bread will not dwell ever in death but will live forever. "Salvation comes from our God, who is seated on the throne, and from the Lamb."

It is appropriate to remind ourselves of our destiny as we celebrate the Feast of All Saints today. We began by asking what God wants. We have said that he wants to share the communion of his Trinitarian life with us. We might have just as well have said that God wants us all to become saints.

We want to avoid slipping into a Protestant key here—that is, to blur the distinction between the sanctity which is the vocation of all Christians and the extraordinary sanctity of those who are saints properly so-called. Although the origins of this feast cannot be traced with certainty, it seems clear that when in the seventh century Pope Gregory III established an oratory for the relics of the saints in St. Peter's, he enjoined that there be celebrated on this day the holy apostles and all saints, martyrs and confessors, and all the just made perfect who are at rest. The second of the four reasons for the institution of this feast given by the Dominican Blessed James of Voragine in his famous book *The Golden Legend* is "to supply for omissions." "We have in fact omitted many feasts," he writes, "not celebrating feast days or making memorials of them.... For one thing the number of [saints] has multiplied until it is almost infinite. Besides that, we are weak and because of our weakness could not put up with so many celebrations." Even if it is clear that it is the extraordinary sanctity of saints properly so-called for which we give God the glory on All Saints' Day, we can with all the more reason be reminded today to commit ourselves with fervor, perseverance, and hope to seek the sanctity that God wants for each one of us as he shares with us nothing less than the communion of Trinitarian life.

"Beloved, we are God's children now; what we shall be has not yet been revealed. We do know that when it is revealed, we shall be like him, for we shall see him as he is."

I pray that all of us who today celebrate this Feast of All Saints will find ourselves together again, that "coming to perfect holiness in the fullness of [God's] love, we may pass from this pilgrim table to the banquet of our heavenly homeland" (Prayer after Communion) with the Holy Mother of God and singing the praise of the Father, Son, and Holy Spirit. Amen.

❧ SERMON 45

Preserved from Sin in View of the Merits of Christ

ON THIS FEAST OF THE IMMACULATE CONCEPTION, it is a joy to salute this great community of Sant'Anselmo, for the Benedictines have been champions of this precious doctrine of our faith and its liturgical celebration for nearly a thousand years. Indeed, the first western theologian to write a defense of the Feast of the Immaculate Conception in the early twelfth century was the Benedictine Eadmer of Canterbury in his *Tractatus de Conceptione sanctae Mariae editum ab Eadmero monacho magno peccatore*—a work that in a remarkable way foreshadows subsequent theological arguments on this theme.

To be sure, not all Benedictines were in favor of the feast or the doctrine. St. Anselm himself, Eadmer's mentor, held for Mary's sanctification in the womb of St. Anne, but, like other theologians before and after, he fell short of affirming her entire freedom from sin from the moment of her conception. Still, English Benedictine communities in Winchester, Canterbury, and elsewhere were noteworthy in their promotion of the feast. So much so that, in the late twelfth century, Pierre de Celle, a monk of Cluny and later bishop of Chartres who opposed the feast, was moved to complain of "English levity" in contrast to "Gallic maturity" in this regard, for, since "England is an island surrounded by water, her inhabitants are understandably affected by the property of this element and are often led to odd and unfounded fancies."

Perhaps Pierre de Celle was unaware that France had in fact played a role in the introduction of the feast to England in the eleventh century, for it was in Normandy that English Benedictines first encountered it. The Normans themselves found the feast celebrated in the Byzantine Magna Grecia.

It was precisely in defense of the celebration of the *feast* of the conception of Mary that Eadmer wrote. This is a point of no small interest in the home of a distinguished faculty of the liturgy, and as a theologian I am bound to acknowledge it. The faithful sensed that any hint of sin was incompatible with the one who bore the Son of God.

Eadmer was well aware that in the recognition of this mystery, popular devotion was ahead of theology. A long theological development was necessary before the popular piety of the people of God would be resoundingly vindicated in the solemn definition of the dogma of the Immaculate Conception in 1854. When I mentioned that I would be preaching here today, a Capuchin friar said to me that, just as it is natural for each of us to desire the most beautiful mother in the world, so it was fitting that God, the all-powerful Father, would chose for the earthly nativity of his only-begotten Son, the most perfectly beautiful Mother. Thus, as the pious faithful have always recognized, the Church must venerate Mary's Immaculate Conception. The words of the angel to Mary, "Hail, full of grace" are not limited temporally as if to exclude even the initial moments of her life. On the contrary, she would not have received the complete fullness of grace had her soul been even for an instant in the condition of spiritual death which is the consequence of original sin. As Saint Augustine famously remarked: "The honor of the Lord does not permit that the question of sin be raised in connection with the Blessed Virgin Mary."

Still, throughout the centuries of theological debate, the central issue was not so much the plenitude of grace that the Holy Mother of God enjoys but the need to include this privilege within the single economy of salvation in Christ. A homily is not the place to recount the intricacies of this fascinating debate, but we must note the critical insight of Duns Scotus who affirmed that Mary is *preserved* from sin in view of the merits of Christ, whereas we sinners are *liberated* from sin by Christ's merits. Advancing an argument that can be found in embryo in Eadmer, Duns Scotus asserted that the sovereign mode of salvation is not to heal a wound already suffered but to protect from injury before its infliction. Associating his Mother with himself in the work of salvation, it was fitting for the perfect Redeemer to preserve his Mother from all sin, original and actual.

The central theological point is of great importance to each one of us. No one, not even the Blessed Virgin Mary, falls outside the divine plan for the salvation of the human race. After the Fall, innocence and sinlessness cannot be seen as parallel possibilities for us—alongside sin and guilt—which were somehow realized in our Lady. Her *preservation* from sin, no less than our *liberation* from sin, must be ascribed to the saving power of the passion, death, and resurrection of our Lord Jesus Christ.

Recall that Eadmer identified himself as author of his work on the Immaculate Conception by adding the words *monacho magno peccatore* (monk and great sinner). We must surely say the same of ourselves—great sinners (*magni peccatori*). As we honor our Lady today, as we acclaim her Immaculate Conception, let us throw ourselves upon the mercy of God—the God who, as we are repeatedly reminded in the season of Advent, forgets our sins and gives us the hope of salvation in the Incarnation of his only Son.

Let us give Eadmer the last word: "If Jeremiah was sanctified in his mother's womb because he was to be a prophet among the Gentiles, and if John, who was to go before the Lord in the spirit and power of Elijah, was filled with the Holy Spirit from his mother's womb, who would dare to say that the one and only mercy seat of the whole world, the most sweet couch of the Son of God Almighty, was deprived of the illumination of the grace of the Holy Spirit from the first instant of her conception?"

❧ SERMON 46

Roses and an Image

ROSES AND AN IMAGE—not words, or at least not many words—
are the central features of the apparitions of our Lady at Tepeyac
which occurred during the octave days of the feast of the Immaculate
Conception in 1531.

The roses were intended as a sign for Bishop Zumárraga who would
presumably have recognized them as a species native to Castile. A miracle that could not have failed to impress the bishop: Castilian roses in
mid-winter Mexico, roses picked on a barren hillside and arranged in
Juan Diego's arms by our Lady herself. "There is no rose of such virtue
/ As is the rose that bore Jesu: / Alleluia," to quote a fifteenth-century
English Advent carol. The roses of Guadalupe make us think of the
expectant Mary, the Advent Mary, who directs our gaze to Christ and
the mystery of his coming to save us. Roses from a mid-winter hillside
signal the unexpected, the sheer grace of Christ's coming, for which
we cannot really prepare and for which grace alone makes us ready. To
quote the second stanza of the English carol: "For in this rose contained
was / Heaven and earth in little space: / *Res miranda*."

The miraculous image of Guadalupe, measuring 6.5x3.5 feet, was
imprinted on the rough cloth of Juan Diego's tilma. It is an image that
is miraculous in two respects: first, because the vegetable fiber of the
cloak, which normally begins to decay after about twenty years, has
remained perfectly intact for nearly five hundred years; and, second,

because, not only are there no brush strokes, but it would be next to impossible to paint such an image on a fabric of this kind. Our Lady says of it: "This sacred image will be known as the Entirely Perfect Virgin Holy Mary of Guadalupe." In a 1688 work on the apparitions, Franciscan Fray Geronimo Valladolid captured the significance of the image nicely when he wrote: "This Virgin as she is portrayed needs no writing because she herself is a writing on a piece of cloth." In other words, the image itself communicates its meaning like a pictograph. Prior to the Spanish conquest of Mexico, the language of the Aztecs, Náhuatl, was written entirely in hieroglyphics. Like this ancient language, the image of our Lady is a pictograph which is itself Mary's message to us.

As a pictograph, the image can be understood in connection with the word "Guadalupe" which is neither a place name (as one might suppose) nor a Náhuatl term. Rather, it corresponds to the Náhuatl expression, *te coatlaxopeuh*, which, when pronounced, would sound to Spanish ears like "Guadalupe." Roughly translated, it means "to crush the stone serpent." The reference here is to the Aztec god, Quetzacoatl, often pictured as a feathered serpent, an object of worship and human sacrifice for over two thousand years. In this perspective, the title of the image turns out to be: "the Entirely Perfect Virgin Holy Mary *who crushes the stone serpent.*" The crescent at Mary's feet represents the serpent being crushed. It is the image itself, in effect, that is powerful in overcoming the serpent—not just the old religion of the Aztecs but, if we think of the words of Genesis (3:14–15), evil itself. The image as a whole has the power to accomplish this. As in a true pictograph, every detail contributes something to the overall message. The sun rays behind our Lady, for example, signify that human beings are more important than the sun god to whom they were routinely sacrificed in the old religion.

The Advent setting of Guadalupe is striking. The incarnate One whose coming we anticipate in this holy season is the Word, the perfect image of the God in human flesh. God sends, not a message expressed in words, but his only-begotten Son in the flesh. Like the image of

Guadalupe, the incarnate son is the image of God: he is the divine message in himself. "By that rose we may well see / That he is God in Persons three: / *Pari forma*."

So roses and an image are central to the apparitions of Guadalupe and to its Advent setting. The unexpected and "impossible" roses remind us of the sheer grace of the Incarnation, and the image itself reminds us of the awesome immediacy of the divine presence in Christ the Incarnate Son.

The feasts of the Blessed Virgin Mary always point us to the central mysteries of our faith. They always point us—as she would do were she the preacher today—to Christ. Mary wants to shape us in these mysteries, to "mother" us in them as brothers and sisters of her divine Son and thus as sharers in the communion of the Blessed Trinity. So it is that, today, from Alaska to the Tierra del Fuego, above and below the Rio Grande, we can all embrace as our Mother "the Entirely Perfect Virgin Holy Mary of Guadalupe," the Queen of the Americas.

❧ SERMON 47

What Sort of King Is This?

WHAT SORT OF KING IS THIS?—born in a borrowed stable, preaching from a borrowed boat, rejected by his putative subjects, and executed as a felon and buried in a borrowed tomb. Here, today, we behold him interrogated by the procurator of a minor Roman jurisdiction who, with understandable perplexity, asks, "Are you the king of the Jews?"

"What sort of king is this?" Pilate must be thinking. Are we not a little perplexed ourselves? The readings do not help us much. There are places in the Gospels where we read of Jesus being surrounded by people hanging on his every word, where an excited crowd is ready to proclaim him king, where he is transfigured in glory before the amazed eyes of his disciples, where he rides triumphantly into the city of Jerusalem with palm branches at his feet. Would not any one of these gospel passages have been more suitable for this Sunday of Christ the King than one in which he stands meekly before Pontius Pilate?

But our perplexity would not be allayed by a different selection of biblical texts. The problem goes deeper. Could not Jesus have secured a more receptive hearing for his message of love and justice for the oppressed? Why did he not come among us as the son of an earthly king, or indeed as the son of the Roman emperor? Then he would have been the most powerful man in the world, a real king, with armies, governors, senators, secretaries, counselors—people who could execute his plans effectively. What is more, he would have won over many followers.

"If you are the king of the Jews," jeered the onlookers at Calvary, "come down from the Cross and save us and yourself!" But he didn't come down from the Cross, did he? And injustice, tyranny, crimes, warfare, sin, and every kind of mischief thrive in our midst. What kind of victory is this, and what kind of king?

Today's liturgy presses these questions upon us, and Christ himself provides the answer: "My kingdom does not belong to this world. If my kingdom did belong to this world, my attendants would be fighting to keep me from being handed over to the Jews." "Then you are a king?" says Pilate. "You say I am a king. For this I was born and for this I came into the world, to testify to the truth," Jesus replies. If his kingdom belonged to this world, we would cling to the lies that so attract us. Why is this? Because if Christ had come arrayed with the symbols and instruments of worldly power, we would have been confirmed in our illusions—our entrenched belief that evil can be overcome by the means that worldly power affords. But God, in his mercy, wants to show us the true nature of the darkness in the human heart. Hence Christ's words to Pilate signaling the nature of his kingship—"I came into the world to testify to the truth"—as well as the identity of his subjects—"everyone who belongs to the truth listens to my voice."

What kind of king is this? This is the king who overcomes the power of sin and death from the inside, who attacks this power at its deepest roots, who allows himself to be crushed by all the concentrated sin of the human race from the beginning to the end of time, who is literally *killed* by this sin, and who nonetheless wins a definitive victory over sin and death by his passion, death, and resurrection.

Confronted with the reality of our alienation from him—and the proliferation of evil that this entailed—God, in his omnipotence, could surely have found other ways to reconcile us to himself and to overcome the evil of sin. But in his mercy he chose a way to save us that, we must suppose, was adjusted, adapted, to our nature. That he chose to send his only Son to suffer and die for our sake tells us something about the reality of our condition. If such was the remedy, what must the harm have been?

Christ's kingship testifies to the truth of the human condition and to the reality and efficacy of God's merciful condescension in our regard. The injustice, tyranny, crimes, warfare, and mischief that thrive in our midst are the result of sin, and they cannot be overcome by programs or remedies, no matter how well-intentioned or well-organized, that come from within the created order. The persistent error of Arianism and all its numerous offspring, in the end, is precisely this: to think that our salvation can come from ourselves. The truth lies elsewhere. "My kingdom is not here."

What kind of king is this?—the king who rules first of all in our hearts and souls and bodies. Christ is our first ally in the interior struggle that St. Augustine calls "a praiseworthy battle [that] acts to keep what is better from being overcome by what is worse. The struggle is to keep desire from conquering the mind and to keep lust from conquering wisdom. This is the steadfast peace in which you ought to develop in yourself, that what is better in you may be in charge of what is worse. The better part in you...is the part in which God's image is found."

As we are transformed by the grace of Christ the King at work in us, we experience within ourselves the tranquility and peace of his reign. "What is more king-like," asks St. Leo, "than to find yourself ruler over your body after having surrendered your soul to God?"

What sort of king is this, my brothers in Christ? Just the sort of king we really need.

* * *

Pope Pius XI instituted the feast of Christ the King in 1925 with his encyclical *Quam Primus*—significantly, to mark the 1600th anniversary of the Council of Nicaea. Recognition of the reign of Christ—according to Pope Pius—was the surest remedy against the destructive forces unleashed by the first world war and already gathering strength for the second. In order "to promote as fully as possible the royal dignity of our Redeemer," he wrote, "there seems to us that there would be nothing more appropriate than the institution of a special and proper feast of

Christ the King." May Christ's eternal and universal reign rule in our hearts, as the Preface of today's Mass declares, "the reign of truth and of life, the reign of holiness and of grace, the reign of justice, of love, and of peace." Amen.

❧ PART V ❧
Holy Orders

❧ SERMON 48

Daniel's Example

As you are admitted to candidacy this evening, my brothers, we can assure you that, generally speaking, you are not likely to be called upon to read the handwriting on the wall, as Daniel was. In other important ways, however, Daniel provides a model of what will be required of you and how you must prepare yourselves for the now imminent call to priestly orders.

Over the centuries the figure of Daniel has fascinated painters, poets, and musicians who have found irresistible the stories of his wise judgment in saving Susannah from her false accusers, of his uncanny ability to interpret for Nebuchadnezzar his two dreams and, in today's reading, the handwriting on the wall for his less fortunate son Belshazzar, and lastly of Daniel's escape from the lions' den. Daniel has been no less a central figure in the rabbinic and Christian theological traditions. Josephus, for example, devoted more attention to Daniel than to any other prophet, and, on the Christian side, many patristic and medieval authors wrote commentaries on the book of Daniel— among them, St. Jerome and St. Albert the Great.

St. Augustine saw Daniel as representative of the celibate life, while St. Jerome saw him as the preeminent prophet of the Incarnation. These are indications that prompt me to regard as providential rather than simply coincidental the fact that this year the rite of admission to candidacy at the Beda falls during a week when Daniel figures prominently in the daily lectionary. Your own situation, my brothers, is not unlike that of Daniel. He found himself among a group of Judean boys chosen by the king's chief eunuch, Ashpenaz—"boys of royal or noble descent," the king demanded, "without any physical defect, of good appearance, versed in every branch of wisdom, well-informed, discerning, suitable for service at the royal court." Something very much like this has happened to you in the past few years.

Like Daniel and his fellows, you have been chosen for service. Pointing to the need for workers in the harvest, Christ encouraged his listeners—not to throw themselves immediately into the task—but first to ask the Lord of the harvest to send workers into his harvest. The Church has understood this to mean that no one enters into Christ's priestly service who has not been called, chosen, and sent. The ordained ministry is not like a career which one self-selects, but a divine vocation and grace to which one is called and strives to be faithful.

Like Daniel and his fellows, you have been chosen because you seem to possess the qualities necessary to serve the King of the universe. It is for the Church and her pastors to determine one's aptitude for this ministry. After a period of discernment and initial formation, you and your superiors have good reasons to believe that you have been chosen by God to share in the priesthood of Jesus Christ. As King Belshazzar said to Daniel, "I am told that the spirit of God Most Holy lives in you, and that you are known for your perception, intelligence, and marvelous wisdom." We in effect say the same to you today. This holy rite of admission to candidacy marks in a formal way the ecclesial judgment that one's vocation is indeed authentic and that one possesses the qualities necessary for the ordained ministry.

With this formal recognition of your candidacy, you enter into a new and deeper phase of formation and testing to prepare you, God willing, for the singular seal of the Holy Spirit in the Sacrament of Holy Orders. You must strive to be like Daniel whose renunciation of fine foods has been taken by both the literary and the theological tradition to represent the renunciation of earthly pleasures and the embrace of a holy and pure life. You will live now for Christ alone. Like Daniel, you know that you cannot succeed in this way of life apart from the grace of God, and, like Daniel, your confidence in this grace should never waver.

About today's text, St. Jerome wrote that, for Daniel, "there was a need not only for reading the inscription but also for interpreting what had been read, in order that it might be understood what these words were announcing." Like Daniel, you must be steeped in the wisdom of God, that comes to you both as God's gift and as the fruit of your own labors of study and reflection. Thus, your theological formation is an essential element in your preparation for the reception of Holy Orders. Perhaps more than ever, the Church today needs priests who can make sense of the whole ensemble of the divine mysteries as they have been revealed to us in Christ, preserved in Scriptures and Tradition, and taught by the Magisterium—priests who can grasp the inherent intelligibility of these mysteries and communicate them effectively and persuasively. These mysteries, at their core, concern the otherwise unimaginable and inconceivable truth that the triune God, who has no need of company, desires to share the communion of Trinitarian love with us. This "handwriting" needs good readers and interpreters.

According to the deep patterns of figuration and typology which divine providence has woven into the fabric of the Sacred Scripture, Daniel can be recognized as prefiguring Christ. In many cases where I have drawn a parallel between Daniel and yourselves, I could well have spoken about the parallel between yourselves and Christ. Your service of the Church—*in persona Christi*—requires of you a more profound form of the imitation of Christ that is required of every one of his disciples. Holy Orders will constitute you ontologically as men who can speak and act *in persona Christi capitis*. This future ontological "enhancement," so to speak, at the core of your being must be matched by a transformation at every level of your character and personality. To be sure, perfect conformity to Christ the High Priest is the work of a lifetime for every priest. But you must begin now to cultivate a disciplined and recollected life, in which the Liturgy of the Hours, the Holy Sacrifice of the Mass, meditation, the Rosary, and spiritual reading are indispensable elements of your everyday schedule. In this way, on the day of your ordination to the priesthood, there will be a "fit," so to speak, between the sacramental transformation of your inner being and the ever-growing conformation of your entire selves to Christ the High Priest.

St. Jerome advises us: "We should follow the example of a man like Daniel, who despised the honor and gifts of a king and who without any reward even in that early day followed the Gospel injunction: 'Freely have you received, freely give' (Matthew 10:8)." Therefore, when you are called by name, come forward and declare your intention before the Church assembled here.

❧ SERMON 49

The Prayers of the Gardener

ON TUESDAY, following an in-flight explosion, a hot air balloon crashed near Luxor in Egypt, killing nineteen tourists—"cremating" them, as the media gruesomely reported. The pilot and a passenger survived. Were those nineteen greater sinners than the two who survived?

In today's Gospel our Lord cites instances like this—catastrophes everyone has heard about. He anticipates what his hearers might be thinking: Do these events have some religious or moral significance? Were the Galileans whose blood Pilate mixed with their sacrifices greater sinners than all other Galileans, or were the eighteen people upon whom the tower in Siloam collapsed greater sinners than all the inhabitants of Jerusalem?

His response to the questions he poses is brief and deceptively simple. The lesson to be drawn from these events is most surely *not* that those who perished were greater sinners than those who survived or were entirely unaffected. Rather it is this: If we do not repent, all of us will perish. In fuller terms the point is that since all of us are sinners, and the end of life can be so unexpected, then there can be no reason to postpone repentance. Nothing is to be gained by procrastination. If we knew that our lives were going to come to an end on such and such a day in the future—say, ten years from now—then we could delay repentance until a safe interval before that date. But we do not know this. Death will be as unexpected for us as for those who perished in these catastrophes.

Our Lord underscores precisely this point by means of the parable of the fig tree. Though the fig tree has been barren for three years, the owner of the orchard agrees to give it a reprieve: one more year. Likewise, God is patient with our procrastination, with our failure to bear the fruit of true repentance, but not indefinitely so. "With fear and trembling," says St. Gregory the Great, "should we hear the words...'cut it down'.... He who will not by correction grow rich unto fruitfulness, falls to that place from whence he is no longer able to rise by repentance."

But there is a bright side to today's sobering Lenten message—as it happens something wonderfully apt on this occasion of the Institution of Acolytes. It is to be found in the humble figure of the gardener in the parable of the fig tree. For it is at his suggestion—we might well say his intercession—that the owner of the orchard gives the barren fig tree yet another year. "Let us not then strike suddenly," says St. Gregory Nazianzen, "but overcome by gentleness, lest we cut down the fig tree still able to bear fruit, which the care perhaps of a skilful dresser will restore." Not only does the gardener put in a good word for the fig tree, but he has a plan for improving its chances of bearing fruit in the coming year: to dig around the tree and fertilize it, to give it special care.

The figure of the gardener is easy to miss, but in the rich tradition of patristic commentary on this parable he gets a lot of attention. A particularly significant reading of the parable sees him as representing Christ who implores the Father to allow him to water the tree with his teaching and his sufferings so that it will yield the fruit of repentance and good works.

This reading counterbalances the sharp warning contained in the whole passage. The prolongation and exquisite tenderness of divine patience with us is assured by the incarnation, passion, death, and resurrection of Christ who stays the pending divine judgment and provides the grace we need to repent of our sins. We are prompted not only to fear and trembling, as St. Gregory rightly says, but also to hope and renewed resolve to open our hearts to Christ and his healing grace. He works at the roots of our fig tree, watering it with his own blood, as it were, to nourish, correct, and guide us to the repentance and love that makes possible our communion with him, with his heavenly Father, and his Holy Spirit. "Christ was born for this," we sang just a few weeks ago at Christmastide, "Christ was born for this."

But there are greater depths to be plumbed here. Listen again to St. Gregory the Great: "By the dresser of the vineyard is represented the order of Bishops, who, by ruling over the Church, take care of the Lord's vineyard." Thus the divine husbandman conjoins to himself laborers in the vineyard to take care of us—and not just as collaborators, but as true instruments of his saving grace, internally united with him to act *in persona Christi capitis*, according to the ancient formula.

Christ established a sacramental economy which may be regarded as an extension of the mystery of the Incarnation itself. The only-begotten Son of God, who came to us in human flesh as our Savior, did not leave us. After he had ascended to the right hand of the Father, he willed to remain with us always, chiefly by his presence in the Holy Eucharist, where he shares with us his body and blood.

What is more, Christ ensured this presence by giving to his disciples, and through them, to their successors, the power of the priesthood to celebrate, in *his* Person, this very sacrifice of his love and his friendship. Bishops and priests are the instruments of this Eucharistic mystery. Through them God wills to pour out his grace—his friendship and love—on us in the Church through the preaching of the Word and the celebration of the Sacraments.

In this way, the divine husbandman continues to be in our midst but in a manner precisely adapted to our human nature, ensuring that the Apostles and their successors chosen from our midst would care for his precious vineyard. The hand of another human being blesses us, pours the water of Baptism on our heads, offers the body and blood of Christ to us in the Eucharist, and is raised in absolution unto the forgiveness of sins. Through these sacramental actions, we see the divine husbandman at work as God bestows his saving grace on us, drawing us into a participation in the communion of love of the Father, Son, and Holy Spirit.

To be sure, as St. Augustine reminds us, "the husbandman who intercedes is every holy man who within the Church prays for them that are without the Church, saying, *O Lord, O Lord, let it alone this year*, that is for that time vouchsafed under grace, *until I dig about it*." Nonetheless, the parable of the fig tree provides a key for understanding a special type of participation in Christ's work as the divine husbandman and thus an insight into what will happen here, dear sons in Christ, as you are instituted in the ministry of acolytes in a few moments.

For you will have a special role in the Church's ministry, in the care and nurturing of the vineyard of Christ. The summit and source of the Church's life is the Eucharist. It is your responsibility to assist priests and deacons in carrying out their ministry, and as special ministers to give Holy Communion to the faithful at Mass and to the sick. Because you are specially called to this ministry, you should strive to live more fully by the Lord's sacrifice and to be conformed ever more perfectly to Christ himself. Strive to understand the deep spiritual meaning of what you do, so that you may offer yourselves daily to God as spiritual sacrifices acceptable to him through Jesus Christ. In performing your ministry bear in mind that, as you share the one bread with your brothers and sisters, you form one Body with them. Show a sincere love for Christ's Mystical Body, and especially for the weak and the sick. Be obedient to the commandment which the Lord gave to his Apostles at the Last Supper: "Love one another as I also have loved you."

In this way, you will begin to share in the unique role of Christ himself who came to save sinners and bring them back to God, and to incorporate the Holy Priesthood and its special assistants—its acolytes—into this work of salvation. Be confident of the divine mercy that has been poured into your own hearts for the sake of repentance and the forgiveness of sins. May God make you fit instruments of this mercy in all your dealings with those whom you serve, in imitation of the divine husbandman, never losing hope in his power to make the barren tree bring forth the fruit of faith, repentance, and love. Amen.

❧ Sermon 50

Transfigured in Christ

"From the cloud came a voice, 'This is my beloved Son. Listen to him.'" This beloved Son, out of an almost incomprehensible love, the Father has given to us—first at Bethlehem, then on Calvary, and now, daily, in the Eucharist. The future God has in view in this astonishing outpouring of love can be glimpsed in the mystery of the Transfiguration—the future for his Son, for us, and, as it happens today, for our new acolytes.

In the Transfiguration, Peter, James, and John witness a remarkable transformation in the countenance of Christ. The ordinary Jesus who is their companion and master is transformed before their eyes in a dazzling display of glory. They are at a loss even to describe what they see. Jesus's clothes become whiter, as St. Mark quaintly puts it, than any bleach could make them. In fact, what they see is not so much a transformation that changes Jesus into something that he had not been beforehand, but rather a disclosure that reveals his true nature. For a fleeting moment, the veil that conceals his glory from their sight is removed and they behold the glory of God's only Son.

The "great reason for this Transfiguration," Pope St. Leo says, is "to remove the scandal of the Cross from the hearts of his disciples, and to prevent the humiliation of his voluntary suffering from disturbing the faith of those who had witnessed the surpassing glory that lay concealed." In other words, when the disciples later beheld Christ dead on the Cross, they would not despair or lose heart. Those who had been to the top of Mount Tabor would be prepared for the events at the top of Mount Calvary: they would know that beneath the appearance of death and defeat lay the reality of victory and life. Appearances to the contrary notwithstanding, as we might say, the Cross constitutes a victory over sin and death, a victory that would be confirmed and made manifest in the Resurrection on the third day—*Christ Jesus who died, or rather, was raised.*

But, according to St. Leo, there is another reason for the Transfiguration. Not only does our Lord want to sustain the faith of his disciples in the face of events that will sorely try it. In the Transfiguration, he reveals not just his own hidden glory, but our future glory as well. "The whole body of Christ," St. Leo says, is "to understand the kind of transformation that it would receive as his gift. The members of that body were to look forward to a share in that glory that first blazed out in Christ their head." Naturally, especially from the point of view of the more senior among us, we seem to be drifting toward decrepitude rather than rising to glory! But again, appearances to the contrary notwithstanding, "all of us, with unveiled faces, seeing the glory of the Lord as though reflected in a mirror, are being transformed from one degree of glory to another" (2 Corinthians 3:18).

In the Transfiguration, the whole mystery of our salvation is laid before us. God in his amazing love for the human race gave his beloved Son first of all at Bethlehem in order that, for men to be born of God, God did not hesitate to be born of man. What is more, "he who did not spare his one Son but handed him over for us all, how will he not also give us everything else along with him?" On Calvary, he did not withhold his beloved Son from the passion and death that would definitively remove the obstacles posed by sin and death to the grace of our sonship—the filiation that draws us into the communion of divine love of the Father, Son, and Holy Spirit. The transformation in us that makes this possible is really a conformation to Christ. We are being refashioned so that "the glory of Christ, who is the image of God" (2 Corinthians 4:4) will shine forth in us: that the Father might see in us what he sees and loves in Christ.

Configuration to Christ, adoptive sonship to the Father in the Holy Spirit, and communion with one another in them: this is the future that God, that great adventurer of love, has laid out before all Christians in the Transfiguration.

Dear sons in Christ, as you are instituted in the Ministry of Acolytes this morning, consider the profound significance that the Transfiguration holds for priests and thus for every candidate for ordination to the priesthood. The Sacrament of Holy Orders—for which service in the instituted ministries of reader and acolyte is a prerequisite—involves a perfect configuration to Christ that is nothing less than an interior transformation of one's very being. When our Lord breathed upon the disciples in his first appearance to them, it was to show, according to St. Cyril of Alexandria, "that the gift of the Holy Spirit necessarily attends those who are ordained by him to be apostles of God.... Transforming them into something other than they were before, Jesus consecrates them by actual sanctification, making them partakers in his nature, through participation in the Spirit and in a sort of strengthening of the nature of humanity into a power and glory that is superhuman." Dear brothers, your institution as acolytes marks an important milestone along your path to Holy Orders and thus to a more perfect configuration to Christ in the priesthood that is centered on the Eucharist and the sacramental life of the Church.

As men chosen for the Ministry of Acolytes, it will be your responsibility for the time being, to assist priests and deacons in liturgical celebrations, especially the Holy Sacrifice of the Mass, and to distribute communion when required. You will perform these functions more worthily if you participate "in the Holy Eucharist with increasingly fervent devotion" and receive "nourishment from it." In *Ministeria Quaedam*, Pope Paul VI wrote: "As one set aside in a special way for service at the altar, the acolyte should learn all matters concerning public divine worship and strive to grasp their inner spiritual meaning: in that way he will be able each day to offer himself entirely to God, be an example to all by his gravity and reverence in church, and have a sincere love for the Mystical Body of Christ, the people of God, especially the weak and the sick." Follow the Lord's command to his apostles at the Last Supper: "Love one another as I also have loved you."

At the very heart of the Ministry of Acolytes is the celebration of the Holy Eucharist, which is the summit and source of the life of the Church. In the divine plan of salvation, the sacraments and especially the Holy Eucharist constitute the primary means by which our configuration to Christ is accomplished over the course of our lifetimes. The Eucharist is like a second Transfiguration, according to St. Peter Julian Eymard. "Whereas on Tabor Jesus had rent the veil that covered his divinity, here he conceals even his humanity and transfigures it into the appearances of bread...compressing himself in the very small space of the Host.... Do you see him in this transfiguration of love and humility? The Eucharistic transfiguration did not take place...in glory but in secret and in a state of humiliation; glory will come as a result of it."

Like the Eucharistic transfiguration, our growing configuration to Christ is something hidden. "Beloved, we are God's children now; what we will be has not yet been revealed. What we do know is this: When he is revealed, we will be like him, for we will see him as he is" (1 John 3:2). Dear brothers, give yourselves everyday ever more fully to the grace of the Holy Spirit at work in your hearts that is promised by the Transfiguration, transforming you from one degree of glory to another until the glory of Christ shines forth in you.

❧ SERMON 51

Teacher, Priest and Shepherd

WE GIVE GLORY AND PRAISE TO GOD, and invoke the intercession and wisdom of their patron saints this morning, as we prepare to ordain our brothers Jerome Augustine Zeiler, Jordan Joseph Schmidt, Augustine Marie Reisenauer, Michael Dominic O'Connor, and Justin Marie Brophy to the sacred priesthood of Jesus Christ. Because these our Dominican brothers, and your relatives and friends, are now to be advanced to the Order of priests, I ask you to consider carefully the nature of the rank in the Church to which they are about to be raised.

It is true that God has made his entire holy people a royal priesthood in Christ. Nevertheless, our great High Priest, Jesus Christ, chose certain disciples to carry out publicly in his name, and on behalf of the human race, a priestly office in the Church. For Christ was sent by the Father and he in turn sent the Apostles into the world, so that through them and their successors, the Bishops, he might continue without interruption to exercise his office of Teacher, Priest, and Shepherd. Indeed, priests are established co-workers of the Order of Bishops, with whom they are joined in the priestly office and with whom they are called to the service of the people of God.

This Holy Priesthood may therefore be regarded as an extension of the mystery of the Incarnation itself. The only-begotten Son of God, who came to us in human flesh as our Savior did not leave us as orphans after his passion, death, and resurrection.

After he had ascended to the right hand of the Father, he willed to remain with us always, first of all by his presence in the Holy Eucharist, where he shares with us his body and blood, and remains present for our loving adoration. Christ ensured this by giving to his disciples, and, through them, to their successors, the power of the priesthood to commemorate, *in persona Christi*, in *his* Person, this very sacrifice of his love and his friendship for us *as if we had been present at the Lord's Supper* on that Thursday evening centuries ago. Of this sacrifice, St. Justin Martyr, the patron saint of one our ordinands, wrote: "For not as common bread and common drink do we receive these; but in like manner as Jesus Christ our Savior, having been made flesh by the Word of God, had both flesh and blood for our salvation, so likewise have we been taught that the food which is blessed by the prayer of his word, and from which our blood and flesh by transmutation are nourished, is the flesh and blood of that Jesus who was made flesh." Priests are the instruments of this Eucharistic mystery. Through them God wills to pour out his grace—his friendship and love—on us in the Church through the preaching of the Word and the celebration of the Sacraments.

In this way, the Son of God continues to be in our midst in a manner adapted to our human nature—by sending his only Son who in turn commissioned the Apostles and their successors—so that we might receive his word and his grace from other human beings. The hand of another human being blesses us, pours the water of Baptism on our heads, offers the body and blood of Christ to us in the Eucharist, and is raised in absolution unto the forgiveness of sins. Through these visible and tangible sacramental actions, God bestows his invisible grace on us, drawing us into a participation in the communion of love of the Father, Son, and Holy Spirit.

To take up this ministry is no easy task. As St. Augustine wrote: "To lead a life of leisure, free from care, little force would be needed to make me do that. There could be nothing more enjoyable than rummaging about the divine treasure chest, with no one to plague me, but preaching, arguing, rebuking, building God's house, having to manage for

everyone—who would not shrink from such a heavy burden?" But, after
mature deliberation, our brothers have shown their readiness to embrace
this burden, and are now to be ordained to the priesthood so as to serve
Christ the Teacher, Priest, and Shepherd, by whose ministry his body,
that is, the Church, is built and grows into the people of God, a holy
temple. In being configured to Christ the eternal High Priest and joined
to the priesthood of the Bishops, they will be consecrated as true priests
of the New Testament, to preach the Gospel, to shepherd God's people,
and to celebrate the sacred Liturgy, especially the Lord's sacrifice.

And now, dear brothers who are about to be raised to the priesthood, recall with me the words of the Fundamental Constitutions
of the Dominican Order: "Made cooperators of the episcopal order
by priestly ordination, we have as our special function the prophetic
office by which the Gospel of Jesus Christ is proclaimed everywhere
both by word and example, with due consideration for the conditions
of persons, times, and places so that faith is awakened or penetrates
more deeply all life in the building up of the body of Christ, which is
perfected by the sacraments of faith."

Dear brothers, you are to be raised to the Order of the Priesthood.
For your part you will exercise the sacred duty of teaching in the name
of Christ the Teacher, and in imitation of our blessed founder, St.
Dominic. Impart to everyone the word of God which you have received
with joy. Meditating on the law of the Lord, see that you believe what
you read, that you teach what you believe, and that you practice
what you teach. Imitate Blessed Jordan of Saxony, the successor of St.
Dominic, about whom the *Lives of the Brethren* record that "the word of
God fell from his mouth with such spirit and fervor that his equal could
hardly be found, for it was clearly the result of a most rare grace. A
remarkable ease showed itself in his sermons and familiar conversations,
so that whatever and with whomsoever he found himself, whether in
the company of religious, clerics, cardinals or prelates, nobles, soldiers,
students, or persons of any condition whatever, his flow of language was
the same with them all, and was enlivened with apt and happy examples, and it was on this account that all were eager to catch his every

word as the word of God." Likewise, dear brothers, let what you teach be nourishment for the people of God. Let the holiness of your lives be a delightful fragrance to Christ's faithful, so that by word and example you may build up God's holy Church.

What is more, you will exercise in Christ the office of sanctifying. By your ministry the spiritual sacrifice of the faithful will be made perfect, being united to the sacrifice of Christ, which will be offered through your hands in an unbloody way on the altar, in union with the faithful, in the celebration of the sacraments.

Understand, therefore, what you do and imitate what you celebrate. As celebrants of the mystery of the Lord's death and resurrection, strive to put to death whatever in your members is sinful and to walk in newness of life.

And, when you gather others into the people of God through Baptism; when you forgive sins in the name of Christ and the Church in the Sacrament of Penance; when you comfort the sick with holy oil and celebrate the sacred rites, when you offer prayers of praise and thanks to God throughout the hours of the day, not only for the people of God but for the world—remember that you are taken from among men and appointed on their behalf for those things that pertain to God. Therefore, carry out the ministry of Christ the Priest with constant joy and genuine love, attending not to your own concerns but to those of Jesus Christ.

As Pope Benedict XVI declared recently: "Two things, above all, are asked of us: there is a need for an interior bond, a configuration to Christ, and at the same time there has to be a transcending of ourselves, a renunciation of what is simply our own, of the much-vaunted self-fulfillment. We need, I need, not to claim my life as my own, but to place it at the disposal of another—of Christ. I should be asking not what I stand to gain, but what I can give for him and so for others. Or to put it more specifically, this configuration to Christ, who came not to be served but to serve, who does not take, but rather gives...."

Finally, dear sons, exercising for your part the office of Christ, Head and Shepherd, while united with the Bishop and subject to him, strive to bring the faithful together into one family, so that you may lead them to God the Father through Christ in the Holy Spirit. Keep always before your eyes the example of the Good Shepherd who came not to be served but to serve, and who came to seek out and save what was lost.

May your lives be marked especially by the same fervent zeal for souls that was manifest in the life of St. Dominic. Listen again to the words of Pope Benedict: "We are concerned with the salvation of men and women in body and soul. And as priests of Jesus Christ we carry out our task with enthusiasm. No one should ever have the impression that we work conscientiously when on duty, but before and after hours we belong only to ourselves. A priest never belongs to himself. People must sense our zeal, through which we bear credible witness to the Gospel of Jesus Christ. Let us ask the Lord to fill us with joy in his message, so that we may serve his truth and his love with joyful zeal," in the Father, the Son, and the Holy Spirit. Amen.

❧ Sermon 52

Priesthood at the Heart of the Dominican Vocation

Our Lord commanded us to pray to the master of the harvest to send laborers into the harvest, and we have prayed. Seated before us in the sanctuary are the answers to our prayers.

My dear brothers who are to be ordained priests, we rejoice with you as, by the grace of God, you are blessed to be the eight hundredth anniversary ordination class. This year we celebrate that very important day—December 22, 1216—when our Holy Father St. Dominic obtained from Pope Honorius III the bull of confirmation for his new Order of Preachers.

As you receive the Sacrament of Holy Orders today, recall that the priesthood is at the heart of your Dominican vocation. St. Dominic was a priest himself who had exercised his priestly ministry as a canon of the cathedral of Osma where he also lived in community under a religious rule. This model of the religious priest or the priestly religious was at least in part the inspiration for his new foundation. In the words of the *Fundamental Constitution* of our Order: "The Order's nature as a religious society derives from its mission and its fraternal communion. Since the ministry of the word and of the sacraments of faith is a priestly function, ours is a clerical order, in whose mission the co-operator brothers too share in many ways, exercising the common priesthood in a manner specific to them."

Dear brothers, your years of priestly formation unfolded in the setting of the fraternal communion of the Dominican Order. In effect, you were preparing for the priesthood at the same time you were learning to be Dominicans. This twofold formation intertwined at every point until today when, by the laying of hands, you will be made sharers in Christ's work of mediation through which, as St. Thomas says, you will, with Christ, both communicate "divine things to the people" and offer to God the prayers of the people and to some degree "make reparation to God for their sins." The abundance of divine grace you have received in your Dominican and priestly formation brings you to this wonderful moment.

We believe that the great High Priest, Jesus Christ, chose certain disciples to carry out publicly in his name, and on behalf of the human race, a priestly office in the Church. For Christ was sent by the Father and he in turn sent the Apostles into the world, so that through them and their successors, the Bishops, he might continue without interruption to exercise his office of Teacher, Priest, and Shepherd. Indeed, priests are established co-workers of the Order of Bishops, with whom they are joined in the priestly office and with whom they are called to the service of the people of God. This Holy Priesthood is thus an extension of the mystery of the Incarnation itself. The only-begotten Son of God, who came to us in human flesh as our Savior did not leave us as orphans after his passion, death, and resurrection.

After he had ascended to the right hand of the Father, he willed to remain with us always, first of all by his presence in the Holy Eucharist, where he shares with us his body and blood, and remains present for our loving adoration. Christ ensured this by giving to his disciples, and through them, to their successors, the power of the priesthood to commemorate, *in persona Christi*, in *his* Person, this very sacrifice of his love and his friendship for us *as if we had been present at the Lord's Supper* on that Thursday evening centuries ago. Of this sacrifice, St. Justin Martyr wrote: "For not as common bread and common drink do we receive these; but in like manner as Jesus Christ our Savior, having been made flesh by the Word of God, had both flesh and blood for our salvation, so likewise have we been taught that the food which is blessed by the prayer of his word, and from which our blood and flesh by transmutation are nourished, is the flesh and blood of that Jesus who was made flesh." Priests are the instruments of this Eucharistic mystery. Through them God wills to pour out his grace—his friendship and love—on us in the Church through the preaching of the Word and the celebration of the Sacraments.

In this way, the Son of God continues to be in our midst in a manner adapted to our human nature—by sending his only Son who in turn commissioned the Apostles and their successors—so that we might receive his word and his grace from other human beings. The hand of another human being blesses us, pours the water of Baptism on our heads, offers the body and blood of Christ to us in the Eucharist, and is raised in absolution unto the forgiveness of sins. Through these visible and tangible sacramental actions, God bestows his invisible grace on us, drawing us into a participation in the communion of love of the Father, Son, and Holy Spirit.

After mature deliberation, dear brothers, you have shown your readiness to embrace this service, and are now to be ordained to the priesthood so as to serve Christ the Teacher, Priest, and Shepherd, by whose ministry his body the Church grows into the people of God. In being configured to Christ the eternal High Priest and joined to the priesthood of the Bishops, you will be consecrated as true priests of the New Testament, to preach the Gospel, to shepherd God's people, and to celebrate the sacred Liturgy, especially the Lord's sacrifice.

Dear brothers who are about to be raised to the priesthood, recall another passage of the *Fundamental Constitution* of the Dominican Order: "Made cooperators of the episcopal order by priestly ordination, we have as our special function the prophetic office by which the Gospel of Jesus Christ is proclaimed everywhere both by word and example, with due consideration for the conditions of persons, times, and places so that faith is awakened or penetrates more deeply all life in the building up of the body of Christ, which is perfected by the sacraments of faith."

You are to be raised to the Order of the Priesthood. For your part you will exercise the sacred duty of teaching in the name of Christ the Teacher, and in imitation of our blessed founder, St. Dominic. Impart to everyone the word of God which you have received with joy. Meditating on the law of the Lord, see that you believe what you read, that you teach what you believe, and that you practice what you teach.

Imitate Blessed Jordan of Saxony, the successor of St. Dominic, about whom the *Lives of the Brethren* record that "the word of God fell from his mouth with such spirit and fervor that his equal could hardly be found, for it was clearly the result of a most rare grace. A remarkable ease showed itself in his sermons and familiar conversations, so that whatever and with whomsoever he found himself, whether in the company of religious, clerics, cardinals or prelates, nobles, soldiers, students, or persons of any condition whatever, his flow of language was the same with them all, and was enlivened with apt and happy examples, and it was on this account that all were eager to catch his every word as the word of God."

What is more, you will exercise in Christ the office of sanctifying. By your ministry the spiritual sacrifice of the faithful will be made perfect, being united to the sacrifice of Christ, which will be offered through your hands in an unbloody way on the altar, in union with the faithful, in the celebration of the sacraments. Understand, therefore, what you do and imitate what you celebrate. As celebrants of the mystery of the Lord's death and resurrection, strive to put to death whatever in your members is sinful and to walk in newness of life.

When you gather others into the people of God through Baptism, when you forgive sins in the name of Christ and the Church in the sacrament of Penance, when you comfort the sick with holy oil and celebrate the sacred rites, when you offer prayers of praise and thanks to God throughout the hours of the day, not only for the people of God but for the world—remember that you have been taken from among men and appointed on their behalf for those things that pertain to God. Therefore, carry out the ministry of Christ the Priest with constant joy and genuine love, attending not to your own concerns but to those of Jesus Christ.

Finally, dear brothers, exercising for your part the office of Christ, Head and Shepherd, while united with the Bishop and subject to him, strive to bring the faithful together into one family, so that you may lead them to God the Father through Christ in the Holy Spirit. Keep always before your eyes the example of the Good Shepherd who came not to be served but to serve, and who came to seek out and save what was lost. May your lives be marked especially by the same fervent zeal for souls that was manifest in our Holy Father St. Dominic and in countless other holy priests and bishops of the Order of Preachers in the eight hundred years of grace that have been granted to us through the merciful love of God, the Father, the Son, and the Holy Spirit. Amen.

❧ SERMON 53

I Have Chosen You

"I T WAS NOT YOU WHO CHOSE ME, but I who chose you." This is our faith, dear brothers and sisters: that these seven friars—our brothers, and your beloved sons—have been chosen by Jesus Christ, the great High Priest, to carry out publicly in his name, and on behalf of the human race, a priestly office in the Church. "No one takes this honor upon himself but only when called by God, just as Aaron was." For just as Christ was sent by the Father, he in turn sent the Apostles into the world, so that through them and their successors, the Bishops, he might continue without interruption to exercise his office of Teacher, Priest, and Shepherd. Indeed, priests are established co-workers of the Order of Bishops, with whom they are joined in the priestly office and with whom they are called to the service of the people of God.

This Holy Priesthood is an extension of the mystery of the Incarnation itself. The only-begotten Son of God, who came to us in human flesh as our Savior, did not leave us as orphans after his passion, death, and resurrection.

After he had ascended to the right hand of the Father, he willed to remain with us always, first of all by his presence in the Holy Eucharist, where he shares with us his body and blood, and remains present for our loving adoration. Christ ensured this by giving to his disciples, and through them, to their successors, the power of the priesthood to commemorate, *in persona Christi*, in *his* Person, this very sacrifice of

215

his love and his friendship for us *as if we had been present at the Lord's Supper* on that Thursday evening centuries ago. Of this sacrifice, St. Justin Martyr wrote: "For not as common bread and common drink do we receive these; but in like manner as Jesus Christ our Savior, having been made flesh by the Word of God, had both flesh and blood for our salvation, so likewise have we been taught that the food which is blessed by the prayer of his word, and from which our blood and flesh by transmutation are nourished, is the flesh and blood of that Jesus who was made flesh." Priests are the instruments of this Eucharistic mystery. Through them God wills to pour out his grace—his friendship and love—on us in the Church through the preaching of the Word and the celebration of the Sacraments.

In this way, the Son of God continues to be in our midst in a manner adapted to our human nature—by sending his only Son who in turn commissioned the Apostles and their successors—so that we might receive his word and his grace from other human beings. The hand of another human being blesses us, pours the water of Baptism on our heads, offers the body and blood of Christ to us in the Eucharist, and is raised in absolution unto the forgiveness of sins. Through these visible and tangible sacramental actions, God bestows his invisible grace on us, drawing us into a participation in the communion of love of the Father, Son, and Holy Spirit. These are the fruits of the Paschal Mystery for whose service you have been chosen. "It was not you who chose me, but I who chose you and appointed you to go and bear fruit that will remain."

After mature deliberation, dear brothers, you have shown your readiness to embrace the service to which you have been called, and are now to be ordained to the priesthood so as to serve Christ the Teacher, Priest, and Shepherd, by whose ministry his body the Church grows into the people of God. In being configured to Christ the eternal High Priest and joined to the priesthood of the Bishops, you will be consecrated as true priests of the New Testament, to preach the Gospel, to shepherd God's people, and to celebrate the sacred Liturgy, especially the Lord's sacrifice.

This configuration to Christ is an interior transformation of your very being. When, during his first appearance to the disciples, our Lord breathed upon them, it was to show, according to St. Cyril of Alexandria, "that the gift of the Holy Spirit necessarily attends those who are ordained by him to be apostles of God.... *Transforming them into something other than they were before,* Jesus consecrates them by actual sanctification, making them partakers in his nature, through participation in the Spirit and in a sort of strengthening of the nature of humanity into a power and glory that is superhuman."

You are to be raised to the Order of the Priesthood. For your part you will exercise the sacred duty of teaching in the name of Christ the Teacher, and in imitation of our blessed founder, St. Dominic. Impart to everyone the word of God which you have received with joy. Meditating on the law of the Lord, see that you believe what you read, that you teach what you believe, and that you practice what you teach.

What is more, you will exercise in Christ the office of sanctifying. By your ministry the spiritual sacrifice of the faithful will be made perfect, being united to the sacrifice of Christ, which will be offered through your hands in an unbloody way on the altar, in union with the faithful, in the celebration of the sacraments. Understand, therefore, what you do and imitate what you celebrate. As celebrants of the mystery of the Lord's death and resurrection, strive to put to death whatever in your members is sinful and to walk in newness of life.

When you gather others into the people of God through Baptism, when you forgive sins in the name of Christ and the Church in the sacrament of Penance, when you comfort the sick with holy oil and celebrate the sacred rites, when you offer prayers of praise and thanks to God throughout the hours of the day, not only for the people of God but for the world—remember that you have been taken from among men and appointed on their behalf for those things that pertain to God. Therefore, carry out the ministry of Christ the Priest with constant joy and genuine love, attending not to your own concerns but to those of Jesus Christ.

As you receive the Sacrament of Holy Orders today, recall that the priesthood is at the heart of your Dominican vocation: "Made cooperators of the episcopal order by priestly ordination, we have as our special function the prophetic office by which the Gospel of Jesus Christ is proclaimed everywhere both by word and example, with due consideration for the conditions of persons, times, and places so that faith is awakened or penetrates more deeply all life in the building up of the body of Christ, which is perfected by the sacraments of faith."

St. Dominic was a priest himself who had exercised his priestly ministry as a canon of the cathedral of Osma where he also lived in community under a religious rule. This model of the religious priest or the priestly religious was at least in part the inspiration for his new foundation: "The Order's nature as a religious society derives from its mission and its fraternal communion. Since the ministry of the word and of the sacraments of faith is a priestly function, ours is a clerical order, in whose mission the co-operator brothers too share in many ways, exercising the common priesthood in a manner specific to them."

Dear brothers, your years of priestly formation unfolded in the setting of the fraternal communion of the Dominican Order. In effect, you were preparing for the priesthood at the same time you were learning to be Dominicans. This twofold formation intertwined at every point until today when, by the laying of hands, you will be made sharers in Christ's work of mediation through which, as St. Thomas says, you will, with Christ, both communicate "divine things to the people" and offer to God the prayers of the people and to some degree "make reparation to God for their sins." The abundance of divine grace you have received in your Dominican and priestly formation has brought you to this wonderful moment.

Finally, dear brothers, exercising for your part the office of Christ, Head and Shepherd, while united with the Bishop and subject to him, strive to bring the faithful together into one family, so that you may lead them to God the Father through Christ in the Holy Spirit. Keep always before your eyes the example of the Good Shepherd who came not to be served but to serve, and who came to seek out and save what was lost. May your lives be marked especially by the same fervent zeal for souls that was manifest in our Holy Father St. Dominic and in countless other holy priests and bishops of the Order of Preachers. May you always remember Christ's words to you, "It was not you who chose me, but I who chose you and appointed you to go and bear fruit that will remain," and serve him faithfully through the grace and the merciful love of God, the Father, the Son, and the Holy Spirit. Amen.

PART VI
Occasional Sermons

❧ SERMON 54

A Day of Thanksgiving and Praise to Our Beneficent Father

IT MAKES PERFECT SENSE that Thanksgiving Day should be marked with a proper liturgical celebration by the Catholic Church in the United States. For, despite its essentially civil character, it has always possessed a significant religious dimension that even the acid of secular modernity has been unable to eradicate. The liturgy invites us to see this day through the eyes of faith.

Sparing you the details of the long and interesting history that clearly reflects the religious character of Thanksgiving Day, if we come directly to the presidential proclamation that in 1863 officially established it as a national holiday, we hear Abraham Lincoln, still "in the midst of a civil war of unequaled magnitude and severity," recounting the many blessings that the nation has enjoyed and then declaring: "No human counsel hath devised nor any mortal hand worked out these great things. They are the gracious gifts of the Most High God, who, while dealing with us in anger for our sins, hath nevertheless remembered mercy. It has seemed to me fit and proper that they should be solemnly, reverently and gratefully acknowledged as with one heart and voice by the whole American People. I do therefore invite my fellow citizens in every part of the United States, and also those who are at sea and those who are sojourning in foreign lands, to set apart and observe the last Thursday of November next, as a day of Thanksgiving and Praise to our beneficent Father who dwelleth in the Heavens."

This was not the first Thanksgiving holiday. Days of thanksgiving had been interwoven with days of fast and "humiliation" stretching back all the way to the 1590s among the Spanish colonists in the southwest and to the 1620s among the English colonists in the northeast. The religious element in these celebrations was always clear, so much so that, when in 1808 Thomas Jefferson declined to proclaim a day of thanksgiving, fasting, and prayer, his explanation for not doing so makes the point explicitly: "I consider the government of the United States as interdicted by the Constitution from intermeddling with religious institutions, their doctrines, discipline, or exercises.... Certainly no power to prescribe any religious exercise, or to assume authority in religious discipline, has been delegated to the general government.... But it is only proposed that I should recommend, not prescribe a day of fasting and prayer. That is, that I should indirectly assume to the United States an authority over religious exercises, which the Constitution has directly precluded them from...the civil powers alone [that] have been given to the President of the United States...[who has] no authority to direct the religious exercises of his constituents." For Jefferson, who had a keen sense for these things, there was no doubt about the religious meaning of Thanksgiving Day.

Although among the most eloquent and moving of the genre, Lincoln's words nonetheless express religious themes that have been commonplace in presidential Thanksgiving Day proclamations over the years, at least until very recently. Viewing this day through the eyes of faith, these proclamations express two themes that are striking: the thanks we owe to God for his personal providence in our regard, and the assurance of divine mercy when we repent of our sins.

Lincoln's proclamation in the first place encourages us to see all the blessings of our lives as "the gracious gifts of the Most High God." Civil war notwithstanding, Lincoln attributes to God that peace with other nations has been preserved, that order has been maintained, that the laws have been respected and obeyed, that farming and industry have not been interrupted, that the population of the nation has increased, and that "the country...is permitted to expect continuance of years with a large increase of freedom." Each of us will have a list of blessings that partly coincide and partly diverge from Lincoln's, but we can take to heart his caution not to "forget the source from which they come"— some bounties indeed "of so extraordinary a nature that they cannot fail to penetrate and soften even the heart which is habitually insensible to the ever watchful providence of Almighty God."

In the perspective of faith, the various good things that we have received or that have happened to us are not simply part of the natural order of things but are expressions of the personal interest and providential care that God has for each one of us. Although leprosy is a terrible and rare affliction, and to have been cured of leprosy was surely a miraculous and rare benefit, the Gospel encourages us to acknowledge that our situation is nonetheless comparable to that of the ten lepers, only one of whom returned to give thanks for something which the other nine seem to have taken for granted. Thanksgiving Day reminds us not simply that we must be thankful for particular blessings (a moral lesson), but more importantly that everything is a gift of God (an ontological truth): our lives, our families, our well-being, our good qualities, our vocations, above all our communion with the Blessed Trinity in grace, and sometimes even our trials.

In the second place, Lincoln does not hesitate to remind us of sin and divine mercy. This theme is not unique to him. Notwithstanding the pervasive deism of his times, a robust Christian faith peeks through James Madison's 1814 proclamation of a day of public humiliation, fasting, and prayer on which "all may have an opportunity of voluntarily offering at the same time in their respective religious assemblies their humble adoration to the Great Sovereign of the Universe, of confessing their sins and transgressions, and of strengthening their vows of repentance and amendment." Madison wrote this during the War of 1812.

For his part, Lincoln writes in a time of terrible crisis as well, and he explicitly links civil strife with sin when he recommends to the American people "that while offering up the ascriptions justly due to [God] for... singular deliverances and blessings, they do also, with humble penitence for our national perverseness and disobedience, commend to his tender care all those who have become widows, orphans, mourners, or sufferers in the lamentable civil strife in which we are unavoidably engaged, and fervently implore the interposition of the Almighty Hand to heal the wounds of the nation, and to restore it as soon as may be consistent with the Divine purposes to the full enjoyment of peace, harmony, tranquility and Union."

This conjunction of thanksgiving for God's gracious gifts with repentance for sin and the remembrance of divine mercy is a striking and rarely sounded note in Thanksgiving Day celebrations. There is a Christian realism at work here, echoed in Sirach's blessing where a prayer for gladness of heart and peace is followed by the words: "May he entrust to us his mercy and may he deliver us in our days."

We cannot expect Madison or Lincoln to explain this implicit conjunction of thanksgiving and repentance, but faith rushes in to make all things clear. What is this Eucharistic sacrifice if not the celebration of the victorious passion, death, and resurrection of our Lord Jesus Christ that heals the wounds of the sin that torments us and our world—a victory for which we daily offer up hymns of praise and thanksgiving? The Eucharistic sacrifice enacts this conjunction of thanksgiving and repentance, of blessing and mercy. Not for nothing are we moved by the words of past presidents on Thanksgiving Day, and, more importantly, ready and willing to mark the day with a proper liturgical celebration of the Holy Sacrifice of the Mass.

* * *

For us, who are sojourning in a foreign land, the celebration of the one national holiday that does not really travel well prompts bittersweet feelings of nostalgia and homesickness. But surrounded by friends we do our best to do it justice. Fortified by this Eucharistic feast, we anticipate the Thanksgiving Day banquet to follow as well as the heavenly banquet to come, recalling the words of the whispered prayer at the purification of the sacred vessels after Holy Communion: "What has passed our lips as food, O Lord, may we possess in purity of heart, that what has been given to us in time may be our healing for eternity." Amen.

❧ SERMON 55

Thanksgiving, A Christian Holiday

ON FRIDAY, NOVEMBER 28, 1884, an upstate newspaper in New York reported from Baltimore that "special services of Thanksgiving were held and a Thanksgiving sermon preached at the cathedral yesterday morning." Since "the date set apart as a legal holiday by the President of the United States...has not [heretofore] been observed by the Catholic church," the article continued, Thursday's event was "indicative of action having been taken by the Plenary Council that has favored the recognition by the Church of that day as a Church holiday."

Thanksgiving is so dear to us and the reasons for celebrating it so obvious that we may well wonder why Catholics at first declined to observe the holiday. The Church was willing to celebrate special days of thanksgiving mandated by the state or federal government—for example, for the restoration of national peace at the conclusion of the Civil War—but had resisted the notion of an annual civil holiday so markedly Protestant in origin. Perhaps nineteenth-century Catholics remembered that, following the drastic reduction of religious holidays during the English Reformation, Puritans had wanted to abolish the observance of all liturgical feast days (including Christmas and Easter). In place of these Catholic holy days, they preferred to establish specific days of thanksgiving (for happy events regarded as signs of divine blessing) or days of fasting (after disasters viewed as acts of divine judgment). In fact, the holiday we now celebrate in late November emerged precisely from such days of fasting and thanksgiving that had been observed in all the American colonies during the seventeenth and eighteenth centuries. Thus it transpired that Catholic pastors for a long time simply refused to observe the originally Puritan but now civilly mandated "holy day" of Thanksgiving.

But by the time the Catholic bishops of the nation gathered for the Third Plenary Council of Baltimore, the roots of the Thanksgiving holiday in Reformation controversies and Protestant practice had perhaps come to seem less significant than the simple fact that, according to the sermon preached on that Thanksgiving Day in 1884, "whether as Catholics or as Americans, [we] can never lack reasons for thankfulness." What is more, "the duty of religious thankfulness is constantly urged by the Church." Thus could the bishops gathered in council "gladly hearken" to "the appeal made by the civil authorities of our country, requesting all citizens to cease from work and business on this day and to raise their thoughts to God, while they bring to mind the great and numberless blessings which he continues to shower upon them and upon their country."

Twenty-first-century Catholics are more likely to question the ceremonial deism behind the public observance of Thanksgiving than we are the Puritanism that might have troubled contemporaries of the American bishops gathered in Baltimore in 1884. But our faith and our experience leave us in no doubt about one thing: the bishops were right to encourage Catholic observance of Thanksgiving Day. As the preacher that day declared: "The practice, which, with us, has now grown to be national, of appointing one day in the year for general thanksgiving to God, the Creator and Giver of all good, has seemed to the Fathers of the Third Plenary Council of Baltimore consonant with the principles of faith and with the promptings of the heart of a Christian people, and they have, therefore, determined to recognize and commend, in a public and solemn way, a custom which declares our dependence upon God, both as a nation and as individuals, while it tends to strengthen the spirit of gratitude and to increase our confidence in his all-wise and Fatherly Providence."

"And now, bless the God of all, who has done wondrous things on earth." With the Fathers of the Third Plenary Council of Baltimore, our faith discerns the common basis in Sacred Scripture that we share with those Pilgrims of long ago who after a year of hardship followed by bounty were moved to declare days of thanksgiving in the fall of 1621. In calling for these days, William Bradford, their governor, was likely inspired by the Jewish Feast of Tabernacles which was celebrated for a week in mid-October after Yom Kippur and the harvest. Like the Hebrews, the Pilgrims brought offerings of harvest fruits in thanksgiving for God's saving deeds in leading them out of Egypt into a land of plenty.

But there is something more. Christ is our Day of Atonement and our Feast of Tabernacles. Behind the Puritan abolition of holy days lay a failure to grasp the quasi-sacramental efficacy of the Catholic liturgical year. In this annual round of feasts and seasons, Christ leads the Church ever anew to retrace his path—his *passio*—from Bethlehem to Golgotha and then to Easter, and thus to share in the particular grace of these mysteries. In our time the Church has gone beyond the Third Plenary Council of Baltimore and drawn this civil holiday into the liturgical year: Thanksgiving Day thus recovers its authentic christological significance.

Christ's is the perfect sacrifice of thanksgiving re-enacted every day in the Eucharistic sacrifice recalling his passion, death, and resurrection. Christ's perfect sacrifice of thanksgiving gives meaning and substance to our own acts of thanksgiving which, without him, would always fall short. It gives meaning and substance also to our celebration of Thanksgiving Day. We are citizens of a nation that sets aside a time to suspend ordinary activities for the purpose of pausing to take stock of our many personal and collective blessings and to give thanks to God for them. From the perspective of Catholic faith, we can understand—as the Fathers of the Third Plenary Council of Baltimore surely did—that it is the passion, death, and resurrection that gives to our thanksgiving on this civil holiday a special value in the sight of the Father who sees and loves in our thankfulness today what he sees and loves in that of his only-begotten Son. "Ten were cleansed, were they not? Where are the other nine? Has none but this foreigner returned to give thanks to God?" Precisely because we are conscious of the many blessings we have received, we want to be numbered not among the nine who failed to give thanks but with the one who did. As Christ healed them from their leprosy, so in him "through his death and resurrection, we find our ultimate redemption, freedom from sin and every blessing." We can never lack reasons for thankfulness.

❧ SERMON 56

Martyrdom as Configuration to Christ

W E GIVE THANKS TO GOD TODAY for the blessed martyrs, illustri-
ous alumni of this college, who attained that perfect configuration to
Christ for which he himself commanded all of us to strive: "If anyone
wants to be a follower of mine, let him renounce himself and take up
his cross everyday and follow me."

With the martyrdom of Father Ralph Sherwin, who was the first,
a pattern of ritualized violence was established from the start. Upon
receiving the sentence of death he was inspired to intone the Easter
antiphon *Haec est dies*: "This is the day the Lord has made, let us rejoice
and be glad." On the day of his execution at Tyburn, Father Sherwin
proclaimed that, "if to be a Catholic, if to be a perfect Catholic, is to
be a traitor, then I am a traitor." As he was dying, he gasped, "Jesu,
Jesu, Jesu, be to me a Jesus." As he passed from this world, the crowd
exclaimed: "Good Mr. Sherwin, the Lord God receive your soul."
Procession to the gallows, prolonged public humiliation, the harangues
of their accusers, their protestation of their faith in Christ, brutal death
by hanging followed by mutilation of their bodies, the jeers or the
prayers of the crowd: over the years these elements repeat themselves in
the martyrdom of Sherwin's fellow Venerable alumni.

The pattern of ritualized violence that we discern in the martyrdom of these forty-four mostly young English priests between the
years 1581 and 1679 bears striking parallels with that of thousands of

martyrs in the first three centuries of the Christian history. In the *Acts of the Martyrs of Lyons and Vienne*, for example, the author (possibly St. Irenaeus) wrote: "The governor brought the blessed martyrs before the tribunal to make a show and spectacle of them before the crowds," and "though their spirits endured much throughout the long agony, they were in the end sacrificed."

Repeated many times in every part of the Roman Empire, this public *spectacle* became for Christians a kind of "public *liturgy* ultimately aimed at the defeat of powers opposed to God and at the conversion of the world." At the center of this public liturgy was the re-enactment of the sacrifice of Christ. Servaise Pinckaers has written: "[E]arly Christians commonly thought of martyrdom as a reproduction of the Passion of Jesus, so much so that they brought out so prominently in their martyrologies all the detailed similarities between the death of the martyr and that of Christ: the essential core of martyrdom is the proclamation of faith in Jesus as the Son of God—that is, the Christian's adoption of Jesus's own testimony about himself."

Moreover, Christ is so absolutely central to the liturgy of martyrdom that he is made present—as a eucharistic sacrifice, in effect, to the eyes of faith. In the words of Karl Rahner, "If in the liturgy of the Mass the death of the Lord and our death in him is mystically celebrated and if, in this celebration, the Church attains the perfect ritual fulfilment of her nature, the same thing happens in death by Christian martyrdom in which the Lord continues until the end of time to suffer and to triumph…." Just recall Sherwin's final words: "Jesu, Jesu, Jesu, be to me a Jesus."

Martyrdom in the Church must thus be distinguished from any other type of voluntary death for an ideal, an ideology, or a cause. Christian martyrdom is not merely one of the many cases in the world of "defending one's convictions to the death." Nor is martyrdom simply an instrument for the dissemination of the Christian message of the faith or for the consolidation of the identity of the Christian community. "In martyrdom…we have an indissoluble unity of testimony and what is testified, guaranteed by God's gracious dispensation. Here there is accomplished with absolute validity and perfection what is testified: authentic Christian life as victorious grace of God. The testimony makes present what is testified and what is testified creates for itself its own authentic attestation." The liturgical and indeed quasi-sacramental character of Christian martyrdom opens up for us something massively important at the core of our celebration and our appropriation of the mystery of this great feast. Not for nothing did the story of the martyrs of this college begin with the words of the Easter antiphon on the lips of the first martyr: *Haec est dies quam fecit Dominus, exaltemus et laetemur in ea.* For in martyrdom we have not only a praiseworthy heroic witness to the faith, but, "in procession before the world," a witness in which the very content of the witness is made present. Thus in Christian martyrdom, the perfect configuration of the martyr to Christ is by grace both achieved and revealed.

As we celebrate today the martyrdom of Saint Ralph Sherwin and his fellow Venerable alumni, we can see in the spirituality of martyrdom the primordial spirituality of all Christian life. "To all Jesus said, 'If anyone wants to be a follower of mine, let him renounce himself and take up his cross every day and follow me. For anyone who wants to save his life will lose it; but anyone who loses his life for my sake, that man will find it. What gain, then, is it for a man to have won the whole world and to have lost or ruined his very self?'" Here Christ is addressing not only potential martyrs, but all of us. Only the perfect image of God who is the Person of the Son could constitute the principle and pattern for the transformation and fulfilment of every human person who has ever lived. And the more we are conformed to his image, the more authentically do we become our true selves.

"The Christian ideal of sanctity emerges directly from the spirituality of martyrdom." It is this profound truth that is not merely witnessed to but is actually realized and made manifest in the death of Christian martyrs. To become sharers in the communion of divine life, we must become like the Son so that the Father sees and loves in us what he sees and loves in Christ. We become conformed to Christ in order to be "at home" in the shared life of the Father, Son, and Holy Spirit. Above all, "if you can have some share in the sufferings of Christ be glad, because you will enjoy a much greater gladness when his glory is revealed." Certainly during episodes of suffering, trial, and self-denial, but not only in them, taking up the Cross each day encompasses the whole of every Christian's life. Throughout this continuous *sequela Christi*, the Holy Spirit is at work shaping in us—Christian martyrs and all the rest of us as well—a transformation that is finally nothing less than a perfect configuration to Christ. This is the meaning of Christian sanctification.

Rightly could Origen say to his community: "I have no doubt that in this community there are a number of Christians—God alone knows them—who before him, according to the testimony of their consciences, are already martyrs, who are ready, as soon as it is asked of them, to shed their blood for Christ. I have no doubt that there are amongst us many who have already taken their cross upon themselves and have followed him." And rightly too may a preacher dare to make Origen's words his own today in the chapel of the Pontifical Seminary of Martyrs. "Your feast day is not indeed in the calendar," declared St. Augustine, "but your crown is ready and waiting for you."

❧ SERMON 57

The Mystery of the Eucharist

ACCORDING TO ST. JOHN'S GOSPEL, the first people to hear Christ proclaim the Eucharist found that the message surpassed their understanding. Some embraced the mystery in faith, but others were put off by it. When they heard Christ say: "I am the living bread that came down from heaven. Whoever eats of this bread will live forever; and the bread that I will give for the life of the world is my flesh," they asked, incredulously, "How can this man give us his flesh to eat?" (John 6:51–52)

How can this be indeed? Although we want to embrace Christ's affirmation in faith, it is instructive to consider how perfectly natural this question is from the human point of view. It is one that is frequently voiced when human beings hear about something that God is said to have done or to be doing. With regard to the Eucharist, it is asked: How can Jesus be really present under the appearances of bread and wine? How can he give us his flesh to eat and his blood to drink? How can the Eucharist be a sacrificial offering? And so on. The initial question "how can this be?" unfolds into a series of questions about the Eucharist.

But suppose that we look at things with the eyes of faith, in the light of the mystery of faith. Suppose that instead of maintaining a human point of view we adopt the divine point of view. Suppose that we approach these questions as the great theologians of the Catholic tradition have. Suppose, in short, that we look at the Eucharist in the way God looks at it. When we do this, we may find that our troubling "how can this be?" becomes an awestruck and faith-filled "why not?" We could say that the mystery of the Eucharist becomes "understandable" in some sense we when we see it precisely for what it really is, namely, a mystery of faith.

In the first chapter of the encyclical *Ecclesia de Eucharistia*, Pope John Paul II wanted to show the profound interrelationship of the mystery of faith, the Paschal mystery and the Eucharistic mystery. In the simplest terms, we can say that the Eucharistic mystery is the re-presentation of the Paschal mystery and that, surpassing human understanding as they do, both mysteries are part of the single mystery of faith and thus can only be received in faith. The divine gift of faith, bestowed on us in Baptism and nurtured through the sacramental life of the Church makes it possible for us to enter into this mystery of faith.

Fundamental to this mystery of faith is the divine desire to share the communion of Trinitarian life with human beings. No one has ever desired anything more than the triune God desires this. God himself has revealed to us (for how could we otherwise have known about it?) that it is this divine desire—more properly, intention and plan—that lies at the basis of everything: creation, incarnation, redemption, sanctification, and glory. To look at everything through the eyes of faith—to adopt, as it were, a "God's eye view"—is to see everything in the light of this divine plan. Looking at things this way—looking at them the way God himself has taught us to do—we understand why we were created, why the Word became flesh, why Christ died and rose from the dead, how the Holy Spirit makes us holy, and why we will see God face to face. We were created so that God could share his life with us. God sent his only-begotten Son to save us from the sins that would have made it impossible for us to share in this life. Christ died for this, and, rising from the dead, gave us new life. To become holy is to be transformed, through the power of the Holy Spirit at work in the Church, into the image of the Son so that we may be adopted as sons and daughters of the Father. Glory is the consummation of our participation in the communion of the triune God—nothing less than seeing God face to face. The mystery of faith is, finally, a mystery of love.

The Catholic tradition has not hesitated to describe this participation in the divine life as a true friendship with God. Given this truth of our faith, is it not in a sense appropriate that God should be moved to send his only-begotten Son into the world and, in the breathtaking divine condescension of the incarnation, to take up a human existence to be known and loved among us as Jesus of Nazareth? Was it not fitting, as the Scriptures say, that the Son of Man should offer his life to his Father on the Cross in a reconciling sacrifice of love for our sake?

For St. Thomas Aquinas, it is but a short step from the incarnation to the Holy Eucharist: "It is a law of friendship that friends should live together…. Christ has not left us without his bodily presence on our pilgrimage, but he joins us to himself in this sacrament in the reality of his body and blood." In effect, Aquinas is saying that it makes sense, given what we know about God's plan to bring us into the intimacy of his divine life, to leave us the extraordinary gift of the real and substantial presence of his Son in the Eucharist. In the light of the entire mystery of faith, we can see the Eucharist as the gesture of our divine friend. Pope John Paul II writes: "It is pleasant to spend time with him, to lie close to his breast like the Beloved Disciple and to feel the infinite love present in his heart."

But there is more. This is a friendship that expressed itself in the ultimate sacrifice of love in which Christ gave his body and blood up for our sake. When he instituted the Eucharist at the Last Supper, "Jesus did not simply state that what he was giving them to eat and drink was his body and blood; he also expressed its sacrificial meaning and made sacramentally present his sacrifice which would soon be offered on the Cross for the salvation of all." By overcoming the effects of sin, the sacrificial passion and death of Christ and his glorious resurrection—the Paschal mystery—restored our friendship with God. In this connection, the Holy Father makes a striking point: "This sacrifice is so decisive for the salvation of the human race that Jesus Christ offered it and returned to the Father *only after he had left us a means of sharing in it* as if we had been present there." Not only does our divine friend want to stay with us; he wants to do so precisely in virtue of the power of the Paschal mystery which guarantees what must now, always and everywhere, be a reconciled friendship won at the price of his blood. No wonder that Pope John Paul II could write: "What more could Jesus have done for us? Truly, in the Eucharist, he shows us a love which goes 'to the end' (cf. John 13:1), a love which knows no measure."

❧ SERMON 58

No One Receives Who Has Not First Adored

Four times during the celebration of the Eucharist the priest elevates the sacred host and the precious blood of the Lord. The first elevation occurs during the consecration when the priest raises the sacred host, and then the chalice containing the precious blood. The second moment occurs when, at the conclusion of the Eucharistic prayer, the priest raises the host and the chalice together just before the recitation of the Lord's Prayer. Then, before the distribution of Holy Communion, the priest presents the sacred host and the precious blood to the entire congregation with the words "Behold the Lamb of God...." And finally, in a more personal moment, each communicant is invited to behold and adore the sacred host just before receiving the Body of Christ.

These moments of "elevation" are the basis of Eucharistic exposition and adoration, revealing the intrinsic connection between the Eucharistic sacrifice of the Mass and Eucharistic devotion to the Blessed Sacrament. Christ, who was raised up on the Cross for our sake, who rose from the dead and ascended to the right of the Father, is raised up again at Mass so that we may look on him and be saved. In the solemn exposition of the Blessed Sacrament, this "being raised up for our sake" is prolonged and extended. We can say then that, in exposition, adoration, and benediction of the Blessed Sacrament, we have *the contemplative extension or prolongation of the Eucharistic sacrifice itself.* The Christian faithful who behold, adore, and receive Christ in the sacrament of the altar desire to continue, in a more contemplative and protracted manner, to look with love on Christ present in the Blessed Sacrament.

Beholding. When St. Thomas Aquinas discusses exposition and benediction, he asks whether Christ is made more present to us when the sacred host is removed from the tabernacle and placed inside the monstrance for our adoration. Aquinas responds in the negative: How could the door of the tabernacle separate us from Christ? When the sacred host is enshrined in the monstrance in exposition, according to St. Thomas, it is not that Christ becomes more present to us, but rather it is that *we become more present to him.* In beholding him exposed to us in the monstrance, our attention is more focused and concentrated, and thus we become more present to him.

All of us recognize this. In a church or chapel where the Blessed Sacrament is exposed on the altar, the mood is one of palpable, even intense, silence, reverence, and concentration. This prolonged beholding is the school of contemplation in which we become ever more conformed to the divine mystery. We may recall the words of St. Albert the Great: By gazing on what is good, we become good. This experience of contemplative prayer is in a real sense a foretaste of the experience of heaven itself where we will be able to gaze upon Christ in all his glory.

Adoring. In beholding him, we also adore him. *Tantum ergo sacramentum veneremur cernui:* "Let us bow down in adoration before so great a sacrament." It is the most natural, instinctive response we have to seeing the Blessed Sacrament exposed: we cannot resist falling to our knees. In his homily at the conclusion of World Youth Day 2005, our Holy Father Pope Benedict XVI provided a profound reflection on the meaning of the word "adore" when he pointed out that it signifies both submission to God and the communion of love—in effect, a submission that becomes love.

Receiving. And love, of course, leads to communion, both in the sense of our ever-deepening interior union with Christ, but also in the sense of receiving him in holy communion as our very food.

Thus, we have the three moments of Eucharistic adoration: beholding, adoring, and receiving. St. Augustine says somewhere: "No one receives the flesh who, beholding him, has not first adored him." These words show how participation in the sacrifice of the Mass leads to Eucharistic adoration, which itself leads us back to the Eucharistic sacrifice. Beholding and adoring first during the Mass itself, we then literally receive Christ as food in holy communion. During Eucharistic adoration, our beholding and adoring engender an interior reception of Christ at the same time that they prepare us for a deepened participation in the Eucharistic sacrifice and the reception of holy communion. Beholding, adoring, receiving: three moments leading us to communion—the communion which God the Father, Son, and Holy Spirit wants to share with us.

"Whoever loves me will keep my word, and my Father will love him, and we will come to him and make our dwelling with him" (John 14:23). Christ reveals to us that the triune God desires to share his life with us in the most intimate manner. The Catholic tradition has not hesitated to describe this participation in the divine life as a true friendship with God. Given this truth, is it not in a sense appropriate that God should be moved to send his only-begotten Son into the world and, in the breathtaking divine condescension of the incarnation, to take up a human existence to be known and loved among us as Jesus of Nazareth?

For St. Thomas Aquinas it is but a short step from the incarnation to the Holy Eucharist: "It is a law of friendship that friends should live together.... Christ has not left us without his bodily presence on our pilgrimage, but he joins us to himself in this sacrament in the reality of his body and blood." In effect, Aquinas is saying that it makes sense, given what we know about God's plan to bring us into the intimacy of his divine life, to leave us the extraordinary gift of the real and substantial presence of his Son in the Eucharist. In the light of the entire mystery of faith, we can see the Eucharist as the gesture of our divine friend.

But there is more. This friendship is a reconciled communion made possible by the ultimate sacrifice of love in which Christ gave his body and blood up for our sake. By overcoming the effects of sin, the sacrificial passion and death of Christ and his glorious resurrection—the Paschal mystery—restored our friendship with God.

In this connection, Pope John Paul made a striking point: "This sacrifice is so decisive for the salvation of the human race that Jesus Christ offered it and returned to the Father *only after he had left us a means of sharing in it* as if we had been present there." Not only does our divine friend want to stay with us; he wants to do so precisely in virtue of the power of the Paschal mystery which guarantees what must now, always and everywhere, be a reconciled friendship won at the price of his blood.

* * *

Our celebration of the Eucharist and our veneration of the Blessed Sacrament today fall thrice fold under the patronage of our Blessed Lady: We are gathered in this great Dominican church of Santa Maria sopra Minerva on May 13, a day which commemorates both the apparitions of the Blessed Mother at Fatima in 1917 and the title, given by Saint Peter Julian Eymard in 1868, Our Lady of the Blessed Sacrament. Mary is the mother of our divine friend and Eucharistic Lord, who holds a chalice in one hand and a host in the other. Under her tutelage we learn to behold, adore, and receive her son. As we celebrate this Eucharist today and extend our veneration of Christ in the Blessed Sacrament to the streets of the city of Rome, may her intercession unite us ever more closely to him, and lead us to the city that has "no need of sun or moon to shine on it, for the glory of God [gives] it light, and its lamp [is] the Lamb" (Revelation 21:23). Amen.

🍃 SERMON 59

The Vision of Dominican Theological Education

"SON THOUGH HE WAS, Christ learned obedience from what he suffered." Learned? Obedience? Suffering? How can such things be attributed to the Son of God? Inevitably, this passage from the Epistle to the Hebrews would be at the center of the great christological debates that occupied the attention of bishops and theologians in the early Church. Theodoret of Cyr devoted a whole book just to the interpretation of the fifth chapter of Hebrews from which this passage is drawn. Eventually, as you know, in 451 the Council of Chalcedon affirmed the distinction of Christ's human and divine natures even as they are united in his person. This resolution came about largely because of the famous letter to the council sent by Pope St. Leo the Great—known traditionally as Leo's *Tome*—in which he laid down rules for speaking about the person and natures of Christ. One could say things about the person of Christ that could not be said about the natures. Thus, Jesus is God, but human nature is not divine. Christ, not his divine nature, learned obedience through suffering. And so on. No wonder the Fathers acclaimed Pope Leo's letter with such enthusiasm. "In Leo," they declared, "Peter has spoken."

But this immensely important clarification of christological language and doctrine was in service of something even greater, the message of salvation itself, here deftly summarized in our passage from Hebrews: "Son though he was, Christ learned obedience from what he suffered; and when perfected, he became the source of eternal salvation for all who obey him, designated by God as high priest according to the order of Melchizedek."

In his commentary on the Epistle to the Hebrews, St. Thomas remarks that, while the other letters of St. Paul treat of the grace of the New Testament either "as it regards the whole Mystical Body of the Church" or "as it pertains to the principal members of the Church," this epistle "treats of the excellence of Christ...of grace insofar as it regards the Head, that is Christ...from whom life flows into the whole body." The epistle does this through an extended and elaborate theological argument tracing the exquisite web of typology and prefiguration without which the Paschal Mystery—the mystery of the passion, death, and resurrection of Christ—would in effect be unintelligible. Jesus of Nazareth, "delivered to us as Christ and Lord," is identified as the prefigured saving High Priest so that, according to Pope Leo (not in the *Tome* but in a sermon) "what had been foretold through so many ages by numerous signs, numerous words, and numerous mysteries would not be open to doubt in these days of the gospel. That way, the birth of the Savior—which was to exceed all wonders and the whole measure of human intelligence—would engender in us a faith all the more steadfast, the more often and the earlier it had been proclaimed beforehand."

Dear graduates, as the Pontifical Faculty prepares to confer upon you well-earned degrees in Sacred Theology, allow me to suggest that the pattern of reflection and argument manifest in the Epistle to the Hebrews is in many ways replicated in the Dominican theological education you have received. You learned to view the mysteries of the Catholic faith as a complex and interrelated whole that reflects the infinite and inexhaustible richness of the Divine Truth itself—or, as one could justly say, *himself.* No facet of this mystery—whether it fall in what we have come to call moral theology or in dogmatic theology—can be understood apart from the whole "mystery of great compassion" (1 Timothy 3:16).

The Epistle to the Hebrews is remarkable for the way that it deploys all the riches of the Scripture to show, in effect, why the Son had to learn obedience through suffering. Listen to St. Leo again: "Our origin, corrupted right after its start, needed to be reborn with new beginnings. A victim had to be offered for reconciliation, a victim that was at one and the same time related to our race and foreign to our defilement. In this way alone could the plan of God—wherein it pleased him that the sin of the world should be wiped away through the birth and passion of Jesus Christ—in this way alone could the plan of God be of any avail for the times of every generation."

The mystery of our salvation is endlessly intelligible because it draws us into the inexhaustibly intelligible mystery of God. Dominican theological education trains us to see all the elements of this mystery in their interconnected unity, and never to field solutions to individual problems that threaten the coherence and truth of the whole or any part of it. As you are awarded these degrees today, realize that they mark just a stage—a milestone certainly—but a stage nonetheless in your continuing pursuit of divine wisdom. Your teachers, who have been happy to certify that you are ready to move on, would be the first to acknowledge this. These degrees also entitle you to act as teachers of sacred theology. Train your students in the obedience to the truth which you have learned from Christ our Redeemer who, "son though he was, learned obedience from what he suffered; and when perfected... became the source of salvation for all who obey him."

❧ SERMON 60

The Paralytic as Everyman

WHEN THE CROWD SEES the paralytic man stand up and start walking home on his own two feet, they are awestruck. To be sure, it is easier to cure the body than it is to cure the soul, but the crowd cannot *see* the man's sins being forgiven. They are impressed by what they *can see*, and that is a paralytic standing on his feet and walking off on his own power.

The crowd is awestruck, but the scribes are scandalized. They shared the common view that physical illness was due to personal sin. When they heard Jesus say to the paralytic, "Your sins are forgiven," the scribes reasoned that he had committed blasphemy in claiming to do what only God can do. Our Lord turns their argument against them. By curing the paralytic, he demonstrates to them that, since he has the power to cure the *effects* of sin (which they believed disease to be), then he clearly must have the power to cure the *cause* of disease (which they believed personal sin to be). "With the same free power with which the Son of Man later tells the paralytic to rise and walk, he first forgives him his sins. And he does the second in order that you may know that he has the power to do the first."

The crowd is awestruck and the scribes are scandalized. What about the paralytic? Notice that he did not ask to have his sins forgiven. The paralytic does not thank Jesus for his pardon for he was more anxious for the cure of his body than his soul.

The paralytic, the scribes, the crowd—all focused on the physical healing. We are very much like them—indeed, we are even more acutely preoccupied with physical well-being than they. Our culture places such a high premium on youth, health, and beauty that it is difficult for us to concentrate on the immeasurably more important spiritual qualities of conversion, forgiveness, virtue, and holiness. Physical infirmities, disfigurement, disease, incapacity—we dread these far more than we do the interior paralysis caused by sin and vice.

Pope Benedict XVI says: "The paralyzed man is the image of every human being whom sin prevents from moving about freely, from walking the path of good and from giving the best of himself. Indeed, by taking root in the soul, evil binds the person with ties of falsehood, anger, envy, and other sins and gradually paralyzes him." It is this spiritual paralysis above all that Christ wants to heal. As is evident in all the miracle stories recounted in the Gospel, Christ wants to bring something more than physical well-being to those whom he cures: he wants to bring them to faith and conversion, to an interior transformation directed to communion with God and with one another in him. This interior healing can only take place if we ask for it: if we join Christ's victory over our sins by confessing them to him and receiving his pardon.

The healing that is Christ's gift to us is the key not only to our personal happiness, but to peace and justice in society. "Today… humanity is marked by sin which prevents it from rapidly progressing in those values of brotherhood, justice, and peace that with solemn declarations it had resolved to practice." It is one of the most powerful temptations of our time to think that our resolutions and efforts will bring peace and justice to the world when in fact, "only God's love can renew the human heart, and only if he heals the heart of paralyzed humanity can it get up and walk. The love of God is the true force that renews the world."

With the paralytic, summoned by Christ's word of forgiveness we *arise* from our sins through contrition, we *take up our bed* through prayer and penance, and we *walk toward home* to eternal life with God.

St. Matthew concludes the story of the cure of the paralytic by noting: "At the sight, a feeling of awe came over the crowd, and they praised God for giving such authority to men." We can do the same. Christ gave the power to forgive sins to the Apostles and their successors. Priests exercise this power, not in their own name, but in Christ's name, *in persona Christi*. It is Christ himself whom we face when we confess our sins and it is he who utters the words of absolution. That is why the priest says, not "*Christ* absolves you," but "*I* absolve you"—the priest speaks in the first person, so fully is he identified with Christ himself. "A feeling of awe came over the crowd, and they praised God for giving such authority to men."

These words are directly relevant to the ecclesial setting of our penitential service this evening. Tomorrow—in the first consistory of the pontificate of Pope Benedict XVI—a former archbishop to many of you and a friend to all of us, William Joseph Levada, will join the apostolic collaborators in the Petrine Ministry who constitute the College of Cardinals.

The College of Cardinals dates back nearly a thousand years to 1150 when Pope Blessed Eugene III organized it in its present form, as a college with a dean (the bishop of Ostia) and three orders of members (bishops, priests and deacons). These three orders in fact reflect something of the complex history of the role of cardinals in the Church, that spans a series of developments stretching back to the days when the very first successors of Peter ordained *priests* to head the principal churches of Rome, appointed *deacons* to administer alms in the main regions of the city, and consecrated the seven *bishops* who occupied the suburbican sees surrounding the city. In addition to their liturgical functions in the great basilicas of Rome—including this one—the cardinal bishops, priests, and deacons came increasingly to exercise crucial administrative functions, as the chief advisors to the popes in meetings called "consistories" from the ninth century and, from the eleventh century, as the exclusive electors of the Roman pontiff in sessions called "conclaves."

While our thoughts and prayers go out to him as he joins this ancient and sacred body, Archbishop Levada himself particularly wanted this evening to be a special moment of preparation—particularly through a vigil of prayer and the Sacrament of Penance—so that we would be attuned to the deep spiritual significance of the exciting events in which we will participate in the coming days.

The Holy Father, the cardinals, the bishops, the priests, and the deacons of the Church: they are the instruments through whom God willed to pour out his grace on us in the Church through the preaching of the Word and the celebration of the Sacraments. In this way, God adapted himself to our human nature—by sending his only Son who in turn commissioned the Apostles and their successors—so that we might receive his word and his grace from other human beings. The hand of another human being blesses us, pours the water of Baptism on our foreheads, offers the body and blood of Christ to us in the Eucharist, and is raised in absolution unto the forgiveness of sins. Through these actions, God's grace is bestowed on us.

The cardinals have a distinctive place in this magnificent economy of grace as the special collaborators of the Successor of Peter and the Vicar of Christ. There have been about three thousand of them (since people started counting), seven of whom are canonized saints, among whom is the martyr St. John Fisher. Pay close attention to what the Holy Father says tomorrow before he imposes the red berretta on each of them: he reminds them that the color red is meant to signify their readiness, *even to the point of shedding blood*, to promote the Christian faith, the peace and tranquility of the people of God, and the liberty and diffusion of the Catholic Church. When, as it surely will, a feeling of awe comes over you and the crowd during tomorrow's ceremony, praise God for giving such authority to men.

❧ SERMON 61

Mary's Fiat in the Life of the Priest

WHEN WE LISTEN TO THE STORY of the Annunciation our attention is irresistibly drawn to its climax—to Mary's *fiat*. And so it should be. If the angels in heaven—themselves in no need of salvation—waited with baited breath for Mary's response to Gabriel, how much more are we keen to hear the words that launch the epoch of our salvation? We want Mary to say *yes*, to embrace the divine will, to accept the coming of the Holy Spirit upon her. And she does, fulfilling the original divine decree whereby she would give the world the Son of God in his human nature, and thus becoming the *Theotokos*. "A branch shall sprout from the root of Jesse, and the glory of the Lord will fill the whole earth, and all flesh will see the salvation of our God in her."

This happy occasion heightens for us the significance of Mary's *fiat*. For, in this celebration of the Eucharistic Sacrifice, we joyfully mark the anniversary of the priestly ordination of our dear brother and friend, Cardinal William Levada, who, with fifty-three of his classmates, received Holy Orders here at the Altar of the Chair fifty years ago today. We can say that they pronounced their own *fiat* before the whole Church on that day. This striking parallel between the Annunciation and the priesthood was drawn by Pope John Paul II when he wrote: "Since the solemn invocation of the Holy Spirit and the eloquent gesture of humility during our priestly ordination, the *fiat* of the Annunciation has resounded through our life."

Prostrate on the sanctuary floor as the Church invokes the power of the Holy Spirit and the intercession of all the saints, the candidate for ordination prepares his heart and soul, his whole being, to embrace with obedience and humility the unique configuration to Jesus Christ the High Priest that God wills to confer upon him in the Sacrament of Holy Orders. In this way, the priest's initial and lifelong *fiat* may be likened to that of Mary, who, according to John Paul II, "became ever more open to the will of the Lord and, by the power of the Holy Spirit...conceived Christ, the salvation of the world. This first obedience pervades her entire life on earth and reaches it climax at the foot of the Cross. The priest is called to match the *fiat* of Mary at all times, allowing him to be led by the Spirit as she was."

Nonetheless, while in the end her *fiat* is absolute and unqualified, Mary's initial reaction to Gabriel's message manifests a certain hesitation. She asks, "How can this be, since I have no relations with a man?" In response to this question the angel Gabriel proceeds to unfold the mystery of the virgin birth, and the immense grace which Mary is to receive. That for which she justly feels unready will be accomplished in her by the Holy Spirit. Moreover, our faith tells us that, in a deeper sense, her very being had been made ready beforehand by God who, in virtue of the foreseen merits of her Son's passion, death, and resurrection, preserved her from all sin, original and actual. How fitting is the celebration of the feast of the Immaculate Conception of the Blessed Virgin early in the season of Advent. Where no earthly preparations could suffice, God himself prepared the way for the Incarnation of his only-begotten Son.

To be sure, our Lady was not totally passive in this transaction of grace. Aquinas affirms that, while it could not strictly be said that Mary merited the Incarnation, it is nonetheless true that "by the grace given her she merited such a degree of purity and sanctity that she could fittingly be the mother of God." "Tell me, angel," St. Augustine asks, "whence has Mary [received] this favor? I already told you [replies Gabriel] when I saluted her: Hail full of grace."

Mary's hesitant question to the angel Gabriel directs our attention to a fundamental law of the entire economy of salvation. For she—the holiest human being who ever lived—nonetheless expresses just the sort of reaction we all have when confronted with the news that God is about to do something unexpected for us. Our natural reaction is: But I am not ready for this. In Mary's case, the angel in effect dismisses her hesitation by affirming that what is about to happen does not depend on her readiness but on the grace already at work in her. There are no conditions or requirements within our—or her—capacity to fulfill that would have made the world ready for the Incarnation of the Son of God. Our worries about being unready are answered somewhat impatiently by the prophet Isaiah. "Listen, O house of David! Is it not enough for you to weary men, must you also weary God? The virgin shall conceive and bear a son, and shall name him Emmanuel." If God had waited until we were ready—or worse still, worthy—for this, he would still be waiting, and so, my dear brothers and sisters in Christ, and so would we. This divine condescension was an act of sheer, super-abundant grace, and, apart from the prevenient grace that prepared for it, neither we nor even our Blessed Lady herself could have been ready for it. This "grace that goes before grace," as it were, prevails throughout the economy of salvation.

We can see, then, that not only Mary's *fiat*, but also her hesitant question regarding her apparent unreadiness, are profoundly significant for every priest. For, I ask you my brother priests, as we knelt on the day of our ordination and felt the weight of the laying on of hands upon our heads, is there one of us who regarded himself as ready or, dare I say it, worthy of the grace of Holy Orders? And now as the years have passed—fifty, forty, thirty, twenty, ten, as the case may be—since that day of our ordination, have we ever felt ready to speak and act in Christ's name or worthy of the abundant graces we have received? In the face of the overwhelming divine love of which we have daily been the object, we can do no better than to utter Mary's simple, humble and obedient *fiat*.

This is true not only for the priests and bishops among us, but also for all the Christian faithful. Before the wonders of divine grace at work within us, who can say more than: "Let it be done to me according to your word"? But it is especially and pointedly true for us priests whom God has willed to unite to his only-begotten Son as unworthy instruments in the economy of salvation itself. By the sacrament of Holy Orders, we have been configured to Christ in order to act in his name, as the tradition has it, *in persona Christi capitis ecclesiae*—he who, according to today's O Antiphon, is none other than the *clavis David et sceptrum domus Israël.* "O Key of David, and scepter of the house of Israel, who opens and no one closes, who closes and no one opens: come, and lead out of prison the captive who sits in darkness and the shadow of death." To this work of salvation, particularly its radically sacramental efficacy, Christ the High Priest joins to himself priests according to his own image, made worthy by his grace to have a share in the power of the keys which by right is his alone.

Thus it is that, with Mary, we can say no more than: "*Fiat!* Let it be done to us according to your word."

Dear friends in Christ, in giving thanks today to God for the blessings that have come to us through the *fiat* of Cardinal Levada and his classmates uttered fifty years ago, we give glory to the Father, Son, and Holy Spirit for the original *fiat* of the Blessed Virgin Mary which brought to us the Savior who is Christ the Lord. Amen.

❧ SERMON 62

Light Immortal, Light Divine

IN ANTICIPATION OF THE OFFICIAL OPENING of the Supreme Court term tomorrow, we unite in prayer today in this solemn liturgy in order to invoke the Holy Spirit upon the distinguished justices, the judges, attorneys, and lawmakers, professors and students of the law, the law clerks and paralegals, and upon all others who serve us in the various sectors of the legal profession. We give thanks to God for their precious service, and we humbly pray, "Holy Spirit, Lord of light / From the clear celestial height / Thy pure beaming radiance give."

The annual invocation of the Holy Spirit at the start of the judicial year in Washington reflects a seven hundred-year-old tradition honoring the sacred character of the law and the vital civic role of its guardians. Indeed, the practice of celebrating a Red Mass—"red" because of the color of both the liturgical vesture and the traditional judicial robes—at the opening of the judicial term is as old as the legal profession itself. According to historian James Brundage, the emergence of a distinctive legal profession in the West dates roughly to the thirteenth century—precisely when the first recorded celebrations of the Red Mass occurred in Paris in 1245 and in Westminster in 1301. It may well be that the widespread practice of celebrating a votive Mass of the Holy Spirit at other similar occasions—like the start of the academic year—originated with the tradition of the Red Mass.

J. AUGUSTINE DI NOIA, O.P.

The celebration of the annual Red Mass signals the profound esteem which the Church has for the Supreme Court and the legal and judicial institutions of this nation, for the invocation of the Holy Spirit on this occasion springs from nothing other than the Trinitarian faith which is at the very center of her faith. "Whoever loves me will keep my word, and my Father will love him, and we will come and make our dwelling with him." Christ teaches and the Church proclaims that God, the Father, Son, and Holy Spirit, desires to share the communion of Trinitarian life with creaturely persons, that—in the famous formulation of St. Irenaeus—God who is without need of anyone gives communion with himself to those who need him. Christ teaches us, moreover, that it is the Holy Spirit who plays a critical role in fitting individual persons and the Church herself for this high destiny. "The Advocate, the Holy Spirit, that the Father will send in my name...will teach you everything and remind you of all that I told you." Thus we can pray: *Veni Sancte Spiritus!* Come Holy Spirit! "Thou, on us who evermore / Thee confess and thee adore, / With thy sevenfold gifts descend. / Give us comfort when we die; / Give us life with thee on high; / Give us joys that never end."

What should we be praying for as we invoke the Holy Spirit on the justices and on all the rest of us during this Red Mass? As St. Paul reminds us, the Holy Spirit himself helps us to ask for the right things: "The Spirit comes to the aid of our weakness; for we do not know how to pray as we ought, but the Spirit himself intercedes with inexpressible groaning." We have already heard some verses from the ancient "Golden Sequence" for Pentecost Sunday, the *Veni Sancte Spiritus*; let us turn to it again to learn more of what we can expect when the Church invokes the Holy Spirit in this solemn setting.

Veni Sancte Spiritus! Come Holy Spirit! "Thou, of all consolers best, / Thou the soul's delightful guest, / Dost refreshing peace bestow; / Thou in toil art comfort sweet; / Pleasant coolness in the heat; / Solace in the midst of woe." In praying to the Holy Spirit, for, among other blessings, consolation, peace, and solace, the Church understands the nearly overwhelming complexity of the climate which envelops the practice of law and the administration of justice today.

And perhaps not just today. It was precisely such complexity that gave rise to the legal profession in the thirteenth century as popes, kings, and bishops found it impossible to carry out their duties without expert legal advice. You will be amused to learn that, during this period, there was lively debate about whether popes should be elected from the ranks of theologians or of canon lawyers: as a theologian, it pains me to report that learned opinion favored the election of qualified lawyers to the See of Peter.

In all seriousness, no informed observer can fail to acknowledge that the social and cultural pluralism of our times—not to mention the relentless and sometimes pitiless public scrutiny to which you are subjected—makes the work of judges and lawyers today very hard indeed. The Church prays that, amidst the clamor of contending interests and seemingly intractable moral disagreements, the Holy Spirit will help you to maintain your personal integrity and professional equilibrium. Not for nothing, then, do we invoke the Holy Spirit today with these poignant words. *Veni Sancte Spiritus!* Come Holy Spirit! "Heal our wounds, our strength renew; / On our dryness pour thy dew; / Wash the stains of guilt away. / Bend the stubborn heart and will; / Melt the frozen, warm the chill; / Guide the steps that go astray."

The words of the prophet Ezekiel recall another important element in our invocation of the Holy Spirit today. "I will put my Spirit within you," he says, "and make you live by my statutes, careful to observe my decrees." Positive law rests on certain principles the knowledge of which constitutes nothing less than a participation in the divine law itself: the pursuit of the common good through respect for the natural law, the dignity of the human person, the inviolability of innocent life from conception to natural death, the sanctity of marriage, justice for the poor, protection of minors, and so on. The legal profession is entrusted with the discernment and administration of justice and the rule of law according to an objective measure—in effect, according to principles—not of our own making. A consensus about these principles inspired the founders of modern democracies, and although it was profoundly influenced by Judaism, Islam, and Christianity (think of

Averroes, Maimonides, and Aquinas), this consensus was understood to transcend religious and cultural differences. Thus, it follows that the invocation of the Holy Spirit in the Red Mass is a prayer for light and guidance. Among the things for which we ardently pray is the wisdom to affirm and maintain those profound truths about human nature that are at the foundation of the common life we treasure in this great nation. "Holy Spirit, Lord of Light ... / Come thou light of all that live ... / Light immortal, light divine."

At the deepest level, our invocation of the Holy Spirit here today manifests the conviction that the democratic state does not so much *confer* the most fundamental human rights and the duties of citizenship as *acknowledge* their existence and source in a power beyond the state, namely in God himself. Your presence here today bears eloquent witness to the enduring power of this conviction.

Yet, as she invokes the guidance and consolation of the Holy Spirit today, the erosion of this conviction is a source of deep concern for the Church. The alternative view—until recently more or less successfully resisted by democratic societies like ours—is the idea that man can find happiness and freedom only apart from God. This exclusive humanism has been exposed as an anti-humanism of the most radical kind. Man without God is not more free but surely in greater danger. The tragic history of the last century—as Pope John Paul II and Pope Benedict XVI have unceasingly reminded us—demonstrates that the eclipse of God leads not to greater human liberation but to the most dire human peril. That innocent unborn human life is now so broadly under threat has seemed to many of us one of the many signs of this growing peril. Gabriel Marcel said somewhere that in our time "human flesh has undergone such intolerable outrage that it must receive some kind of reparation in glory... The world today can be endured only if one's spirit is riveted on [the] hope of the resurrection...If this hope were shared by a greater number, perhaps, respect for the flesh and for the body, so terribly lacking in our time, would be restored." Thus, along with wisdom and light, today we must also beg the Holy Spirit for the gift of hope in the resurrection.

Our enactment of this ancient ritual of the Red Mass joins us to the generations of judges and lawyers who pursued their professions conscious of their need for divine grace and guidance, for enlightenment, for consolation, for refreshment, for solace, for healing, for comfort, for hope. May these wonderful blessings of the Holy Spirit be yours today! *Veni Sancte Spritus!* Come Holy Spirit! "Come, thou Father of the poor, / Come with treasures which endure… / Light immortal, light divine, / Visit thou these hearts of thine, / And our inmost being fill." Amen.

❧ SERMON 63

The Man Born Blind

PEOPLE WHO LACK ONE SENSE often develop a heightened sense of perception in other senses. People who lack sight, for example, can be said to "see" more things than sighted people can: they can smell, or hear, or feel things that the sighted hardly notice. We who are convinced that we "see" everything can be said to be "blind" to many things that people without sight actually can "see" well. In the story of the healing of the man born blind, the Pharisees—the educated elite who should see—turn out to be blind, while the man born blind sees with the eyes of faith becomes the teacher of the Pharisees who say "we see."

In a sermon on this story, St. John Chrysostom said: "There is a twofold vision and a twofold blindness: the one of sense, and the other of understanding." Clearly then, the man born blind can be said to see more than the Pharisees do because he has received from our Lord not only the gift of physical sight—the vision of sense perception—but also the gift of faith—the vision of true understanding. Lacking this faith, the Pharisees are blind in their understanding, while the man born blind, and now possessed of this understanding, sees himself and the world around him in a completely new light. He now knows that Jesus is the Messiah who brings the word and the reality of love, grace and communion with the Father, Son, and Holy Spirit to the whole human race.

What else can this mean for us who, in the grace of Baptism, have received the gift of faith but that we must look at the human reality with the eyes of faith in order to understand it truly? Only with the faith that we and the man born blind receive from Christ can we see the full truth about the human person and about human society, for we learn to look upon these realities in the way that God looks at them. The message that Christ brings to us and to the world involves not the suppression of human nature and human goods but their total realization.

The all-encompassing range of this vision makes us universalists not sectarians. We see things now in the perspective of the divine desire to bring all human beings into the communion of the Blessed Trinity. We learn to regard the persons who come to us as patients, or clients, or students, or penitents as called to communion with the triune God and with one another in him. What higher destiny can there be than this one? Who promises something higher, broader, more universal than this? The message which the Church receives from Christ and is bound to proclaim to the world does not impose constraints on the human race but sets it free to pursue a destiny that is unimaginably greater than anything we could generate on our own and that our culture, with all its undeniable richness, could offer us. Adherence to this message does not turn us into narrow sectarians or zealots, dwelling in an intellectual ghetto and trying to impose our narrow values on the wider public culture. On the contrary, the faith we have in God explodes our narrow understanding and opens us to the broadest possible and most comprehensive vision of what it means to be human.

The Rose Mass this morning gives us the opportunity to face up to something that may make us uncomfortable. Catholic health care professionals at times feel a certain unease when they have to uphold Catholic principles on a series of issues—abortion, contraception, sterilization, use of fetal stem cells, euthanasia, as if the Catholic identity of their institutions depended on a series of so-called "prohibited services." This experience of unease exposes a critical challenge: to learn to see the convictions that come from faith not as an embarrassing constraint forcing us to approach our secular partners and the wider public in an apologetic mode, but, on the contrary, as a message that the world is dying to hear and, one could say, dying from not hearing.

If like the man born blind, we have learned to see ourselves and others with the eyes of faith, then we must embrace Catholic moral principles and articulate the practical consequences of a vision of the dignity of the human person that we have learned from Christ—not as an embarrassing constraint but as a liberating gift which we are eager to share with others. Rather than preferring the blindness of the Pharisees, we must learn to see, like the man born blind, with the eyes of faith.

Before he meets Christ, the man is blind both "in sense" and "in understanding" and needs to be healed of his physical and spiritual blindness. We are like him. In the spiritual sense, we are all born blind and we are healed by the grace of Baptism. *Once you were in darkness and now you are in the light.* No more than did the man born blind can we take our new healed condition for granted. Our awareness that we were once blind ourselves—*born blind* like that man in the Gospel—is central to our appreciation of the precious gift we have received from Christ in being able to see everything with the eyes of faith.

This awareness will shape our approach to others. We who once were blind approach others who do not share our faith with humility and modesty. We approach them with conviction, but not with arrogance, with the liberating and enabling knowledge of our own unworthiness before the unsurpassable grace and mercy of God. For the very reason that we cannot claim this grace as based in ourselves, it empowers us with the confidence that comes from God himself. The man born blind knew this, and it imparted to his witness a quite remarkable simplicity and boldness.

The man born blind was able to offer a courageous and inspired witness to the gift of faith he had received. Through his wily responses to the Pharisees (as the lawyers in the congregation will no doubt have appreciated!), he becomes their teacher. He is not in the least intimidated by them, by their office, learning, or standing in society. He actually engages them in argument, striving both to grasp the point of their questions and to respond in a way that summons them to the discipleship that he himself has embraced. Like the man born blind, we must be ready to bear witness to our faith in conversation with those who do not share it. What is needed today is an unapologetic but principled kind of witness, arising out of the conviction that faith is a gift to the world that fulfills the deepest human longings. This implies that our level of professional education—which in a body like the John Carroll Society must be very high indeed—should at least be matched, if nor surpassed, by our understanding of our faith and our skill in upholding and communicating it today. Like the man born blind, we must be ready and wily witnesses to our faith in whatever circumstances we find ourselves.

In his example of faith, of awareness of the gift of healing he has received, and of his readiness to bear witness to the truth about Christ, the man born blind shows us how to face the challenges to the Catholic identity of our health care institutions. Christ's final words are somber: "I came to make the sightless see, and the seeing blind." Those who know that they are blind welcome the gift of sight that comes from Christ. Those who say "we see, we see" remain blind. Let us strive with Christ's grace to be found, not among the sighted who remain blind, but among the sightless who have learned to see.

❧ SERMON 64

Christ Tells Us What He Knows

SOMETIMES WE ASSOCIATE PRIDE WITH KNOWLEDGE. Those who seek to know too much might be in danger of having too high an opinion of themselves and their abilities. In Christian tradition these dangers have often, and rightly, been linked.

But we can be misled by linking pride and knowledge in this way. For the Gospel teaches us that, apart from Christ, the danger is not that we aim too high, but that we aim too low. Christ says to us today: "I call you friends because I have made known to you everything I have learned from my Father." In other words, Christ is the Teacher who tells us what it is we have to know, both about God *and* about ourselves, what God knows and reveals through Christ, and through Christ alone. Without Christ, we would never know our true nature and destiny. Christ alone knows, and he tells us what he has learned from the Father. On our own, we could never know the truth about ourselves. By creating us in his own image, as knowers and lovers who seek the infinitely knowable and loveable, God has made us to aim at the highest Good and the greatest Truth, nothing less than himself. The danger, it seems, is not that we will aim too high, but that, in the light of our own limited perspectives, that we will not aim high enough.

How could we know on our own that our destiny is to enjoy the communion of divine love? How could we know on our own that marriage in God's sight is a symbol of the union of Christ with his

Church? How could we know on our own that sex isn't just for the pleasure it provides us but for the union between husband and wife that participates in the creative power of God, that it is procreative and not merely reproductive? How could we know on our own that we are meant to enjoy the communion—the "family life" as it were—of the Father, Son, and Holy Spirit and with one another in them? How could we know on our own that the family itself is a kind of symbol of the Trinitarian union? How could we know these things apart from Christ? The danger here, in all of these matters, is that without Christ we would have thought too little of ourselves, not too much. These are matters that Christ learned from the Father and has made known to us.

One of the primary objectives of the John Paul II Institute of Marriage and Family Studies is to cultivate the learning that Christ received from the Father and, in this way, to transform our knowledge of the human reality, to teach us never to aim too low, but to see ourselves and others as God sees us, within the all-encompassing scope of the divine vision of creation. This is the kind of knowledge that, far from inducing prideful self-congratulation, can only be received and relished as a divine gift.

As such, it is a kind of knowledge that invites a lifetime of study and reflection. St. Augustine makes this clear when he asks (in commenting on the passage of the Gospel of John that we are considering): "How did he make known to his disciples all things that he had heard from the Father when he forbore saying many things because he knew they as yet could not hear them?" To reframe the question in terms of our theme today, we could ask: How can mere humans adopt the divine perspective? How could we ever take in all that God knows? St. Augustine responds to his question in a way that throws light on ours: Christ "made all things known to his disciples" in the sense that "he knew that he should make them known to them in that fullness of which the Apostle speaks, *Then we shall know even as we are known* (1 Corinthians 13:12). For as we look for the death of the flesh and the salvation of the soul, so should we look for that knowledge of all things which the Only-Begotten heard from the Father."

In other words, by making known to us what he learned from the Father, Christ launches us upon a long journey of learning. We could not hear what Christ had to teach us all at once. We could not take it all in. It is not just that it takes us a long time to learn all that Christ teaches us: for our graduates today, who have worked so hard, it undoubtedly seems to have taken a long time to get to this point! But the deeper truth is that they, like ourselves, have only just begun to learn the things that Christ received from the Father and has imparted to us: to know even as we are known, to know ourselves as Christ alone knows us.

When the tradition asks about the nature of the sin of the angels, it has generally given the answer that it was a sin of pride—specifically, the sin of wanting to be like God. By maintaining that we can adopt the divine perspective on ourselves in knowledge, are we not flirting with just this sort of pride? St. Thomas points out that it is not wrong, strictly speaking, to want to be like God. The problem with the angels was wanting to be like God as their due, as if it were something that belonged to them by right, something for which they were worthy. And that was their sin in aiming too high. For ourselves, we will only know ourselves as Christ knows us when we understand that the divine plan is to make us like God as his gift to us. Christ says: "The Father will give you anything you ask in my name." What we must ask in Christ's name is to receive the gift of being like God, of enjoying the life of God as his adopted sons and daughters in the communion of the Blessed Trinity. The knowledge that we seek and that we commend to these young graduates, and to others, is a knowledge that leads to love. St. Gregory the Great said: "He made all things known to them, then, because they burned with the fire of Divine Love. For while we love the heavenly things we hear, we know them by loving them because Love itself is knowledge." The knowledge that comes from Christ leads to love.

* * *

It happens that today we celebrate the feast of the Apostle Matthias, about whom practically nothing is known apart from what we hear today in the Acts of the Apostles. There are many legends about him, many so-called "Gospels" of Matthias and "Acts" of Matthias. But we know nothing about him except that he was one of the companions of Christ and could thus, according to St. Peter, be a suitable candidate to fill out the number of the Twelve after the betrayal of Judas. Beyond this, tradition indicates that St. Matthias spread the Gospel to what is now Turkey and that he was crucified there. According to St. Clement of Alexandria, St. Matthias was known especially for his desire to imitate the passion of Christ in his own body.

The words of the Gospel of John apply strikingly to St. Matthias: "You did not choose me; no, I chose you; and I commissioned you to go out and bear fruit, fruit that will last." How can we fail to hear these words today without thinking that they are addressed directly to our graduates? We pray that the knowledge they have gained during their studies will lead them to seek, not their own honor and glory, as St. Matthias clearly did not, but to bear fruit that will last. Amen.

❧ Sermon 65

A Suitable Place

Sometime in 1220 St. Dominic began a letter to the convent of Dominican nuns in Madrid with these words: "Friar Dominic, Master of the Preachers, to the dear prioress and the whole convent of nuns of Madrid. Heath and daily progress. We rejoice greatly and give thanks to God because of your holy lives and because he has liberated you from the corruption of the world. Up to the present you have not had a suitable place for the carrying out of your religious life. But now... by God's grace you possess buildings sufficiently well-adapted for the maintenance of the regular life."

Notice the phrase "a suitable place." It describes St. Dominic's constant goal in his work of establishing the first communities of Dominican nuns. Indeed, throughout the literature recording the histories of these and subsequent communities—and clearly in the history of the founding of this monastery here in Washington, *a suitable place* is the goal passionately, boldly, and persistently sought. This suitability is measured by many factors, some mundane, others intangible. We shall ask "suitable for what?"—not irreverently, of course, but in order to come to a deeper understanding of the Dominican contemplative life that is solemnly inaugurated here today. St. Dominic took an active role in seeking suitable locations for the three monastic foundations: Prouille, Madrid, and Rome. In Madrid, it was fairly easy. In May 1220, he simply moved the friars from their priory there and moved into it a group of women converted by him and the preachers, and living apart from each other since 1218. It was to this newly established community that the letter quoted earlier was addressed. Finding a suitable place for his other monastic foundations was not at all so easy. St. Dominic was intermittently engaged from 1207 until the end of his life in 1221 in the endeavor to establish his first community of nuns at Prouille on a solid basis: bartering for land, securing endowments, overseeing lawsuits, obtaining the necessary protections, and so on. So direct was his involvement that Vicaire could write that St. Dominic "sold, bought, exchanged parcels of land, not without a certain ability for business...in order to establish an unbroken domain" for the monastic enclosure at Prouille. Always the goal is: a suitable place.

And finally, there was San Sisto in Rome to which he devoted much of his energy in the final months of his life. Settling sixty or so nuns who would finally have their suitable place at San Sisto by mid-April 1221 posed quite a challenge to St. Dominic's organizational and diplomatic skills. Here it was not only a matter of securing adequate property, endowment, and protection that engaged his attention. A more subtle challenge awaited him in the form of the celebrated miraculous icon of the Blessed Virgin Mary in the church of the nuns of Santa Maria in Tempulo, one of the groups that was to take vows in the Dominican Order in the new community at San Sisto Vecchio. The icon of the Madonna had always manifested a pronounced unwillingness to be moved from Santa Maria in Tempulo. Once when it was carried off by Pope Sergius III even to so august a setting as the Lateran, it reportedly returned to Santa Maria "flying through the window like a bird." The nuns of Santa Maria in Tempulo agreed to make profession in the Dominican Order and relocate to San Sisto only on the condition that they be released from their vows to him if their famous icon—which would naturally accompany them to their new home—returned to Santa Maria as it had been known to do in the past. On the day when all of the nuns were finally gathered at San Sisto, St. Dominic, accompanied by the cardinals Nicholas of Tusculum and Stefan of Fossanova, and a group of Dominican friars and lay people, all barefooted, carried the icon in solemn procession to San Sisto. There the icon was solemnly installed in the restored basilica. This event was witnessed by seventeen year old Sister Cecilia Cesarini, who recounted this and other miracles of St. Dominic while in her eighties and living in a monastery in Bologna, and was able to report that the icon was still in place with the nuns of San Sisto. There were no lengths to which St. Dominic would not go to find a suitable place for his nuns.

Anyone acquainted with the story of the long pilgrimage that has brought these Dominican nuns to two acres on Sixteenth Street will be struck by the boldness and determination, all focused on the single goal to find a suitable place for the monastic enclosure and the contemplative life it affords. Mother Mary of the Angels and Sister Mary of the Blessed Sacrament left the Dominican monastery in Union City, New Jersey, in 1907 to found a new community in Baker City, Oregon. When, after two years, it became clear that the support needed to sustain the small community was simply lacking in Baker City, Mother Mary of the Angels prayed for guidance and opened the Catholic Directory to the Diocese of La Crosse, Wisconsin. After a visit there, Mother Mary of the Angels was convinced that La Crosse would provide a suitable location for a Dominican monastic community. On July 2, 1909, the community began the arduous trip by rail to La Crosse, nourished on the way with only the six dozen biscuits one of the nuns had baked, along with water and coffee. The first band established itself in a house on Avon Street. A new location on George Street was twice flooded by the waters of the Mississippi in the 1950s and finally proved unsafe for habitation. Under the direction of Mother Mary of the Immaculate Conception, who had come from West Springfield with a group of sisters to augment the La Crosse community, the nuns moved again to South Avenue.

We can sense something of the struggle these nuns faced in the ensuing years from the words addressed to the community in a letter in 1959 from the bishop of La Crosse, John P. Treacy: "Like every good work, there must be a humble beginning, and the more precious the work and the higher the purpose of its founding, the greater must be the sacrifice in accomplishing that work…. Christ's Church itself came to us through much suffering. All our religious orders began with the greatest sacrifices of poor and humble men and women…. No more brilliant example of this is there than the somewhat more humble beginning of the [Dominican Nuns] in La Crosse fifty years ago."

Now in 1985 they have come to this two-acre plot in the great city of Washington, to a suitable location bounded by Sixteenth, and Emerson, and Farragut, and Piney Branch, to this ample and wonderfully designed monastery and chapel. The distance between Union City and Washington—just about two hundred miles—has taken them seventy-eight years and several thousands of miles to traverse, all in the bold and untiring pursuit of a suitable place. It is no surprise, surely, that their story reminds us of St. Dominic's similar quests for the nuns of Prouille, Madrid, and Rome.

What makes a location suitable? Above all, it must be suitable to the celebration of the sacred liturgy—the Liturgy of the Hours and the Holy Eucharist—which are at the very heart of the Dominican monastic life and which require an ample and well-fitted chapel. The buildings, the grounds, the setting—as an ensemble they must afford the tranquility needed for a life of silence, prayer, work, study, and community in Christ.

Of special importance today is that the location must be suitable for the monastic enclosure. Apart from the Eucharist itself, the most solemn part of today's ceremony will come at the end of Mass when the Archbishop formally erects the papal enclosure here, that space physically marked out by the choir screen, the locked doors of the cloister, the panels in the visiting parlors, and the wooden fence encompassing these lovely two acres. But the monastic enclosure is something more intangible and indeed spiritual than simply the physical space defined by fences and locked doors.

Here lies the deep mystery of the Dominican contemplative life and of the determined pursuit of a suitable place. For, in the person of this successor of the apostles, God himself lays claim to these two acres.

In this place is established in a particularly intense and heightened form a form of life that provides a glimpse of the future of the world and of humankind within it. Far from representing primarily an exclusion or rejection of the world beyond the monastery, the monastic enclosure compresses the whole of human reality with all its infinite longing for union with God and affirms it without reservation. We wrest these two acres of the city of Washington and "enclose" them in order to bring into existence the beginning of the destiny of the whole world. For the enclosure affords—not by human discovery or provision, but by the action of divine grace itself—a place suited to the seeking of union with God as the end that surpasses all others and by which all others are in the end encompassed. This is the high destiny to which every human person is called and which the whole cosmos is stretching to reach. In this suitable place, the end of the world begins to be.

Listen anew to St. Dominic: "Friar Dominic, Master of the Preachers, to the dear prioress and the whole convent of nuns of Washington. Health and daily progress. We rejoice greatly and give thanks to God because of your holy lives and because he has freed you from the corruption of the world. Up to the present, you have not had a suitable place for the carrying out of your religious life. But now… by God's grace you possess buildings sufficiently well adapted for the maintenance of the regular life."

❧ SERMON 66

Free For God Alone

SOMETIME IN 1206, at Prouille, St. Dominic and Bishop Diego gathered a group of women—who at the time were not living together—as the beginning of a community. Shortly before this, when St. Dominic arrived at Fanjeaux and looked out over the vast territory that was the object of his preaching endeavors—the "holy preaching" as it was called—St. Dominic spied Prouille at the convergence of several roads extending out in different directions. At the time, Prouille was uninhabited except for a small chapel. Perhaps there, in the vision of the famous Seignadou, St. Dominic saw not only this great work of preaching, of drawing this people from their errors to the crucified Savior, but also the new Order that he was yet to found but which began in a real way with that community. We now understand that this was the foundation of Dominican monastic life.

A great deal of research and controversy surrounds the issue of what happened in 1206 and what it signified. Perhaps there is not such a great mystery. Consider what St. Dominic did afterwards, founding contemplative communities at Bologna, at Madrid, at San Sisto in Rome. As Blessed Cecilia wrote, "They had no other master to instruct them about the Order." St. Dominic had a clear intention in what he was doing when he gathered together those women at Prouille. Indeed, by the end of the century, there were already one hundred and forty-one monasteries—seventy-five of them in

Germany alone. Surely this is a sign of the clarity of St. Dominic's original conception.

But what did he intend? "These women, free for God alone, he associated with his 'holy preaching' by prayer and penance." Care is needed here. There is always a temptation to assign some practical purpose to monastic life. Surely it is correct to say that one purpose of Dominican monastic life is to pray for the "holy preaching." Thus, over these eight hundred years, the friars could rely on the prayers of the nuns: the nuns are praying for us, and we can count on that.

But if we conclude that this is what St. Dominic had in mind, we would fall short of the mark. Here is something that may at first seem a little rash, but turns out to be eminently defensible: Dominican monastic life is that state of being to which the "holy preaching" is meant to bring its hearers. Consider this passage from the Fundamental Constitutions of the Nuns: "It is God who now makes them dwell together in unity and on the last day will gather into the Holy City a people acquired as his own. In the midst of the Church their growth in charity is mysteriously fruitful for the growth of the people of God. By their hidden life they proclaim prophetically that in Christ alone is true happiness to be found, here by grace and afterwards in glory."

What is this but a description of the gathered communion of the faithful around God, living "free for God alone" as all contemplative religious live. If this is true, then it follows that the Dominican nuns strive to live now in that state to which we are all called eventually to dwell—to be together with God and with one another in him.

Dear sisters in St. Dominic, resist with all your might any proposal to provide monastic life with a practical purpose. Many people ask about the nuns, "Well, what are they *doing*? What contribution to they make? They should be doing something useful." These questions open up a tempting line of reasoning, and history shows that many, even contemplatives, have fallen for it. The friars count on you to resist it. We try to help you to resist it, but we are not immune to the temptation to articulate a practical purpose for your existence. Praying for the friars, indeed, praying for the whole Church, is not enough. What did everyone say about St. Dominic? That he spoke only to God and about God. When he gathered women together in the great cities of Europe, it was very clear what these monasteries were meant to be. Surely he did not think of them in a primarily utilitarian way. What these communities make us think of is God. What we see in them is that to which we are all called, and to which the "holy preaching" must lead others.

So on that day in 1206, when St. Dominic and Bishop Diego gathered that first group of Dominican women together, this man who spoke only to God and about God surely intended to found communities who sole purpose was to be "free for God alone."

❧ Sermon 67

Christe the Good Samaritan

Over a hundred years ago, on January 25, 1903, my father Giacomo was baptized in this church. At the age of 20, he departed for the United States with his sister, Anna, and her husband, John Gaudio. Like so many Italians seeking a better life in those days, he left behind his mother and father, Rachele and Giuseppe, and, as things turned out, he was never able to return before his death in 1959.

You can imagine what a tremendous joy it is for me to return to Irsina, to this very cathedral, to celebrate the first anniversary of my ordination as archbishop. On July 11, 2009, in Washington, the basilica of the Immaculate Conception was full of my family and friends and Dominican brothers. Today, this duomo di Santa Maria Assunta is filled with so many family and new friends—with the priests, the mayor, the officials, and the residents of Irsina—who with me, may give fervent thanks to God for the many gifts we have received from his abundant mercy—especially for the gift of my episcopal ordination and for the gift of this blessed reunion with the family of my father in the place of his birth and his baptism.

And, of course, it is natural for us to rejoice in the company of the family and friends whom we love. But—turning now to today's Gospel—Our Lord teaches us that our love must extend beyond family and friends. As St. Jerome says: "Some think that their neighbor is their brother, family, relative or kinsman. Our Lord teaches who our

279

neighbor is.... Everyone is our neighbor, and we should not harm anyone. If, on the contrary, we understand our fellow human beings to be only our brother and relatives, is it then permissible to do evil to strangers? God forbid! We are neighbors, all people to all people, for we have one Father."

As we have just heard, after our Lord has said that we should love our neighbor as ourselves, the lawyer asks, "Who is my neighbor?" In response, our Lord tells the story of the Good Samaritan in which we learn that we must consider every man as our neighbor.

But we must look more deeply as this familiar story. For, while at the beginning the lawyer asks "Who is my neighbor?"—at the end of the story Christ asks "Which of these three seems to you to have been neighbor to the man who fell into the hands of the robbers?" In other words, in the story of the Good Samaritan, Christ intends to teach us, not only that we must consider every man as our neighbor, but what it means to be the neighbor to another. Christ invites us to look into our own hearts, to see whether we know what it is to be a neighbor, to see whether we possess the qualities necessary to be a true neighbor to another—the readiness, the foresight, the generosity, the charity necessary to take care of someone in need. The remarkable conduct of the Good Samaritan—even with respect to a Jew with whom he would ordinarily not associate—makes us pause and think deeply about ourselves, and how we should act in such circumstances. "Go and do likewise."

But we know ourselves well enough to realize that it is not easy to go and do likewise. Often we are too selfish, too lazy, too absorbed with our own affairs, too oblivious to the needs of others. More is necessary than just the desire or even the determination to imitate the Good Samaritan. He acts with spontaneity and ease. He shows no reluctance. He knows immediately what must be done, and does it without considering the cost to himself. The parable presents us with a man of a certain virtuous character, who would act in this way not only on this occasion but in every similar circumstance.

Thus, when our Lord tells us to go and do likewise, he is saying: *Go and become the kind of person who can do likewise.* This means that we must be converted and transformed. To *act* like the Good Samaritan really means to *become* like the Good Samaritan: someone who possesses the readiness to do the good, who experiences ease in accomplishing it, and who enjoys satisfaction in its performance—in other words, one who has become a person of virtue.

And now we come to the deepest level of this parable of the Good Samaritan. For, my dear friends in Christ, it is the whole human race and thus we ourselves who are the man left by the roadside in desperate need, and it is the Lord who is the Good Samaritan.

Listen to what St. Ambrose has to say: "When he turned aside to worldly sins, Adam fell among thieves...[who are] the angels of night and darkness...who first steal the clothes of spiritual grace.... He received a mortal wound by which the whole human race would have fallen if that Samaritan, on his journey, had not tended his serious injuries."

Again, listen to words that St. Augustine preached concerning this parable: "Robbers left you half-dead on the road, but you have been found lying there by the passing and kindly Samaritan [who is Christ himself]. Wine and oil have been poured on you. You have received the sacrament of the only-begotten Son. You have been lifted up onto his mule. You have believed that Christ became flesh. You have been brought to the inn, and you are being cured in the Church."

At its deepest level, therefore, the parable teaches us that, because of the salvation Christ accomplished for us by his death and resurrection when we were lost, our ability to imitate the virtues exhibited by the Good Samaritan depends absolutely on the grace of Christ at work in us. He is not only the model and example for us—the Good Samaritan who helps others. He is the source and cause of all the virtues that we need to live a holy and blessed life, and, in the end, to be truly neighbors to all those who need us as we travel the roads and pathways of life.

✳ ✳ ✳

At the end of our reflection, allow me to thank his Excellency, the Archbishop of Matera for his presence. Excellency, I express the congratulations of the whole community as you approach the anniversary of your priestly ordination in this coming week.

Dear friends in Christ, one year ago I was ordained bishop in the Basilica of the Immaculate Conception, and today I celebrate the first anniversary of that happy day in this cathedral of Santa Maria Assunta—titles that mark the beginning and the end of the earthly life of our Blessed Lady. From start to finish, let us live our lives always under her protection, and, like the Good Samaritan, let us show to others a generous measure of the love we have received from her Son through the Holy Spirit. Amen.

❧ SERMON 68

Matilda Carucci Di Noia (1911–2007)

THERE ARE NO WORDS in which to express my family's profound gratitude to all of you who have joined us today to commend my mother to the mercy of God in the sure hope of the resurrection of the dead. When I left Rome on Wednesday, I put a packet of about twenty letters into my bag. They were letters my mother had written to me over the years. Naturally, as I reread them over these days since her death, they brought back many memories. They are full of concern for me, for my brother and sister, for her beloved grandchildren, for her own brothers and sisters, and for her friends. She recounts things that she has been doing and wonders, politely, about things she thinks I should be doing. There are requests that I pray for people who are ill or celebrate Mass for people recently deceased. And so on.

I was particularly touched—and I know that the friars here will be as well—by a letter she wrote to me on April 27, 1981, after spending Holy Week and Easter (one of the many such visits over the years) at the Dominican House of Studies in Washington: "It was very nice to spend some time with you. It was good to attend all those morning and evening prayers, plus the Holy Week Services. I enjoyed being there and thank you for inviting me. But I felt very strange when I got back: I missed everything."

I do not mention these letters now in order to introduce a eulogy in my mother's honor today. If that were my intention, she would be the

first to reprove me. My mother's letters—and indeed her whole life—
do reflect her goodness, her generosity, her prayerfulness, her love. But,
with the unshakeable faith in our Lord that characterized her entire life,
she would surely want us to look not at herself but at *him*. For the Mass
of Christian Burial is not chiefly to celebrate the good qualities of the
deceased or our fond memories of them—important and precious as
these are—but to commend them to the mercy of God in the sure hope
of the resurrection of the dead. This is what we are doing today in this
church where she attended daily Mass for so many years: we commend
our mother and grandmother, our sister and aunt, our cousin and friend,
to the mercy of God in the sure hope of the resurrection of the dead.

We turn to another precious set of letters in order to do so—those
of St. Paul to the churches, in particular this morning to his letter to
the Romans: "Are you not aware that we who were baptized into Christ
Jesus were baptized into his death?" St. Paul asks. "We were indeed
buried with him through baptism into his death, so that, just as Christ
was raised from the dead by the glory of the Father, we too might live
in newness of life." These words explain why my mother, as much as
all the rest of us, needs the mercy of God and needs us to call it down
upon her. Without the passion, death, and resurrection of Christ, we
would still be in our sinful state, unreconciled with God. But through
our participation in his sacred paschal mystery, we die not only in our
bodies, but we also die to our sins and thus is the mercy of God poured
out upon us.

Hence the words of the book of Wisdom: "The souls of the just are
in the hand of God and no torment shall touch them. They seemed, in
the view of the foolish, to be dead.... But they are in peace." Because
we receive the mercy of God through our participation in the death and
resurrection of Christ, we possess the sure hope of the resurrection from
the dead for my mother and for ourselves. "I am the resurrection and
the life; whoever believes in me will never die. Do you believe this?" our
Lord asks us. Each one of us must respond as his friends do. "Yes, Lord.
I have come to believe that you are the Messiah, the Son of God, the
one who is coming into the world."

My mother entered the hospital on December 23. Thus, her final days coincided almost exactly with the Christmas–Epiphany season that concluded on Sunday. This cannot have been accidental, but rather an expression of the supreme delicacy with which divine providence directs our lives and answers our every prayer. Did she not receive, in this manner, the answer to her own favorite prayer? "Hail and blessed be the hour and the moment when the Son of God was born of the most pure Virgin Mary, at midnight, in Bethlehem, in piercing cold. In that hour, O my God, hear my prayers and grant my desires."

It is almost impossible to mourn for my mother's death. Her life is complete. She has attained that fullness of life with God that she so ardently desired and that is the aim towards which our own lives must be directed. Behind her she leaves, in the words of Cardinal Bertone's letter, a "legacy of goodness." But she also leaves behind her a void. That is the source of our pain and sorrow. But we must fill it in the way that we would have: with prayer and service in the name of Christ.

Among the great loves of her life were the Blessed Virgin Mary and the Dominican Order. In her letter of July 27, 1980, written shortly after my assignment to the faculty of the Dominican House of Studies, after noting with pleasure that the proper title of the community is the Priory of the Immaculate Conception, she writes: "May the Blessed Mother be always close to you and protect and inspire you always."

And then there are the Dominicans. Almost to the day, the final year of her life was spent in the bosom of the Order of Preachers. She was warmly welcomed by the Dominican Sisters of Hawthorne at St. Rose's Home in Lower Manhattan, where she often received visits from the Dominican friars from both St. Vincent Ferrer and St. Catherine of Siena priories, and from St. Joseph Rectory and from Our Lady of Lourdes.

The hope that is prompted by this love for our Lady and for the Order is captured in the image on the front of the programs for today's Mass—the Dominicans in heaven gathered under Mary's mantle. Taken from one of the panels of Sylvia Nichols's magnificent stained glassed windows in the new chapel of Providence College, this image depicts a dream in which St. Dominic, upon arriving in heaven, is upset that he cannot find any of his nuns or friars there. When he goes to our Lady in distress, she sweeps open her mantle, and, lo and behold, St. Dominic finds sheltered within its folds all his beloved friars and nuns. Commending her to God's mercy today, in the sure hope of the resurrection, our prayer is that my mother will find her place in heaven with the Dominicans under Mary's mantle. Amen.

❧ SERMON 69

Rachel Angela Di Noia Benischek (1939–2015)

THE CHURCH GATHERS US in the Holy Sacrifice of the Mass today to commend to the mercy of God the soul of our beloved sister Rachel whose passing has saddened, and even shocked us. It was so completely unexpected. Who among us has not been thinking of the words of Christ that conclude the Gospel passage we have just heard? "You know not the day nor the hour." We need to ponder the meaning of these words.

Consider this: We all conduct our lives according to some sort of schedule that organizes our time. Adjustable to the seasons, the weather, the calendar, other people's schedules, and so on, we organize our days and weeks to maximize what we can accomplish in the time allotted. None of us thinks about the possibility that we will not be here tomorrow or the next day, or next week. My calendar is already full up to December. There is nothing wrong with this way of proceeding. On the contrary. Our responsibilities to our children, our students, etc., demand that we plan our time wisely.

But the really important thing to remember is that our timetables and schedules are embraced by another. There is another all-encompassing plan that embraces our individual plans, and that is the plan of divine providence for each one of us. This is a plan that arises from the loving wisdom of God according to which God undertakes to draw us ever closer to him over the course of our lifetimes, and in the end to let us rest in the company of the Father, Son, and Holy Spirit.

We need to see our individual plans within the context of this over-arching—and loving—divine plan for each one of us.

Just about three weeks ago, Rachel fell in St. Catherine's Church while attending the farewell Mass of Fr. Jordan Kelly, and broke her hip. In hindsight, we now see that moment in the light of a series of events that led finally to the end. We see that at that moment, she really fell into the arms of the Dominicans and their associates at St. Catherine's, who would shortly be joined by the Carmelite Sisters for the Aged and Infirm during her post-surgery sojourn at Mary Manning Walsh Home which admitted her despite being technically "all full." Rachel enjoyed the care and attention of excellent doctors and nurses from some of the best health care institutions in the world. But—unbeknownst to them or to any of us—her life was moving toward its climax. Looking back, we can see it. I noted the uncanny calm of her voice whenever we spoke on the telephone. Did she sense that her hour was coming?

To us, her death seemed untimely. It came too soon. But in God's providence for her, the time had come. Her time. We know not the day nor the hour, but God does. In our time frame, there are the shocks and surprises of the unexpected, but not in God's. If we may dare to view things from God's perspective—as our faith prompts us to do—we see that the time had come for God to take her to himself. What shock is there in this? This is what our faith teaches us to expect.

To see this clearly—or to be invited to see it—is a great grace for us. Even in our sorrow at Rachel's passing, she would want us to see that it is the special grace of this moment.

❧ SERMON 70

Eileen Patricia Nolan (1939–2017)

In HIS LOVING PROVIDENCE God took Eileen to himself on Tuesday of the First Week of Advent this year. And now just as the nine days of solemn preparation for Christmas Day are about to begin tomorrow, her family and friends gather in this Mass of Christian Burial to commend her soul to his mercy. "See what love the Father has bestowed on us": in this moment of sorrow and loss, God turns our minds and hearts to the coming mysteries of the Incarnation always close to Eileen's heart.

For Eileen loved Christmas. Some of my fondest memories of her—and I suspect this is true for many of you as well—revolve around Christmastide. On a snowy Friday night now well over twenty years ago Eileen and I found ourselves stuck in a snow drift somewhere on the New Hampshire turnpike traveling to Kennebunkport, Maine, for the enchanting Christmas prelude weekend that we both loved. She calmly said a prayer, and we were soon on our way again. We all have warm memories of her Seward Square apartment decorated for Christmas. Christmas at the Dominican House of Studies, Christmas with her beloved family, Christmas with dear Father O'Sullivan and her St. Peter's friends: these were times that filled Eileen's heart with joy.

I can still hear her saying to me: "Fr. Di Noia, you know love comes down from heaven at Christmas." And what is Christmas about if not the great act of divine love that we call the Incarnation? The only-begotten Son of God, by the power of the Holy Spirit, became incarnate in the womb of the Blessed Virgin Mary so that the Father, who loves us more than we can imagine, might give us a share in the life of the Blessed Trinity. "See what love the Father has bestowed on us." The Son of God became a son of man so that we the sons and daughters of man could become the children of God. "Beloved, we are God's children now." "O amazing goodness!" wrote St. Augustine. "He was born the only Son, yet would not remain so; but grudged not to admit joint heirs to his inheritance." According to the Venerable Bede, "the grace of our creator is so great that he has allowed us both to know him and to love him, and moreover to love him as children love a wonderful father."

This was Eileen's faith, as it is ours. "Beloved, we are God's children now," we read in the first letter of John. There follow the most extraordinary lines in the Scriptures about the life to come: "What we shall be has not yet been revealed. We do know that when it is revealed we shall be like him, for we shall see him as he is." If she has not already, Eileen will soon see the fulfillment of this promise with her own eyes.

When Father Charles Farrell was elected prior of the Dominican House of Studies in 1981, he showed the wisdom of an experienced superior when he said to me, his sub-prior at the time: "We have to do something about the food." He wanted to replace the mediocre food service company that we had inherited, and somehow God led him to the Nolans' Capitol Hill wine and cheese shop. It was love at first sight. Eileen came to the Dominican House as Director of Food Services for the next twenty-nine years. Her own early life as a Dominican sister of the Congregation of Our Lady of the Rosary made her a perfect fit. This former Sparkill Dominican understood and loved the Dominican Order. She had the Dominican spirit in her heart. She was one of us. Yes, she was a consummate food service professional but she did it all with a Dominican flair.

In many ways, this characteristic Dominican sensibility—a firm acknowledgment of the beauty of created things and a recognition of the importance of material things like good food—is rooted in our faith in the Incarnation. The Son of God became a son of man, he took on human flesh, human existence, becoming like us in all things but sin. This Christmas faith was the source of the energy behind Eileen's enthusiastic guidance of the St. Patrick's Day celebration here at St. Peter's as much as her dedicated and loving service to the friars at the Dominican House of Studies over the years. In retrospect, there can be little doubt that Eileen's service contributed to the continuity and stability of the community and the faculty at the Dominican House of Studies during those critical years of development.

"The souls of the just are in the hand of God, and no torment shall touch them. They seemed, in the view of the foolish, to be dead; and their passing away was thought an affliction and their going forth from us, utter destruction. But they are at peace." Eileen's last years were difficult, a time of moving with Christ from Bethlehem to Golgotha as we all eventually must. I remember visiting her while she was recovering some years back in a nursing home in Maryland. Her legs had worn out after all those years of working in the kitchen, but she was always preternaturally cheerful, more interested in talking about me than about her aches and pains.

Eileen's wonderful and devoted family accompanied her in the final journey. For beyond Calvary, we pass with the risen Christ into the life to come where she is now at peace. According to an ancient Christian writer, "Those who have merited to be numbered among the saints shine like the nighttime stars of this creation." Now Eileen will enjoy that fullness of life that Christ made possible by coming to us at Christmas. "Come to me," Christ says to her and to all of us, "all you who labor and are heavy burdened, and I will give you rest. Take my yoke upon you and learn from me, for I am meek and humble of heart; and you will find rest for yourselves. For my yoke is easy, and my burden is light." Eileen will celebrate this Christmas in heaven.

❦ NOTES

THE OCCASION AND LOCATION, lectionary readings and sources of each sermon are provided in the notes that follow. All scriptural passages without parenthesized citations are drawn from the lectionary readings assigned for the celebration. Texts of the Collects or other parts of the Mass cited in these sermons can be found in the *Roman Missal*. For the complete texts and publishing information of hymns quoted in the sermons, see *The St. Michael Hymnal*, 4th ed., Michael O'Connor and Linda Powell Schafer (Lafayette, IN: St. Boniface Parish, 2011). Passages from the Fathers of the Church and some other Christian authors are drawn from various sources: the *Liturgy of the Hours*, especially the Office of Readings; St. Thomas Aquinas, *Catena Aurea: Commentary on the Four Gospels*, 4 vols., ed. Cardinal John Henry Newman (Castletown: Baronius Press, 2009); and *Ancient Christian Commentary on Scripture*, 29 vols., Thomas Oden, gen. ed. (Downers Grove: Intervarsity Press, 1998–2009). For individual Fathers, see: *St. Leo the Great Sermons*, trans J. P. Freeland & A.J. Conway, The Fathers of the Church Series, vol. 93 (Washington, DC: Catholic University of America Press, 1996); and *Forty Gospel Homilies of St. Gregory the Great*, trans. David Hurst (Kalamazoo, MI: Cistercian Publications, 1990).

This book is dedicated to the memory of Father Thomas Dominic Rover, O.P., who was professor of homiletics at the Dominican House of Studies in Washington and at St. Stephen Priory in Dover, MA, from 1957–1968. A native of Washington and an alumnus of Georgetown University college and law school, Fr. Rover entered the Dominican novitiate in 1944 and was ordained a priest in 1951. After studying at Yale University's drama school, he joined Blackfriars Theatre where he wrote four full-length plays. He taught theology at Providence College for many years, and died in Washington in 1998. A volume of Fr. Rover's poetry—*In Defense of Mermaids and Other Poems*—was published in 2014.

*)(*

Preface. The opening quotation from the Second Vatican Council is drawn from the Constitution on the Sacred Liturgy, *Sacrosanctum Concilium*, §35. "Through the course of the liturgical year..." is drawn from the *Introduction to the Lectionary*, §24. The words of Pope Francis are drawn from *Evangelii Gaudium*, §11, as are those in the following paragraph, ibid., §139. The quotation in the final paragraph ("poetic use...) is drawn from Arlene Scott's biographical note at the end of Thomas Dominic Rover, *In Defense of Mermaids and Other Poems: Poems of a Dominican Priest* (Logos Institute Press, 2014), p. 48.

PART I

Sermon 1. His Blessings Flow Far as the Curse Is Found. Christmas Midnight Mass 2012, Dominican House of Studies, Washington, DC. **Lectionary:** Isaiah 9:1–6 / Titus 2:11–14 / Luke 2:1–14. This sermon was previously published online by *First Things* and is reprinted with permission. The opening paragraph is a verse from "Joy to the World." Quotations throughout from the Christmas carol, "In the Bleak Midwinter." Quotations from St. Leo the Great come from his sermon 31 as found in the Office of Readings for December 17. Twenty children were among the twenty-six people who were shot and killed in an attack on the Sandy Hook Elementary School in Newtown,

Connecticut, about two weeks before Christmas on December 14, 2012. (See also Sermon 32 below.)

Sermon 2. Christ Was Born for This. Christmas Midnight Mass 2014, Dominican House of Studies, Washington, DC. **Lectionary:** Isaiah 9:1–6 / Titus 2:11–14 / Luke 2:1–14. Quotations throughout from the Christmas carol, "Good Christian Men Rejoice." The phrase "at midnight, in Bethlehem, in piercing cold" is drawn from an ancient Advent prayer traditionally said from the feast of St. Andrew (November 30) until Christmas Day: "Hail and bless be the hour and moment in which the Son of God was born of the most pure Virgin Mary, at midnight, in Bethlehem, in piercing cold. In that hour, vouchsafe, O my God, to hear my prayers and grant my desires, through the merits of our Savior Jesus Christ and of his Blessed Mother."

Sermon 3. O Marvelous Exchange. Christmas Day 2015, Dominican House of Studies, Washington, DC. **Lectionary:** Isaiah 52:7–10 / Hebrews 1:1–6 / John 1:1–18. This sermon was previously published online by *First Things* and is reprinted with permission. The opening paragraph quotes the *Magnificat* antiphon of First Vespers of the Solemnity of the Mother of God. For "God's infinity…" see Gerard Manley Hopkins, "The Blessed Virgin Compared to the Air We Breathe," lines 18–19; as well as "hand leaves his sight…" ibid., lines 112–13. Verses from the Christmas carol, "Puer Natus Est in Bethlehem." Quotation from St. Athanasius, *On the Incarnation*, 54.3. Quotation from St. Irenaeus, *Against Heresies,* book 5, preface. Passage from St. Leo the Great, sermon 21, 1 and 2.

Sermon 4. No Room for Sorrow. Christmas Day 2016, Dominican House of Studies, Washington, DC. **Lectionary:** Isaiah 52:7–10 / Hebrews 1:1–6 / John 1:1–18. Quotation from St. Leo the Great, sermon 21. Quotations throughout from the Christmas carol, "Hark the Herald Angels Sing." Passage from St. Augustine, *De trinitate*, 13.10. Quotations from St. Leo, sermons 24 and 25. The passage "for what else…" is drawn from *A Letter to Diognetus*, 8. "For unless…" comes from St. Leo, letter 31. "One who was merely…" is from St. Thomas Aquinas, *Summa Theologiae* III, q. 1, a. 2, citing St. Leo, sermon 21. Other quotations come from St. Leo, sermons 24, 25, and 27.

Sermon 5. Let No Tongue on Earth Be Silent. Christmas Day 2017, Dominican House of Studies, Washington, DC. **Lectionary:** Isaiah 52:7–10 / Hebrews 1:1–6 / John 1:1–18. Quotations throughout from the Christmas carol, "Of the Father's Love Begotten." For the opening paragraph and *passim*, cf. Karl Rahner, *Everyday Faith* (New York: Herder and Herder, 1968), pp. 37–42. Cf. St. Augustine, *Tractatus on the Gospel of John*, 2.13 and 15. For "Devils fled…," see St. John Chrysostom, Homily XII, 1. For "No one is excluded…," see St. Leo the Great, sermon 21. For details on the cultural celebration of Christmas, see Gerry Bowler, *Christmas in the Crosshairs* (New York: Oxford University Press, 2017), *passim*. The quotation "Just as stars…," is drawn from Benedict XVI, *Seek That Which Is Above* (San Francisco: Ignatius Press, 2007), p. 23. For "The seeming pretense…," see Rahner, ibid., p. 41.

Sermon 6. He Came to Earth to Lead us to the Stars. Christmas Day 2018, Dominican House of Studies, Washington, DC. **Lectionary:** Isaiah 52:7–10 / Hebrews 1:1–6 / John 1:1–18. For the text of the Christmas Sequence *Laetabundus*, see the Dominican Gradual. "He was a baby and a child…" is drawn from St. Ambrose, *Exposition on the Gospel of Luke*, 2.41–42. Quotations throughout are from the Christmas carol, "See Amid the Winter's Snow." The quotation "Our Lord Jesus Christ…" is from St. Irenaeus, *Against Heresies,* book 5, preface. "He comes to make his blessings flow…" is from "Joy to the World." For "Fodder gives way…," cf. St. Cyril of Alexandria, Homily on Luke, 1. "Break forth, O beauteous…" comes from the carol, "Break Forth O Beauteous Heavenly Light."

Sermon 7. Christ at the Heart of the Holy Family. Holy Family, December 28, 2014, St. Dominic Church, Washington, DC.

Lectionary: Sirach 3:2–6, 12–14 / Hebrews 11:8, 11–12, 17–19 / Luke 2:22–40. The cartoon referenced is by Jules Pfeiffer and appeared in *The New York Review of Books* in the 1970s.

Sermon 8. My Father's House. Holy Family, December 27, 2015, St. Dominic Church, Washington, DC. **Lectionary:** Sirach 3:2–6, 12–14 / 1 John 3:1–2, 21–24 / Luke 2:41–52. "The Father's word..." is drawn from the carol "Puer Natus Est in Bethlehem." The quotation that follows comes from St. Athanasius, *On the Incarnation*, 54.3. See Venerable Bede, *In Lucae Evangelium expostio*, 2:51. See Pope Leo XIII, *Neminem Fugit*, June 14, 1892, §1.

Sermon 9. Christ Manifested to the Whole World. Epiphany, January 8, 2012, Brompton Oratory, London, England. **Lectionary:** Isaiah 60:1–6 / Ephesians 3:2–3a, 6–6 / Matthew 2:1–12. The opening lines are from the carol "Songs of Thankfulness and Praise." For the *inquietudine di Dio*, see Pope Benedict XVI, Homily for the Epiphany of the Lord, January 6, 2012. The quotation "nothing more than..." comes from Alan Torrance, "Being of One Substance with the Father," in *Nicene Christianity*, ed. C. R. Seitz (Grand Rapids, MI: Brazos Press, 2001), p. 57.

Sermon 10. Consecrated to His Father's Service. Presentation of the Lord, Evensong, February 1, 2016, Church of Our Lady of Walsingham, Houston, Texas. **Lectionary:** Samuel 1:20–28a / Romans 8:14–21. While the Christmas season concludes with the celebration of the Baptism of the Lord, nonetheless, because the feast of the Presentation of the Lord links the Nativity of Christ with Eastertide, this sermon is included at this point. Evensong was celebrated on this occasion as part of the events of the ordination, on February 2, 2016, of Bishop Steven J. Lopes as second ordinary of the Personal Ordinariate of the Chair of St. Peter. "Jesus by thy presentation..." comes from the hymn "In His Temple Now Behold Him." The quotation from Pope John Paul II is drawn from the apostolic constitution *Pastores Gregis*, §13.

Part II

Sermon 11. Palm Sunday *and* Passion Sunday. Palm Sunday 2012, St. Dominic's Monastery, Linden, Virginia. **Lectionary:** Mark 11:1–10 / Isaiah 50:4–7 / Philippians 2:6–11 / Mark 14:1–15:47. The quotations of St. Andrew of Crete are drawn from the Office of Readings for Palm Sunday.

Sermon 12. Palm Sunday: Past and Present. Palm Sunday 2013, St. Dominic's Monastery, Linden, Virginia. **Lectionary:** Luke 19:28–40 / Isaiah 50:4–7 / Philippians 2:6–11 / Luke 22:14–23:56. For "not as things past...," see Jordan Aumann, citing Cardinal Bérulle, in *Christian Spirituality in the Catholic Tradition* (San Francisco: Ignatius Press, 1985), p. 226. The quotations of St. Bernard are drawn from the Office of Readings for the feast of the Holy Rosary (October 7). The quotation of St. Andrew of Crete is drawn from the Office of Readings for Palm Sunday. Pope John Paul called Mary the "incomparable model" in *Rosarium Virginis Mariae*, §10. "O God, who is this season..." is drawn from the alternate collect for Saturday of the Fifth Week of Lent.

Sermon 13. God Greatly Exalted Him. Palm Sunday 2014, St. Dominic's Monastery, Linden, Virginia. **Lectionary:** Matthew 21:1–11 / Isaiah 50:4–7 / Philippians 2:6–11 / Matthew 26:14–27:66. For "going of his own accord...," the next quotation, and the quotations in each of the three final paragraphs, see St. Andrew of Crete from Office of Readings of the Liturgy of the Hours for Palm Sunday.

Sermon 14. When Jesus Came to Jerusalem as a Child. Palm Sunday 2015, St. Dominic's Monastery, Linden, Virginia. **Lectionary:** Mark 11:1–10 / Isaiah 50:4–7 / Philippians 2:6–11 / Mark 14:1–15:47. For "Jesus Christ is our high priest..." and for quotations in the final paragraph, see St. John Fisher, Office of Readings for Monday of the fifth week of Lent.

Sermon 15. Exaltation Hidden in Humiliation. Palm Sunday 2016, St. Dominic's Monastery, Linden, Virginia. **Lectionary:** Luke 19:28–40 / Isaiah 50:4–7 / Philippians 2:6–11 / Luke 22:14–23:56. "Ride on!..." and verses in the paragraphs that follow come from the hymn, "Ride on, Ride on in Majesty." "This whole mystery..." is drawn from St. Leo, sermon 52, 2.

Sermon 16. Entering Jerusalem with Christ. Palm Sunday 2017, St. Dominic's Monastery, Linden, Virginia. **Lectionary:** Matthew 21:1–11 / Isaiah 50:4–7 / Philippians 2:6–11 / Matthew 26:14–27:66.

Sermon 17. Every Knee Should Bend. Palm Sunday 2018, St. Dominic's Monastery, Linden, Virginia. **Lectionary:** Mark 11:1–10 / Isaiah 50:4–7 / Philippians 2:6–11 / Mark 14:1–15:47. For "He, to whom divinity...," see St. John Chrysostom, Homily on Philippians; for "He emptied himself...," see St. Gregory of Nyssa, *Against Apollinarius*; for "taking the form...," see St. Augustine, *Contra Faustum;* and for "enhancing the human...," see St. Leo the Great, Epistle 28. "It is obvious..." is taken from St. Gregory of Nyssa, ibid. "The glory of the Father..." is from St. Athanasius, *Against the Arians.*

Sermon 18. Palms and Ashes. Palm Sunday 2019, St. Dominic's Monastery, Linden, Virginia. **Lectionary:** Luke 19:26–40 / Isaiah 50:4–7 / Philippians 2:6–11 / Luke 22:14–23:56. The opening sentence and the final quotation are taken from St. Leo the Great, sermon 62. The theme of the human heart conquered only by Christ the King is common among preachers of Orthodox churches.

Sermon 19. O Happy Fault. Easter Vigil 2013, Dominican House of Studies, Washington, DC. **Lectionary:** The Nine Readings of the Easter Vigil. "For those..." comes from St. Irenaeus, *Against Heresies,* book 4, from the Office of Readings for Wednesday of the second week of Lent. For "Yes, the plan of our salvation...," see the hymn *Pange Lingua.* For "the Passover of our salvation...," see St. Melito of Sardis,

Easter Homily, Office of Readings for Holy Thursday. For "When mankind was estranged…" and for "Christ came in the flesh…," see St. Basil, *On the Holy Spirit*, the Office of Readings for Tuesday of Holy Week.

Sermon 20. Hail the God of My Salvation. Easter Vigil 2014, Dominican House of Studies, Washington, DC. **Lectionary:** The Nine Readings of the Easter Vigil. The *Salvator Mundi* was composed by Arnulf of Louvain (d. 1250) and is quoted throughout. For St. Melito of Sardis, see the Office of Readings for Holy Thursday. For "All that the Son of God…," see St. Leo the Great, sermon 63, 6.

Sermon 21. Mary Magdalen, the *Apostola Apostolorum*. Easter Morning 2015, Dominican House of Studies, Washington, DC. **Lectionary:** Acts 10:34a, 37–43 / Colossians 3:14 / John 10:1–9. The quotation of Pope John Paul II is from *Mulieris Dignitatem*, §16; that of Pope Benedict is from "Women in the Early Church," General Audience, February 14, 2007; that of Pope Francis is from a daily meditation, "The Gift of Tears," April 2, 2013. For "Jesus is Isaac…," see Joseph Ratzinger, *Behold the Pierced One* (San Francisco: Ignatius Press, 1986), p. 119.

Sermon 22. Awake O Sleeper. Easter Morning 2016, Dominican House of Studies, Washington, DC. **Lectionary:** Acts 10:34a, 37–43 / Colossians 3:1–4 / John 20:1–9. The passage from the Ancient Homily is found in the Office of Readings for Holy Saturday. St. Thomas discusses the nature of the sin of the fallen angels in *Summa Theologiae* III, q. 63, aa. 1–3.

Sermon 23. Gazing with Mary on the Risen Christ. Easter Morning 2017, Dominican House of Studies, Washington, DC. **Lectionary:** Acts 10:34a, 37–43 / Colossians 3:1–4 / John 20:1–9. This sermon was previously published in *Nova et Vetera*, Vol. 15, No. 4 (Fall 2017), pp. 979–82, and is reprinted with permission. For "Before her eyes…," see Sedulius, *Paschale Carmen*, V, 361–64. The quotation of Pope John Paul II is from his General Audience, May 21, 1997. For "the eyes of her heart...," see *Rosarium Virginis Mariae*, §10. "O That birth forever blessed..." is from the Christmas hymn, "Of the Father's Love Begotten." "He comes to make his blessings..." is from "Joy to the World." "In Abel he was slain..." comes from St. Melito of Sardis, Easter Homily, Office of Readings for Holy Thursday. "Earth stood hard..." comes from the Christmas carol "In the Bleak Midwinter." "Myrrh is mine...," comes from the Christmas carol, "We Three Kings of Orient Are." For "to be open..." see *Rosarium Virginis Mariae*, §13. "Welcoming the risen Jesus..." and the quotation in the following paragraph are from Pope John Paul II, General Audience, May 21, 1997. For "who in this season..." see the alternate collect for Friday of the fifth week of Lent.

Sermon 24. Light Shines in the Darkness. Easter Morning 2018, Dominican House of Studies, Washington, DC. **Lectionary:** Acts 10:34a, 37–43 / Colossians 3:1–4 / John 20:1–9. "The sons of darkness..."and the next quotations in this paragraph derive from Quodvultdeus, Third Homily on the Creed, 5, 14–17. "The Lord Christ..." is from an Easter homily by St. Augustine.

Sermon 25. The Empty Tomb. Easter Morning 2019, Dominican House of Studies, Washington, DC. **Lectionary:** Acts 10:34a, 37–43 / Colossians 3:1–4 / John 20:1–9. The quotations of St. John Chrysostom are from his *Homilies on the Gospel of John*, 85, 4. For "When Peter and John saw...," cf. St. Thomas Aquinas, *Commentary on John*, c. 20, lect. vi. The quotation of St. Cyril of Alexandria is from his Commentary on John, 12. For "each and every event...," see St. John Chrysostom, Homily on Holy Saturday, 10. The quotation of Pope Benedict XVI is from his *Jesus of Nazareth: From the Entrance into Jerusalem to the Resurrection* (San Francisco: Ignatius Press, 2011), p. 254. The quotations of St. Thomas Aquinas are from *Summa Theologiae* III, q. 55, a. 6, ad 1, and q. 53, a. 2.

Sermon 26. The Sacrament of the Divine Mercy. Divine Mercy Sunday 2013, Basilica of the National Shrine of the Immaculate Conception, Washington, DC. **Lectionary:** Acts 5:12–16 / Revelation 1:9–11a, 12–13, 17–19 / John 20:19–31. The words of Pope Francis are drawn from the Sunday Angelus, March 17, 2013. The quotations of Pope John Paul II are from his encyclical *Redemptor Hominis*, §20.

Sermon 27. The Triumph of Paschal Grace and Divine Mercy. Divine Mercy Sunday 2014, Basilica of the National Shrine of the Immaculate Conception, Washington, DC. **Lectionary:** Acts 2:42–47 / 1 Peter 1:3–9 / John 20:19–31. The words of Pope Benedict are drawn from his Address to the Congregation for the Causes of Saints, December 19, 2009. The quotation is from *Veritatis Splendor*, §18. The quotations of St. Irenaeus are from *Against Heresies*, book 4. For "The heralds of the truth…," see St. Maximus the Confessor, Letter 11, Office of Readings for Wednesday of the fourth week of Lent.

Sermon 28. Divine Mercy: An Easter Gift to the Church. Divine Mercy Sunday 2016, Basilica of the National Shrine of the Immaculate Conception, Washington, DC. **Lectionary:** Acts 5:12–16 / Revelation 1:9–11a, 12–13, 17–19 / John 20:19–31. The quotations from Pope John Paul II are from his Homily on April 22, 2001, and the encyclical *Redemptor Hominis*, §20. The quotations of Pope Francis are from his Homily, February 10, 2016.

Sermon 29. The Saga of Divine Mercy. Divine Mercy Sunday 2017, Basilica of the National Shrine of the Immaculate Conception, Washington, DC. **Lectionary:** Acts 5:12–16 / Revelation 1:9–11a, 12–13, 17–19 / John 20:19–31. For "Jesus did not let…," see St. John Chrysostom, Homilies on John, 86, 2; for "resolved…to appear…," see St. Cyril of Alexandria, *Commentary on John's Gospel*, 12, 1; and for "for the healing…," see St. Augustine, *Tractatus on John's Gospel*. The quotation of St. Gregory the Great comes from Homily 26, and the next quotation is from St. Cyril of Alexandria, *Commentary on John's*

Gospel, 12, 1. For "offers to the doubters'...," see St. Leo the Great, sermon 73, 7. The quotations of St. Cyril of Alexandria are drawn from his *Commentary on the Gospel of John,* 12, 1.

Sermon 30. The Fountain of Divine Mercy. Divine Mercy Sunday 2018, Basilica of the National Shrine of the Immaculate Conception, Washington, DC, **Lectionary:** Acts 4:32–35 / 1 John 5:1–6 / John 20:19–31. The passage quoted in the first paragraph is drawn from St. Faustina Kowalska, *Diary,* §699; for the quotation in the next paragraph, ibid., p. 48. For "Not without purpose...," see St. John Chrysostom, *Homilies on the Gospel of John,* 85.3. For "From the Lord's pierced heart...," see Ratzinger, *Behold the Pierced One,* p. 48. The ancient Christian poet is Romanus Melodus, *Kontakian on Doubting Thomas,* 30.1–3. For "Doubting Thomas...," see Ratzinger, ibid., p. 53, and for "All of us...," ibid., p. 54. "The blood and water..." is from *Catechism of the Catholic Church,* §1225, and "So where were..." is from St. Ambrose, *On the Sacraments,* 2.2. "Christ visits us..." is drawn from St. Cyril of Alexandria, *Commentary on the Gospel of John,* 12.1. The final quotation is drawn from the hymn, "At the Lamb's High Feast We Sing."

Sermon 31. The Wounds of Jesus are Wounds of Mercy. Divine Mercy Sunday 2019, Basilica of the National Shrine of the Immaculate Conception, Washington, DC. **Lectionary:** Acts 5:12–16 / Revelation 1:9–11a, 12–13, 17–19 / John 20:19–31. For "Having seen and touched...," cf. St. Augustine, *Tractatus on the Gosepl of John,* 121. The words of Pope Francis are from his Address, Santiago Cathedral, January 16, 2018. The words of Pope Francis in the next paragraph are drawn from his Homily on Divine Mercy Sunday, 2015, while those of St. Thomas Aquinas are from *Summa Theologiae* III, q. 54, a. 4, ad 2 and ad 3. "Rest in Christ's passion..." is from Thomas à Kempis, *The Imitation of Christ,* Bk. II, 1, 1425; "There the security..." from St. Bernard, sermon 61; and "When it seems to you..." from St. Faustina, *Diary,* §1184. "He preferred..." is from St. Ambrose, Commentary on the Gospel of Luke, 24. The words of Pope Francis are from his

Address to the Stigmatines, February 10, 2018. "The blessed in heaven…" comes from St. Augustine, *De Symbolo*, bk. 2, c. 8. The Advent hymn is "Lo He Comes with Clouds Descending."

Part III

Sermon 32. The Massacre of Innocents. Fourth Sunday of Advent 2012, Basilica of the National Shrine of the Immaculate Conception, Washington, DC. **Lectionary:** Micah 5:1–4a / Hebrews 10:5–10 / Luke 1:39–45. See the note for Sermon 1 above.

Sermon 33. Surprised by Death. Fourth Sunday of Lent 2016, St. Mary's Cathedral, Edinburgh, Scotland. **Lectionary:** Exodus 3:1–8a, 13–15 / 1 Corinthians 10:1–6, 10–12 / Luke 13:1–9. For St. Gregory the Great's comments on the significance of the barren fig tree, see his sermon 31.

Sermon 34. Judge Not and You Shall Not Be Judged. Monday of the Second Week of Lent 2006, Basilica of San Clemente, Rome. **Lectionary:** Daniel 9:4b-10 / Luke 6:36–38. For quotations from St. John Chrysostom and St. Cyril of Alexandria, see *Catena Aurea*, vol. 3 (Luke), 222.

Sermon 35. The Merciful Judge Who Saves Us. Monday of the Fifth Week of Lent 2011, Basilica of the National Shrine of the Immaculate Conception, Washington, DC. **Lectionary:** Daniel 13: 1–9, 15–17, 19–30, 33–62 / John 8: 1–11. The series of quotations in these five paragraphs are all drawn from Karl Barth, *Church Dogmatics* IV.I (Edinburgh: T&T Clark, 1956), pp. 232–34.

Sermon 36. Let Go the Demons. Fourth Sunday of Ordinary Time 2009, Casa Santa Maria, Rome. **Lectionary:** Deuteronomy 18:15–20 / 1 Corinthians 7:32–35 / Mark 1:21–28. For "show clearly…," see St. Augustine, *City of God*, 9.21, and "Faith is mighty…" is drawn from his *Tractatus on the Gospel of John*, 6.21.

Sermon 37. Christ Brings True Peace to Our Hearts. Twentieth Sunday of Ordinary Time 2007, Domus Guadalupe, Rome. **Lectionary:** Jeremiah 28:4–6, 8–10 / Hebrews 12:1–4 / Luke 12:49–53. The final quotation is drawn from the Office of Readings for the Memorial of St. John Eudes (August 19).

Sermon 38. Two Shall Become One Flesh. Twenty-seventh Sunday of Ordinary Time 2009, Pontifical North American College, Rome. **Lectionary:** Genesis 2:18–24 / Hebrews 2:9–11 / Mark 1:2–16. "Adam's sleep…" comes from St. Augustine, *City of God*, 22.17. The passage of Mar Jacob are from his Homilies. "Although the dignity…" is from the *Catechism of the Catholic Church*, §1603. The quotation of Pope Benedict XVI is found in the *International New York Times*, September 28 2009, p. 3. Origen's comment is drawn from his Commentary on Matthew, 14.16.

Part IV

Sermon 39. Consumed by the Holy Mysteries. Feast of St. Thomas Aquinas 2011, Catholic University of America, Washington, DC. **Lectionary:** Ephesians 3:8–12 / John 17:11b–19. This homily was previously published in *Nova et Vetera*, Vol. 9, No. 2 (Spring 2011), pp. 257–59, and is reprinted with permission. "It is a law of friendship…" is drawn from St. Thomas Aquinas, *Summa Theologiae* III, q. 75, a. 1.

Sermon 40. Divine Wisdom in Teaching and Learning. Feast of St. Thomas Aquinas 2018, Pontifical University of St. Thomas Aquinas ("Angelicum"), Rome. **Lectionary:** Wisdom 7:7–10, 15–16 / John 17:11b–19. For the quotation from the inaugural address of St. Thomas Aquinas, see *Rigans montes*, chapter 1. The passage "an imprint…" is from *Summa Theologiae* I, q. 1, a. 3, ad 2, and the "*contemplata aliis tradere*" is from II-II, q. 188, a. 6. This homily owes a great debt to Frederick C. Bauerschmidt's *Thomas Aquinas: Faith, Reason and Following Christ* (New York: Oxford University Press, 2013).

Sermon 41. *Munus Petrinum.* Chair of St. Peter 2012, Santa Maria in Traspontina, Rome. **Lectionary:** 1 Peter 5:1–4 / Matthew 16:13–19. The occasion of this Mass was the pilgrimage of the Personal Ordinariate of the Chair of St. Peter to Rome.

Sermon 42. Bound to the See of Peter. Feast of St. Pius V 2004, Congregation for the Doctrine of the Faith, Palazzo del Sant'Uffizio, Vatican City. **Lectionary:** Acts 20:17–18, 28–32, 36 / John 21:15–17. An English translation of the homily preached at the Mass celebrated by Cardinal Ratzinger for the feast of St. Pius V, patron saint of the Congregation for the Doctrine of the Faith. The main source for this sermon is *Saints of the Rosary* (Dublin: Dominican Publications, Dublin, 1956).

Sermon 43. The Science of the Cross. Feast of St. Teresa Benedicta of the Cross, O.C.D. (Edith Stein) 1997, Basilica of the Shrine of the Immaculate Conception, Washington, DC. **Lectionary:** Hosea 2:16–17, 21–22 / Matthew 25:1–13. The commemoration took place a year before Edith Stein was canonized by Pope John Paul II on October 11, 1998. A slightly different version of this homily was previously published in the *Fellowship of Catholic Scholars Quarterly*, Vol. 21 (1998), pp. 7–9. For details of the life of Edith Stein, see Freda Mary Oben, *Edith Stein: Scholar, Feminist and Saint* (Staten Island: Alba House, 1988).

Sermon 44. The Universal Call to Sanctity. Solemnity of All Saints 2012, Casa Santa Maria, Rome. **Lectionary:** Revelation 7:2–4, 9–14 / 1 John 3:1–3 / Matthew 5:1–12. The quotations in the first paragraphs are drawn from St. Irenaeus, *Against Heresies*, book 4. See James of Voragine, *The Golden Legend* (Princeton: Princeton University Press, 1993), p. 659.

Sermon 45. Preserved from Sin in View of the Merits of Christ. Solemnity of the Immaculate Conception 2011, Abbey Church of

Sant' Anselmo in Aventino, Rome. **Lectionary:** Genesis 3:9–15, 20 / Ephesians 1:3–6, 11–12 / Luke 1:26–38. The words of Pierre de Celle are quoted in Hilda Graef, *Mary: A History of Doctrine and Devotion* (London: Bloomsbury, 1985), p. 251. "The honor of the Lord..." comes from St. Augustine, *De natura et gratia*, 36.42. For discussion and texts of Eadmer of Canterbury, see C. Maggioni, "Dalla Festa della concezione di S. Anna all'Immacolata Concezione della B.V. Maria," *Rivista Liturgica*, Vol. 91 (2004), pp. 781–810.

Sermon 46. Roses and an Image. Feast of Our Lady of Guadalupe 1996, National Conference of Catholic Bishops Chapel, Washington, DC. **Lectionary:** Sirach 24:23–31 / Galations 4:4–7 / Luke 1:39–51. For the interpretation of the image of Guadalupe in the light of Aztec pictography, see Helen Behrens, *America's Treasure: The Virgin Mary's Apparitions to Juan Diego* (Mexico: H. Behrens, 1964).

Sermon 47. What Sort of King Is This? Solemnity of Christ the King 2009, Casa Santa Maria, Rome. **Lectionary:** Daniel 7:13–14 / Revelation 1:5–8 / John 18:33b–37. The quotation of St. Augustine is from sermon 53A, 12; the quotation of St. Leo the Great is from sermon 4. The quotation of Pope Pius XI is from *Quam Primus*, §39.

Part V
Sermon 48. Daniel's Example. Rite of Admission to Candidacy, November 25, 2009, Pontifical Beda College, Rome. **Lectionary:** Daniel 5:1–6, 13–14, 16–17, 23–28 / Luke 21:12–19. The quotations of St. Jerome are drawn from his Commentary on Daniel.

Sermon 49. The Prayers of the Gardener. Institution of Acolytes, Third Sunday of Lent 2013, Pontifical North American College, Rome. **Lectionary:** Exodus 3:1–8a, 13–15 / 1 Corinthians 10:1–6,10–12 / Luke 13:1–9. "With fear and trembling..." is from St. Gergory the Great, Homily 31 on the Gospel of Luke. "Let us not..." is from St. Gregory Nazianzen, Oration 32. "By the dresser..." is from St. Gregory the Great, Homily 31. "The husbandman…" is cited by St. Thomas Aquinas in the volume on Luke, *Catena Aurea*.

Sermon 50. Transfigured in Christ. Institution of Acolytes, Second Sunday of Lent 2018, Pontifical North American College, Rome. **Lectionary:** Genesis 22:1–2, 9a, 10–13, 15–18 / Romans 8:31b-34 / Mark 9:2–10. St. Leo's sermon 51 on the Transfiguration is quoted in the Office of Readings for the Third Sunday of Lent. The passage "that the gift of the Holy Spirit…" is drawn from St. Cyril of Alexandria, *Commentary on the Gospel of John*, 12.21. "Whereas on Tabor…" is drawn from St. Peter Julian Eymard, *The Real Presence*, pp. 279–83.

Sermon 51. Teacher, Priest and Shepherd. Ordination to the Priesthood, Dominican Friars, May 25, 2012, St. Dominic Church, Washington, DC. **Lectionary:** Isaiah 61:1–3 / 1 Timothy 4:12–16 / Luke 22:14–20, 24–30. "For not as common bread…" is drawn from St. Justin Martyr, *First Apology*, 66. The quotation of St. Augustine is from his sermon 339. "Made cooperators…" is from the Constitutions of the Dominican Order, 1. The quotations of Pope Benedict XVI are from his Homily for the Chrism Mass, Holy Thursday 2012.

Sermon 52. Priesthood at the Heart of the Dominican Vocation. Ordination to the Priesthood, Dominican Friars, May 21, 2016, Basilica of the National Shrine of the Immaculate Conception, Washington, DC. **Lectionary:** Acts 10:37–43 / Hebrews 5:1–10 / John 15:9–17. "The Order's nature…" and, later, "Made cooperators…" are from the *Constitutions of the Dominican Order*, 1. The words of St. Thomas Aquinas are from *Summa Theologiae* III, q. 22, a. 1. The quotation of St. Justin Martyr is from the *First Apology*, 66.

Sermon 53. I Have Chosen You. Ordination to the Priesthood, Dominican Friars, May 20, 2017, St. Dominic Church, Washington, DC. **Lectionary:** Acts 10:37–43 / Hebrews 5:1–10 / John 15:9–17. The quotation of St. Justin Martyr is from the *First Apology*, 66. The quotation of St. Cyril of Alexandria is from his Commentary on the Gospel of John, 12.1. "Made cooperators…" and "The Order's nature…" are from the Constitutions of the Dominican Order, 1. The words of St. Thomas are from *Summa Theologiae* III, q. 22, a. 1.

Part VI

Sermon 54. A Day of Thanksgiving and Praise to Our Beneficent Father. Thanksgiving Day 2014, Pontifical North American College, Rome. **Lectionary:** Sirach 50:22–24 / Luke 17:11–19. For the texts of presidential Thanksgiving Day proclamations, see http://www.thanksgivingproclamations.com/.

Sermon 55. Thanksgiving, A Christian Holiday. Thanksgiving Day 2018, Pontifical North American College, Rome. **Lectionary:** Sirach 50:22–24 / 1 Corinthians 1:3–9 / Luke 17:11–19. For approval of the observance of Thanksgiving Day by Catholics, see Melanie Kirpatrick, *Thanksgiving: The Holiday at the Heart of the American Experience* (New York: Encounter Books, 2016), pp. 95–96. The newspaper article from the Dunkirk, New York *Evening Observer* is online. For quotations from the Third Plenary Council of Baltimore (1884), see *Memorial: A History of the Third Plenary Council of Baltimore*, archive.org/stream/thememorialvolum00unknuoft/thememorialvolum00unknuoft_djvu.txt.

Sermon 56. Martyrdom as Configuration to Christ. Martyrs' Day 2017, Venerable English College, Rome. **Lectionary:** 2 Maccabees 7:1–2, 9–14 / 1 Peter 4:12–19 / Luke 9:23–26. Concerning the martyrdom of Father Robert Sherwin, see Christopher Daw, et al., *The Forty-Four Martyrs of the Venerable English College* (Farnsborough: St. Michael Abbey Press, 2000), p. 8. The quotation "The governor brought…" is taken from Robin Darling Young, *In Procession Before The World: Martyrdom as Public Liturgy in Early Christianity* (Milwaukee: Marquette University Press, 2001), pp. 36–37. The quotation "public liturgy…" is taken from ibid., p. 59. The next quoted passage is taken from Servais Pinckaers, O.P., *The Spirituality of Martyrdom*

J. AUGUSTINE DI NOIA, O.P.

(Washington, DC: Catholic University of America Press, 2016), p. 47. The quotation "If in the liturgy of the Mass…" is drawn from Karl Rahner, *On the Theology of Death* (New York: Herder & Herder, 1961), p. 105, and the quotation that follows, ibid., p. 104. "The Christian ideal of sanctity…" comes from Pinckaers, ibid., p. 34. Quotations in the last paragraph come from Origen, *Homily on Numbers* 10.2, and St. Augustine, sermon 306E.

Sermon 57. The Mystery of the Eucharist. Celebration of Corpus Christi, May 13, 2005, Pontifical University of St. Thomas Aquinas ("Angelicum"), Rome. The quotation of St. Thomas Aquinas is from the *Summa Theologiae* III, q. 75, a. 1. The next quotations are from Pope John Paul II, *Ecclesia de Eucharistia*, §25; §12; §11; and §11 again.

Sermon 58. No One Receives Who Has Not First Adored. Eucharistic Procession, Alma Sisters of Mercy, Sixth Sunday after Easter 2007, Santa Maria sopra Minerva, Rome. **Lectionary:** Acts 15:1–2, 22–29 / Revelation 21:10–14, 22–23 / Jihn 14:23–29. The quotation of St. Thomas Aquinas comes from *Summa Theologiae* III, q. 75, a. 1. The quotation of Pope John Paul II is from *Ecclesia de Eucharistia*, §11.

Sermon 59. The Vision of Dominican Theological Education. Solemn Vespers and Conferral of Degrees, May 18, 2012, Pontifical Faculty of the Immaculate Conception, Washington, DC. **Lectionary:** Hebrwes 5:8–10. The quotation of St. Thomas comes from his commentary on the Epistle to the Hebrews, Prologue 4. St. Leo's words come from sermon 23.

Sermon 60. The Paralytic as Everyman. Penance Service, Vigil of the Consistory, March 23, 2006, Basilica of St. Mary Major, Rome. **Lectionary:** Matthew 9:1–8. The quotation "With the same free power…" is from Karl Barth, *Church Dogmatics*, IV.2 (Edinburgh: T&T Clark, 1956), p. 233. The three quotations of Pope Benedict XVI that follow are all from the Sunday Angelus, February 19, 2006.

Sermon 61. Mary's *Fiat* in the Life of the Priest. Fiftieth Anniversary of Cardinal Levada's Priestly Ordination, Tuesday of the Fourth Week of Advent 2011, Altar of the Chair, St. Peter's Basilica, Vatican City. **Lectionary:** Isaiah 7:10–14 / Luke 1:26–38. The quotations of Pope John Paul II are from his *Letter to Priests* (1998), §7. The quotation of St. Thomas Aquinas is from *Summa Theologiae* III, q. 2, a. 11, ad 3, and that of St. Augustine is from his sermon 291.

Sermon 62. Light Immortal, Light Divine. Invocation of the Holy Spirit at the Start of the Judicial Year, October 3, 2010, Red Mass, St. Matthew's Cathedral, Washington, DC. **Lectionary:** Ezekiel 36:24–28 / Romans 8:26–27 / John 14:23–26. Quotations throughout from the Pentecost Sequence, "Veni Sancte Spiritus." The reference is to James Brundage, *The Medieval Origins of the Legal Profession* (Chicago: University of Chicago Press, 2008).

Sermon 63. The Man Born Blind. Fourth Sunday of Lent 1999, The Eighth Annual Rose Mass, St. Patrick's Church, Washington, DC. **Lectionary:** 1 Samuel 16:1, 6–7, 10–13 / Ephesians 5:8–14 / John 9:1–41. St. John Chrysostom discusses the parable of the man born blind in Sermon 76.

Sermon 64. Christ Tells Us What He Knows. Feast of St. Matthias the Apostle 1997, Vespers, Commencement Exercises, Pope John Paul II Institute for Marriage and Family Studies, Basilica of the National Shrine of the Immaculate Conception, Washington, DC. **Lectionary:** Acts 1:15–17, 20–26 / John 15:9–17. The quotation of St. Augustine is from the *Tractatus on John's Gospel*, 56.1. St. Thomas Aquinas discusses the nature of the sin of the fallen angels in *Summa Theologiae* I, q. 63, a. 3. The quotation of St. Gregory the Great is from Sermon 27. St. Clement of Alexandria mentions the Apostle Matthias in his *Stromata*, 3, 4.

Sermon 65. A Suitable Place. Mass of Dedication and Erection of the Monastic Enclosure of St. Dominic's Monastery, May 4 1985,

Washington, DC,. For the letter of St. Dominic to the nuns of Madrid, see Francis C. Lehner, ed., *St. Dominic: Biographical Documents* (Washington: Thomist Press, 1964), pp. 91–92; for Blessed Cecilia Cesarini's account of the miraculous icon of the Madonna of Santa Maria in Tempulo, ibid., pp. 182–83. For the details of St. Dominic's role in the establishment of communities of nuns, see M.-H. Vicaire, *St. Dominic and His Times* (New York: McGraw-Hill, 1964), for Prouille, pp. 113–36; for Madrid, pp. 252–58; for San Sisto, pp. 345–55. The icon of the Madonna remained at San Sisto until 1575 when the community moved to San Domenico e Sisto. When in 1931 this convent became the site of the Pontifical University of St. Thomas Aquinas ("Angelicum"), the icon was transferred to the Dominican Church of Santa Maria del Rosario a Monte Mario. In 2008, the Washington community moved to a permanent home at St. Dominic's Monastery in Linden, Virginia.

Sermon 66. Free for God Alone. Eight Hundredth Anniversary of the Foundation of the Dominican Nuns in 1206, June 15, 2006, Dominican House of Studies, Washington, DC. Blessed Cecilia Cesarini (1203–1290) was the first nun to make profession into the hands of St. Dominic at the monastery of San Sisto in Rome. The quotations are from the Book of Constitutions of the Nuns, 1, IV and V.

Sermon 67. Christ the Good Samaritan. First Anniversary of Episcopal Ordination, July 11, 2010, Duomo di Santa Maria Assunta, Irsina, Italy. **Lectionary:** Deuteronomy 30:10–14 / Colossians 1:15–20 / Luke 10:25–37. The text of the sermon is an English translation of the original Italian. The quotation of St. Jerome is from his Homily on Psalm 14. The quotation of St. Ambrose is from his Exposition of the Gospel of Luke, 7.73. That of St. Augustine is from his sermon 179a, 7–8.

Sermon 68. Matilda Carucci Di Noia (1911–2007). Mass of Christian Burial, January 13, 2007, Church of St. Anthony, Bronx, New York. **Lectionary:** Wisdom 3:1–9 / Romans 6:3–9 / John 11:17–27.

Sermon 69. Rachel Angela Di Noia Benischek (1939–2015). Mass of Christian Burial, August 14, 2015, Church of St. Anthony, Bronx, New York. **Lectionary:** Wisdom 3:1–9 / Thessalonians 4:13–18 / Matthew 25:1–13.

Sermon 70. Eileen Patricia Nolan (1939–2017). Mass of Christian Burial, December 16, 2017, St. Peter's Church, Capitol Hill, Washington, DC. **Lectionary:** Wisdom 3:1–9 / 1 John 3:1–2 / Matthew 11:25–30. The quotation of St. Augustine is from his *Tractatus on John*, 2.13, and that of Venerable Bede is from his *Commentary on 1 John*. The ancient Christian writer is Cassiodorus and the quotation is from his *On the Psalms*.

CLUNY MEDIA

Designed by Fiona Cecile Clarke, the CLUNY MEDIA *logo
depicts a monk at work in the scriptorium,
with a cat sitting at his feet.*

*The monk represents our mission to emulate
the invaluable contributions of the monks
of Cluny in preserving the libraries of the West,
our strivings to know and love the truth.*

*The cat at the monk's feet is Pangur Bán, from the
eponymous Irish poem of the 9th century.
The anonymous poet compares his scholarly
pursuit of truth with the cat's happy hunting of mice.
The depiction of Pangur Bán is an homage to the work
of the monks of Irish monasteries and a sign
of the joy we at Cluny take in our trade.*

"Messe ocus Pangur Bán,
cechtar nathar fria saindan:
bíth a menmasam fri seilgg,
mu memna céin im saincheirdd."

Made in the USA
Middletown, DE
14 December 2019